Praise for David Allen

'Every decade has its defining self-help business book. In the 1940s it was *How to Win Friends and Influence People,* in the 1990s *The Seven Habits of Highly Successful People.* These days we're worried about something much simpler: *Getting Things Done.* That's the title of productivity guru David Allen's pithy 2001 treatise on working efficiently, which continues to resonate in this decade's overworked, overwhelmed, overstretched workplace.' **Time**

'For the last twenty-five years, Allen has been helping people achieve stress-free efficiency, and in doing so has been called one of the world's most influential thinkers on productivity.' **Guardian**

'Allen is remaking the self-help tradition for the information age. Allen's practical suggestions on how to turn thoughts into reality sharply distinguish him from his predecessors.' **Wired**

'David Allen's productivity principles are rooted in big ideas . . . but they're also eminently practical.' **Keith H. Hammonds, *Fast Company***

'. . . elegant in its simple suggestions . . . *Getting Things Done* has fans in nearly every corner of the corporate globe.' ***Business Week***

'The GTD system is a revelation. My life is still as jam-packed as ever, but I feel much more in control, as though I'm tooling around in a well-engineered car that makes doing 80 feel like 50.' **Fortune**

'What a stimulating dose of uncommon sense! These powerful and practical pointers for life are as subtle and rich as they are simple. David Allen is a master at marrying the sensible and the sublime.' **Arianna Huffington**

'This should be required for everyone entering business.' **John Edwin Mroz, East West Institute**

Also by David Allen

Getting Things Done

Ready for Anything

Dear Kirsten & Courtney,

This seems like an eminently sensible approach to maintaining sanity in a frantic world. But read this book back to front - well sort of. Start with pages 125-127 190 192 and then ch9.

Lots of love,
Daddi

MAKING IT ALL WORK

DAVID ALLEN

PIATKUS

PIATKUS

First published in Great Britain in 2008 by Piatkus Books
First published in the US in 2008 by Viking Penguin,
a member of Penguin Group (USA) Inc.

A CIP catalogue record for this book
is available from the British Library

ISBN 978-0-7499-4103-1

Papers used by Piatkus Books are natural, renewable and recyclable
products made from wood grown in sustainable forests and certified
in accordance with the rules of the Forest Stewardship Council.

Mixed Sources
Product group from well-managed
forests and other controlled sources
www.fsc.org Cert no. SGS-COC-004081
© 1996 Forest Stewardship Council
FSC

Typeset by Phoenix Photosetting, Chatham, Kent
www.phoenixphotosetting.co.uk
Printed and bound by CPI Mackays, Chatham ME5 8TD

Piatkus Books
An imprint of
Little, Brown Book Group
100 Victoria Embankment
London EC4Y 0DY

An Hachette Livre UK Company
www.hachettelivre.co.uk

www.piatkus.co.uk

Contents

Preface   ix

1 | Introduction: From Getting Things Done to Making
It All Work   1

2 | The GTD phenomenon   14

3 | Making It All Work—the Process   49

4 | The Fundamentals of Self-Management   60

5 | Getting Control: Capturing   76

6 | Getting Control: Clarifying   103

7 | Getting Control: Organizing   128

8 | Getting Control: Reflecting   161

9 | Getting Control: Engaging   170

10 | Getting Control: Applying This to Life and Work   193

11 | Getting Perspective   200

12 | Getting Perspective on the Runway: Next Actions   209

13 | Getting Perspective at Ten Thousand Feet: Projects   216

14 | Getting Perspective at Twenty Thousand Feet: Areas of
Focus and Responsibility   227

15 | Getting Perspective at Thirty Thousand Feet: Goals and
Objectives   235

16 | Getting Perspective at Forty Thousand Feet: Vision   241

17 | Getting Perspective at Fifty Thousand Feet: Purpose
and Principles   249

18 | Getting Perspective: Gracie's Gardens Revisited   261

19 | Making It All Work—in the Real World   266

20 | In closing . . .   283

Appendix i. Incompletion Trigger List   288

Appendix ii. Natural Planning Model   290

Appendix iii. Project Planning Trigger List   291

Appendix iv. Mastering Work Flow   293

Appendix v. The Weekly Review   295

Appendix vi. Workflow Processing and Organizing   296

Appendix vii. Horizons of Focus   297

Index   299

Preface

Since the publication of my first two books, *Getting Things Done* and *Ready for Anything*, I've had the opportunity to engage with many thousands of people who have adopted their principles and techniques, and have received countless letters and e-mails from readers who have validated the efficacy of the GTD approach. What has emerged for me since is not so much new information but new and deeper perspectives about why that information works as well as it does and how universally it can be applied. This book is my attempt at sharing that awareness, plus expanded instructions for using this material in the broadest possible way.

It was challenging to frame my writing here for both the large audience of people who are familiar with my work and those who may be reading or hearing of these methods for the first time. I am trusting that the inherent power in the information itself will make it valuable for both groups. The first four chapters examine the GTD phenomenon—what it is and why it continues to expand around the world. The rest of the book explores the components of the two core aspects of self-management: chapters 5–10 investigate the dynamics of gaining control, and chapters 11–18 deal with achieving perspective.

For reference I have included several Appendices that describe the key models of the GTD process.

Though many parts of this material can be used for topical reference, the whole is greater than the sum of the parts. I recommend that you absorb the contents as a whole, at your own pace. Though it doesn't get any simpler than this, the power is in the understanding and application of its subtlety.

. . . And Many Thanks to

my wife and partner, Kathryn, for her unfailing love, encouragement, and support;

the many clients, staff, associates, and friends who have aligned with and contributed to this work;

the scores of practitioners of GTD around the world who have provided feedback and valuable insights into the implementation of these models;

my personal counselors, especially Michael Hayes, who have helped me stay connected to my intuition and the bigger picture;

my agent, Doe Coover, whose continued diligence has given my book writing a firm business foundation;

my editor at Viking, Rick Kot, whose intellectual rigor, laborious fine-tuning of my prose, and patience helped nurture the project across the finish line; and

all the other sources of my inspiration—seen and unseen.

Making It All Work

1 | Introduction: From Getting Things Done to Making It All Work

The art of progress is to preserve order amid change and to preserve change amid order.

—Alfred North Whitehead

Much of what sophisticates loftily refer to as the "complexity" of the real world is in fact the inconsistency in their own minds.

—Thomas Sowell

To lead an effective life, we need to be able to make things happen—to engage with our world so it will supply us with the experiences and results we seek. Making the right choices and ensuring their efficient execution have always been key elements of success. An endless stream of books, seminars, consulting, and coaching programs has emerged to facilitate those processes, to remind us how to plan, vision, set goals, clarify values, and motivate ourselves and others; any number of techniques and tools are available to help us get organized, manage our time, and be more efficient.

What's missing is a fundamental understanding of, and effective model for, the dynamics of the process as a whole—a way to make it all work. Is there some coherent method that encompasses that totality yet can be applied to any part of it, at any time?

Indeed there is, and it is the subject of this book. *Making It All Work* is a manual for getting anything and everything on track—from a bloated e-mail in-box to a significant professional challenge or your next vacation. The same principles and practices are applicable to them all, and when these techniques are incorporated across the spectrum of life and work, a wonderful integration takes place. Work takes on a lighter quality, and life itself becomes a successful enterprise.

Approaching work is a game, and one that's fun to play, as long as we know the purpose, the boundaries, the contents, and the rules. When any of those parameters are unclear, we develop unnecessary stress and are ineffective. But if, on the other hand, a bullet-proof, trusted process is in place which you know you can apply whenever needed to clarify and align your thinking and resources—no matter what's going on—it's much easier to experience a heightened sense of freedom and spontaneity with how you spend your time in your job.

Similarly, we need to be more practical, efficient, and effective in much of the rest of our day-to-day experience, incorporating business's best practices into many of the activities that we label as "personal." The business of our lives will be a good one as long as we know the business we're in, the nature of the transactions we must perform, and how to handle those outcomes and actions effectively. The paradox is that when the mechanics of our day-to-day lives are not handled in an effectively engineered fashion, our ability to actually *be* personal is diminished. To serve our families, our individual health and well-being, and our recreational and creative needs optimally, many businesslike behaviors are required.

The game of work and the business of life are really the same thing, when it comes down to the principles and behaviors and techniques that eliminate distraction and foster beneficial focus. And winning at both work and life is not a matter of crossing some distant finish line. It's about internalizing a set of responses and behaviors that are consistently successful when applied to any aspect of life and work that could be functioning better.

In 2001 I published my first book, *Getting Things Done: The Art of Stress-Free Productivity,* which has not only gone on to sell hundreds of thousands of copies in almost thirty languages but has spawned a worldwide following among the widest range of people imaginable, including corporate executives, university professors, software engineers, soldiers, musicians, students, and the clergy. The acronym GTD, as the methodology described in that book has come to be known, has become a standard item in the lexicon of self-management, and a Web search for the term generates literally millions of references.

For several years after *Getting Things Done*'s publication, whenever I was asked, "What's next?" by people enthusiastically implementing its practices, my answer was simply, "Read *Getting Things Done* again!" Its five stages of processing your "stuff" into real outcomes and actions and maintaining a reviewable inventory of your commitments was, is, and always will be the most effective way to get control of your immediate environment and psyche. Likewise, assessing the six distinct Horizons of Focus at which you have agreements and attention was, is, and always will be the way to trust your priority decisions. My experience has shown me, however, that there is still a wide gap between understanding and implementation, and that almost everyone can benefit from applying the models even more effectively and consistently across the whole spectrum of personal and organizational life. The GTD method has been experienced by some of the most sophisticated people in the world as novel, effective, and profound—yet it should be the way we all approach the game of work and the business of life.

There are many layers to the unpeeling of the GTD onion and multiple levels of it to "get." Even some of the greatest advocates of GTD, who feel they really did "get it," and who keep on keeping on with the process in all its fine-tuned details, have still probably not fully tapped the depth and breadth of its power. The most sophisticated users "get" that there is a lot that they have yet to "get." When people first encounter my methods, more control, energy, focus, and creativity are unleashed than they expect. I have struggled over the years with ways to urge GTD users that the more conscientiously they adopt its procedures, the more motivation they will have to apply them in even broader contexts, and to apply them more consistently. Their potential to improve personal and professional environments is remarkable and has only begun to be tapped.

As many have discovered, these principles and processes go far beyond motivational positive-thinking pep rallies and offer, instead, very practical approaches for recognizing and relieving the pressures that can throw us off. Although that message was implicit in *Getting Things Done,* it deserves a much broader exposition. Implementing some of the basic and rather mundane techniques of GTD provided immediate relief from the pain created by the overwhelming input and changing contexts of highly active people. That has been such an unfulfilled need that it has catapulted my model into global awareness and acceptance. Simply having a trusted way to keep from drowning in e-mail can be a critical life preserver. But the issues and the solutions remain significantly larger than that.

People are still desperate for some light at the end of the "over-whelmingly busy" tunnel, and they need a direct and practical guide to find it. Many of the readers of my first book and followers of GTD have acknowledged that they have only just started the process and have only partially implemented it. And among those who jumped in wholeheartedly, a majority has found that they have rather easily "fallen off the wagon."

There has been a widely expressed desire for a more complete explication of GTD principles and how they can be integrated more fully and consistently. Because I have been privy to an extraordinary range and volume of positive feedback for *Getting Things Done* as well as from the thousands of people who have attended our seminars and used our materials, I have been able to achieve another level of insight and an awareness about this body of work, especially the tenets that lie behind the concrete work flow and focus methods. I have come to realize that the principles underlying those techniques have much broader implications and multifaceted applications that go far beyond a mere "personal organizing system." I've known for many years that there was an even greater power inherent in the adoption of these techniques—personally, interactively, and organizationally. But only in the last decade have I begun to extract the essence of how and why that's true. I developed a one-day seminar titled "GTD: The Road Map" explicitly to home in on that understanding and offer universally useful techniques to leverage it. *Making It All Work* presents a practical implementation for accessing that power.

While *Getting Things Done* offered a primer and a simple manual, *Making It All Work* is intended to provide you with a road map—one that will enhance your abilities to process life and work in tandem. The tools for operating your car are different from the manual for fixing it and the map you need to keep you on course and get you where you're going. And though knowing how to drive a car is a highly useful skill, understanding the basics of how a car works provides an underlying freedom and confidence.

Making It All Work is not intended to supplant or change any of the information in *Getting Things Done;* rather, it builds on its principles and applies them to even greater effect. Applying GTD to any degree actually gives a real experience of positive self-management—people experience more control and a more constructive perspective. That has been true for situations as varied as getting a handle on paper strewn all over an office to managing a merger with another division to dealing with the death of a life partner. You need to feel you have a grip on things and are directing them appropriately. You need to have enough of a sense of command of a situation to be able to think constructively beyond survival, and then, when you can think about what you're doing, you need to feel like there is direction and meaning to your focus and investment of resources.

There are many different kinds of situations in which the techniques for achieving greater control and perspective can be constructively applied and the approach that will be most useful in the moment can change frequently. Mid-morning it might make the most sense to clean up your in-basket, while after lunch it could be best to brain-storm a big project. Before your team tries to get organized, it might more appropriately clarify its driving vision. Before your family thinks about its next vacation, it could be more fruitful to complete some key projects. In other words, you won't at any specific point in time ever need or want to be concentrating on everything that needs to be controlled and aligned in your life and work. You will never want to go everywhere on any of your maps. But it will be good to know what works best for a specific problem and which viewing point would serve you best in a particular circumstance.

Each one of the eleven main parts of the models I will present in *Making It All Work* has applications in almost every sector of life. And each segment embodies practical steps that have instant stand-alone value for improving a wide variety of problematic situations, which you can use anywhere, anytime. You don't have to commit to some major "system implementation" to find great merit in understanding a particular technique from any one of the sections. The whole is greater than the sum of the parts, as I think you'll agree, but the fact remains, many people will resist utilizing *any* of these methods if they believe they are all necessarily tied together. Some readers who en-countered the GTD model assumed that such a complete and de-tailed methodology was simply too much to deal with. There's plenty for all of us to explore and expand upon within any part of this over-all set of practices.

There are principles that underlie the principles for getting things done, and an awareness of them offers great value to a much broader spectrum of society than just the audience of "high-performing pro-fessionals" who gravitated toward my earlier writings and teaching. For instance, the first step in gaining control of work flow is to cap-ture everything that has your attention—write it all down, then get it into a trusted "bucket" until you can decide what it means and what you're going to do with it. The underlying principle of clearing the air (externally and internally) by identifying those things that are pulling or pushing on the psyche holds equally true in social situations in which you want to gain more control, such as a conversation with your kids, or in your chamber of commerce committee meeting. Once you really *get* the basic principle of increasing productivity and decreasing stress by keeping things out of your head instead of inside it, you will discover countless ways to benefit from it. If you understand the principles that lie underneath the GTD methods, and how and why they work, then you attain all kinds of freedom to implement those principles in whatever way you want.

For Those Already Familiar with GTD

In my experience, people who have embraced the GTD model seem to fall into three basic categories:

1. Those who *think* they got it, but didn't really get it.
2. Those who got some of it and realize they didn't really apply it like they should.
3. Those who really got it, and really implemented it to an "advanced" level.

(If you're wondering about the group that got it but didn't think it was worth doing, I have to say honestly that I have not heard from or about those people, if they exist at all.) In all the years since the initial publication of *Getting Things Done,* I've never received any feedback complaining that the model doesn't work. Virtually all we hear from readers is that "it's powerful, it's great, just a little bit has made a ton of difference, I've only started, I know it works—but I've just not been able to get myself to fully work it," and so on.

For Group 1—those who believe they've really implemented the GTD model because of their success with a particular part of it—I want to challenge you to take another look into what a total productivity model involves. A common impression of my work is that it provides world-class tips and tricks for getting control of e-mail and paper filing (which it does); because those benefits were so rewarding, many people didn't dig any deeper into the application of, say, the Horizons of Focus, which address the issue of priorities. They also didn't explore why the principles that lay behind those useful techniques were so powerful. Tech-oriented adherents of GTD often got so enthralled with the value of lists—which ones to draw up and how to sort and organize them—that they didn't advance to the next step of understanding the thought processes required to generate what goes *on* the lists or the necessity of making them complete and ubiquitous—practices that are much more central to the process.

For Group 2—the folks who recognize there's huge value in GTD but who haven't been able to get or keep themselves consistently on board with it—I want to rekindle your enthusiasm with a fresh and enhanced exposition of the models and supply more avenues and possibilities for applying its principles. There are many GTD users who have expressed the desire to have more of it "stick," and *Making It All Work* will give you the impetus to make this happen.

For Group 3—the people who caught the game and really did follow through with a thorough adoption of its principles—I want to reinforce your successes and supply more and enhanced ways in which you can utilize what you already know works. As a significant minority of the GTD-aware population, you already have discovered that the real productivity methods have even deeper and richer applications. You are lifelong learners who recognize that you have undertaken a lifestyle curriculum.

For Those Who Are New to GTD

The purpose of *Making It All Work* is to reinforce and deepen the understanding of the core GTD principles—why they work, what positive results can be achieved with an almost infinite range of applications, and what negative consequences ensue when they are ignored.

Familiarity with my previous writings is not a prerequisite for reading and gleaning great value from *Making It All Work,* although you would find *Getting Things Done* a very useful and complementary resource. *Getting Things Done* is full of step-by-step instructions about how best to create a customized productivity system. It contains many practical details and techniques, which won't necessarily be repeated in this book, though I will review the basics of the GTD model and share examples of how people have experienced their own applications of it—mainly as validation of its effectiveness but also to provide a larger context for understanding its implications.

Here I will be stressing and elaborating on the essential underlying components that make the GTD model work, and why they resonate on so many levels with so many people. You will find many valuable nuggets that can be extremely useful across the broad spectrum of your current and future reality.

I will share some of the universal techniques that have emerged in and around GTD. They will likely be able to be improved upon over the coming years, and new ways of working them will certainly be developed. For instance, when the *Star Trek*–ish computer is finally invented that recognizes your voice in all of your common environments, is easily programmable, and is managed by you with vocal commands, you will simply say out loud:

"Computer!"

"Yes, David."

"Bread—sourdough"

. . . and it will be in the grocery bag at your front door in your next semiweekly delivery.

"Computer!"

"Yes, David."

"Area of focus—fun—next time in New York—sculpture exhibits."

. . . and whenever "New York" is on your schedule, you will receive an e-mail with links to sculpture exhibits on those dates. Your automatic review of your areas of focus, interest, and responsibility, which shows up on your computer every six weeks, will likewise include "sculpture exhibits in New York" on the list, under your previously described category of "fun."

As of this writing, the technology exists to create such a system, even if easy accessibility doesn't. But the productive set of behaviors it encompasses—having an idea, and then capturing it in a trusted system that will ensure it is appropriately processed, organized, and fed back to you when and how you want to see it—will be highly functional now and forever. Your task at this time, if you believe such a project might be worth undertaking, is to figure out how you could accomplish those "knowledge-work athletics" on your own.

HOW TO USE THIS BOOK

I highly recommend that you keep a notepad and pen or other recording device close at hand as you continue to read (or listen to) this book. Doing so would be implementing one of the core principles itself—*noticing what you are noticing,* which might be something you would want to do something about, and capturing it when you have the thought. This material has a way of triggering all kinds of direct and indirect thinking, some of which will likely contain the seeds of some very important content for your world in the future. There will be many universes passing through your mind between here and the end of the book—so don't lose the opportunity to mine the gold to be found there!

It's a good practice to have some sort of capture tool at hand whenever you are in a mode to potentially be thinking of anything of value—even if later you do nothing with your notes. Simply having the device available is an "assumed affirmation"—it tees up a part of your awareness to be more focused on potential value. You are "acting as if" there *might* be value, and that, in and of itself, will likely serve as a self-fulfilling prophecy.

Making It All Work will also provide you with the opportunity to do some beneficial self-coaching, as well as present some proven, highly effective models for consulting with others—whether individuals you may be relating to or groups with which you are involved. As I continue to grow and expand in my life and career, I constantly need to remind myself of aspects of this material I need to get focused on and on course in the situations I find myself in. I didn't write this book because I'm already done with this material (heavens, no!)—I'm simply sharing an understanding of some highly effective techniques that we all have and can and will use to great benefit.

I guarantee you will find fertile food for thought here. I have yet to meet any conscious, open, and creative person who wouldn't admit to an interest in and awareness of improvements they could make in being more capable of controlling aspects of their world and keeping the optimum focus for themselves. The contents of this book are not final answers but trustworthy and workable approaches to finding them. And more important, *Making It All Work* will provide a road map for identifying what questions you should be *asking,* and when and how best to execute the resolutions.

AFFIRMING SUCCESS

As Olympic athletes have known for years, it greatly improves perception and performance to visualize a successful outcome to any endeavor, before you actually undertake it. To that end, I suggest you now stop reading or listening for a moment and bring an image to mind of what you'd really like to get out of an exploration of the material in *Making It All Work.*

To begin, think about why you bought this book or audiobook. There are certainly many other choices you could have made and be engaged with right now. What, particularly, attracted you to pick this title? What were you hoping you could get from it?

Let me affirm or expand your options for a moment. What if you had the ability to gain control and perspective whenever you felt you had lost it? How would you feel if you were confident that you had found a totally trusted process to bring you back on track, on top of your game, whenever you felt it was necessary? What risks might you be willing to take, risks that you haven't yet dared, if you really knew you had those skills and tools? What wildly successful experiences could possibly happen for you if you did have that confidence?

I can guarantee you that, with a willingness to experiment, a small amount of focus and discipline, and mastery of a few simple techniques, those kinds of results and even greater ones are achievable. In the course of this book I'll be walking you through many different levels of how you're engaged with work and life. While some of the most significant areas that can be improved will actually be some of the more mundane, such as how you deal with e-mail or how you keep track of family projects, I want to encourage you to not lose sight of the ultimate goal here, which is to always have at your disposal everything you need to right yourself and your various enterprises consistently and to get back on course.

NOT ABOUT THE ANSWERS, BUT ABOUT TRUSTING YOUR ANSWERS

Don't expect *Making It All Work* to provide you with substantive answers to specific questions like: What should I do about changing jobs? Should I commit to another relationship? Should I buy the company? Should we get a puppy? Applying the methods in this book will, however, help you develop the self-assurance to trust your own solutions.

Getting Things Done provided hope, a belief for which the world has recently been starved. It affirmed that there is light at the end of the tunnel and that, with a little guidance, anyone can get back on top of his or her tumultuous world of overwhelming input, rapid change, and infinite options.

Making It All Work will deliver the keys to engender trust, and that's where we all need and want to go. Every decision and, indeed, even every action, is a risk. You could never know enough to know, in the moment, that what you are doing in the moment is the perfect thing to do. In this world there is no magic formula that can be trusted to eliminate all doubt, nor will there ever be. But there are very real and practical things we can do that can minimize those risks and maximize our willingness and capability to engage. Being in a state of freedom and flow is supported by our confidence in what we're doing, given the totality of our awareness.

Nothing is perfect, final, or fixed in this material world. As soon as we are tempted to believe it is, we've probably set ourselves up for disappointment. What we're truly striving for is the permanence that we can count on, amid all the change and flux. And the most permanent, secure, and stable thing we can possess is a foolproof way to deal with impermanence, insecurity, and surprise. A real connection with some greater awareness of the wellspring of our being and our universe will always provide the ultimate relief and resolution. But, as an Arab proverb so appropriately counsels: Trust in Allah, and tie your camel.

2 | The GTD Phenomenon

Just as the tumultuous chaos of a thunderstorm brings a nurturing rain that allows life to flourish, so too in human affairs times of advancement are preceded by times of disorder. Success comes to those who can weather the storm.

—I Ching

Why have the simple formulas described in *Getting Things Done* sparked such a significant buzz? What is it about this set of familiar, easily grasped concepts and behaviors that has triggered such an enthusiastic response?

While there may be reasons of which I'm unaware—sometimes fads and phenomena do spread for no apparent reason—I do know of four factors that have contributed to the growth of GTD's popularity.

First of all, the concepts work, in an understandable and logical way.

Second, they are easily implemented, by anyone, at any time, with common tools everyone has.

Third, the problems that GTD addresses, and the awareness of them, continue to grow steadily and globally.

Fourth, the model corresponds to something deeper and
more intuitive that resonates in the human psyche at
many levels.

The Concepts Work

The GTD model was researched, tested, and honed in the context of
real situations involving real people. For the most part I sought to
discover self-management techniques that worked and then exam-
ined *why* they worked. I believed that if I could identify the principles
that underlay the effectiveness of a particular technique, I could then
apply those principles in an infinite number of ways with any number
of techniques and methods that could help me get more done with
more freedom and focus.

For instance, I became fascinated with the question of why, after
making a big list of everything that was on my mind, I felt differently
about the tasks facing me and why my thinking about them became
much clearer. Nothing had changed in my world per se; all I had
done was to express what was on my mind in an objective way. I
worked with the hypothesis that the reason I felt better was that if an
obligation remained recorded only mentally, some part of me constantly kept thinking that it should be attended to, creating a situation that was inherently stressful and unproductive. By writing it
down, I was able at least to begin to loosen its grip on me. Were these
principles that could be applied anywhere, with anyone, at any time,
and produce the same result?

I followed a similar process to derive the entire core set of principles that constitute GTD, and then I asked myself if there was something about how and why these processes worked that could be
understood at a deeper level and consequently applied in more universal ways to improve things.

It turns out that absolutely everything that was effective within
the original set of methods was connected to a deeper and more
fundamental truth about how things work and how we work them.

Processing "stuff" out of your in-basket reflects the most appropriate way to create a cooperative relationship with anything new in your environment. Organizing and reviewing your inventory of incomplete items in your world relates not only to getting on top of your workload but also to productively manage a big project or your relationship with your parents. Clarifying your areas of focus and responsibility at work facilitates a much greater sense of focus about your work projects; when you apply that across your life, it will increase your balance and integration with your broader life experience. The applications and implications of each part of the GTD model seemed to be limitless.

GTD'S SUCCESS IN THE HIGH-TECH WORLD

Just how well GTD did prove to work is reflected, I think, in the surprising phenomenon of its rapid and viral spread through the technology/IT/blog community. As of this writing there is an average of more than fifty new and unique blog postings a day (just in the English language) referring in some way to GTD. While its principles themselves have very little to do, specifically, with software, computers, or the raft of new technogadgets that have flooded the marketplace, I have some guesses as to why it has been adopted so enthusiastically in this quarter.

I'm about as lazy as anyone on the planet, and nearly every geek and computer-oriented person I know leans in that direction as well. Programmers work long hours trying to design stuff that keeps them from having to work long hours. The nature of computing is to make things easier, faster, more powerful, and more coherent—in other words, to help get more done with less effort. Maximize output with minimum input is the essence of both productivity improvement and GTD principles, so it would seem natural that people attracted to the world of computers would gravitate to ideas that line up with those interests.

Computer programs must deal with all possible cases in their proscribed universes by establishing a coherent set of rules. Similarly, there are no leaks, no bugs, and no ambiguous or overlooked elements in the prescriptions of GTD. The model gives you the formula about what to do with anything and everything you might encounter in daily life—how to accept, evaluate, integrate, organize, and reassess it accordingly. One techie convert to GTD explained to me, "David, you've just laid out all the subroutines that need to be run on whatever shows up in your universe."

Many in the technology world are also eager early adopters. Because GTD represents a new approach to some of the long-standing issues of time management and organization, along with a promise for something most people have never given themselves permission to try to achieve—stress-free productivity—it does require openness and a bit of adventurousness to accept its precepts.

GTD is also system-independent, which means that almost any kind of personal organizing structure or software can be used to implement its principles. Because what I teach is actually not a system but a systematic *approach,* it can be adapted to take advantage of many of the features of software applications that have seldom been used before. Thousands of users of popular enterprise desktop software, such as Microsoft Outlook and Lotus Notes, have rarely had good enough reason to utilize their Task or To-Do functions. But once they see how those features can be configured for GTD, they discover and access a new power in this software. GTD has also established a platform of thinking and organizing that has given rise to literally hundreds of homegrown software applications that have been developed by the techies who wanted to create their own customized spin on it.

WHY OTHER SYSTEMS AND MODELS HAVE FAILED

Perhaps the main reason the world is discovering that GTD works is that it's the first model that has *really* worked: nothing else designed to address the same problems seems to have come close to being as functional. The majority of previous solutions were either inappropriately simplistic, incomplete, or unnatural—or some combination of these.

What people usually mean when they want to "get organized" is that they need to get *control* of their physical and psychic environments. That realistically can't be achieved with one simple activity. You must first capture and then clarify everything that is potentially unclear and out of place in your world before you can organize it appropriately; even after you've done that, you must also have a regular review process. GTD is the first popular system that has coached people to start with a current-reality objective inventory of everything on their mind, before making any value judgments about it.

In a similar vein, other systems have neglected to incorporate all the components that are critical for gaining control and perspective. If a model focused on priorities, it usually didn't deal with effective ways to get the lower-priority issues out of the way as efficiently as possible, without neglecting any commitments. And even if it did champion the value of setting goals, it typically didn't delineate how many different kinds and levels of goals there are with which we operate, each of which requires very different kinds of structures to keep in place.

Overall, every model or system I've researched likewise seems to assume that you can start from scratch with a current, accurate, and total perspective; create commitments and structures based on intelligent and rational thinking from a current, accurate, and total perspective; and maintain a stability and coherence in your implementation of everything that can hold your focus and your actions pristinely to those preconceived goals and plans. Good luck. Ever met anyone who had a life that stable and simple?

Real experience is a lot messier than that. We engage with our world, we have some sense of what's important to us internally, at many different levels, and we try to stay in control and keep our focus as best we can. Not only are we constantly surprised by unexpected input and experience on the outside, we're constantly growing and changing our own perspectives. If you try to overformulate some model of focus and organization that doesn't take that flux into account and give you a way to improve your navigation within it, it won't stick. GTD sticks.

GOOD DESIGN = ELIMINATION OF DRAG

Perhaps the best way to understand why GTD works so effectively is to think, design-wise, about the elimination of drag.

For many years I wondered why it is that the people who need GTD the least are those who are the most interested in it and are inspired to use it. The individuals who hire our coaches to work with them on improving work flow are usually not at the lower rungs of performance; they are more typically already the top producers, most effective leaders, and most efficient people. Why? It is this group that is characteristically most aware of the negative consequences of system hindrance and drag.

If someone is already in his comfort zone and not interested in achieving results more smoothly and expansively, he probably won't be sensitized to any potential performance enhancements, or even deem them necessary or valuable. The popularity of GTD to a large extent has been due to the hunger in the expanding cadres of upper-level performers, in life and work, for a system that really works to reduce friction and increase flow. GTD provides sufficient structure to contain the complexity, although with an organic kind of flexibility that can maintain stability amid an infinite variety of forms of growth, change, and surprise.

The Principles Are Simple and Easily Implemented

You don't have to buy any special product or learn any new skills to begin to "do GTD" instantly. Virtually everything in the process involves familiar behaviors that are both simple and rooted in basic common sense. The only specific requirements are something to write with, a mind that works sufficiently, and a place that can hold the lists you create.

A key reason for the continuing growth of GTD is that its techniques are based on fundamental, universal human principles—not more variable cultural, professional, or psychological differentiations. In the many years I and my staff have been involved in working with this material, we have yet to find any particular category of people that gains more value than any other from an understanding and implementation of GTD. We have applied it with children, CEOs of major corporations, artists, project managers, shop-floor workers, families, students, clergy, and retirees. We have trained Fortune 50 corporations, global not-for-profits, high-tech start-ups, mom-and-pop businesses, and government agencies. We have introduced GTD methods into every type of industry—financial services, utilities, health care, energy, transportation, aerospace, consumer products, technology, and education. We find equal receptivity in Germany, Saudi Arabia, Estonia, Puerto Rico, Canada, and Brazil. And we have found no prevalence in the acceptance of the techniques by personality type, learning style, or sex.

The Problem and Perceived Need Are Growing

If GTD solved a problem that was unique and restricted to a very small population, its popularity would have been limited. Likewise, if it addressed an issue that wasn't especially critical, in the grand scheme of human endeavor, one wouldn't expect it to be widely adopted. The fact is, huge numbers of people are increasingly experiencing greater amounts of stress, a sense of loss of control, and an inability to focus sufficiently. In response to that situation, a recognition of the need for regaining our equilibrium is growing worldwide.

Ultimately what we desire is more freedom, not more work. At the same time we want to be capable of dealing with surprise, which is occurring more frequently than ever before. What we have, in short, is a desperate need to learn how to manage—not information but rather what things mean and how they all relate to each other.

A SURPLUS OF SURPRISE

I've often been asked, "What is it that's new, David, in the world of technology, communication, and information that's causing so much stress?" My answer is pretty simple—"Nothing's new except how frequently everything *is* new."

Change always produces some form of stress, for our entire world is designed to maintain stasis. When something new happens that must be integrated into the existing system and set of data, something else has to give way to make room for it. It's ironic that even the most positive changes often create significant pressures and pains. They require the recalibration of relationships and self-images, and force the upheaval of familiar structures and patterns.

While that's always been true, what's different in today's world is that in the last three days you have probably received more change-producing, project-creating, and priority-shifting input than your parents received in a month . . . and for some of them, in a year. Such upheavals happened relatively so seldom in their world, they just tolerated the stress. You are living in a near-constant state of it, as your adoption of new technology has permitted all kinds of things to be landing in your e-mail and your voice mail, any one of which could undermine what you think your priorities should be.

Whether you are relating to that stream of new inputs as good or bad has a lot to do with your confidence that you can deal with it in a positive, sustainable way, without it simply overwhelming you and your systems, and that you can integrate what it means to you as you recalibrate all of your commitments on the fly. If, on the other hand, you are not up to that task, you'll feel like you're drowning in a sea of confusion and shifting commitments of focus.

NOT INFORMATION, BUT POTENTIAL-MEANING OVERLOAD

Most popular self-help regimens have sought to address two issues that are in fact subtle phantoms: time management and information management. Their solutions have typically involved introducing appropriate design into a given system, the use of a calendar (and a watch), and the adoption of speed, space, sorting, and selecting tools and technology.

Neither of these is actually the cause of our stress, however. You can't really manage time; time just is. What you *can* manage is yourself—

your focus and your actions. Time is what creates the awareness of constraint, which then forces the real issue, which involves where and when you allocate your resources. When you are fully and optimally self-managed, time actually disappears. You're just engaged. There's no sense of lack, conflict, or imbalance in your experience.

The real issue that needs to be addressed, rather, is potential meaning overload. Nature, one of the most complex environments we can experience, is actually relaxing to us, because our minds love infinite complexity and variation. But the data of nature are fundamentally self-evident: the meaning of the sight and sounds of bears, bees, and berries, once you've had a little experience with them, are obvious. A piece of datum like an e-mail, however, is a lot more obtuse, as it involves opening it, reading it, interpreting and evaluating it, and integrating all these subtle inputs and variables into a coherent whole. You are, in effect, confronting daily a hundred or more different *potential* bears, bees, or berries.

Your success in dealing with such stress will lie in your ability to apply effective thinking techniques to each item, quickly, and to develop a way to then move the contents into appropriate buckets. That's what GTD teaches and why it works uniquely in the heat of the current-day realities.

GETTING THINGS DONE IS A LEARNABLE PROCESS, NOT AN INBORN TRAIT

Another factor in the spread of GTD has been the increasing demand for productivity, pure and simple. The world is expecting more and more that people will have an ability to make things happen—to get things done. While inspiration and innovation are crucial, if a company or individual cannot execute the plan, the goal, the vision, all the best ideas and strategies are useless.

But can you really train someone to get things done? Can a definable set of behaviors increase that facility? Popular belief still holds that certain people are by nature more productive, while others just aren't born that way. A similar preconception used to be applied to salespeople, until one day someone woke up and realized that there was a characteristic, identifiable *sales process*. Some individuals understood it more intuitively and spontaneously than others, but it actually involved a particular set of procedures that could be taught, learned, and implemented.

A comparable phenomenon has taken place in the area of creativity and innovation. People were once thought to be either wired to be creative and innovative, or not. Wrong. There actually is an *innovation process*. If someone follows the appropriate prescription of behaviors, he or she will experience an enhanced output of creative and innovative ideas and solutions.

Not surprisingly, there is an analogous process for getting things done—a process that GTD defined. The growing recognition that the process can be learned, shared, and implemented, by both individuals and cultures, has triggered a response that has begun to reverberate around the world.

It Matches Something Fundamental and Intuitive

The final reason that I have identified for the growing recognition of GTD is one that I doubt I can explain in nice, concise terms, for it involves the more subtle arenas of psychology, aesthetics, and spirituality. I don't claim to have any significant expertise in any of these fields, but there is an aspect of GTD and its expression that seems to resonate with something deeper and more meaningful than simply the specifics of the topics and contents with which it coaches people to work. I will be bold enough to suggest that GTD approaches the world in much the same way that art, psychology, and spirituality have: as a framework to understand and experience new levels and depths of truth and reality.

We typically don't interact with our world in a preconceived, linear, logical, top-down manner. We certainly are capable of doing that kind of thinking and analyzing, but we are usually forced to confront a somewhat different reality, one in which things happen that don't fit into clear and rational categories.

We do seem, in a very broad sense, to have a drive, an impulse, something very basic that motivates and guides us, from the inside out. But for most people, most of the time, that drive does not offer a very conscious and objective plan. If you review your life, you may discover that you indeed have had some sort of direction all along, but it probably wasn't clear-cut and obvious as you were moving down the path.

What was true, certainly, is that you were engaged in a constant stream of *experiences*—a vast majority of which were unplanned and unexpected. But you quickly made meaning out of those experiences, that is, you created a relationship to their content. Somehow all along there was a connection between your own internal blueprint and what you encountered in the world.

Assuming that we seek improvements in how we do what we do, then choosing tools and techniques that start with, incorporate, and support this vision of our lives makes for the most productive course of action. GTD deals equally with an incorporation of all the inputs from external sources, and a sensitivity to and recognition of any and all internal directions and impulses. And it doesn't demand that you have any of it figured out when you begin. We relate with our world by accepting, clarifying, sorting, reflecting, and engaging; GTD simply recognizes that underlying formula for the human experience, makes it more conscious, and allows you to leverage that awareness in increasingly dynamic ways.

ABOUT UNCOVERING WHAT'S ALREADY THERE

GTD has never promoted committing to something new and grand, or getting passionately involved in your life. The process simply asks that you identify what's already true for you. We all have enough to do—we've all committed to way more than fifteen of us could possibly finish or fulfill. The assumptions of this model are that you're already endowed with all the creativity, motivation, inspiration, and intelligence that you'll ever need. You simply need to sharpen your ability to recognize what exists, at deeper and more expanded levels, eliminate whatever obstacles prevent their fullest expression, and supply yourself with the tools to be able to capture, form, and express your gifts more fully in the world. GTD has universal appeal because there is no agenda it tries to promote, other than providing the best and easiest ways to return a sense of control and perspective to your life, in case you've slipped behind in either of them.

IT HAS A KIND OF STYLE . . .

GTD has a certain sophistication in providing a context that always seems to give you a map that can reveal what lies ahead of wherever you are. Again, remember that it is not a system, but a systematic approach. Systems will always have a limited life span because, as form follows function, the desired results will continually change, in quality and quantity, and the systems to achieve them must accordingly be undone and redone. An *approach,* however, if it is the right one, will be adaptable and flexible over time, able to support new and expanded content. The GTD model is unique in granting equal weight to everything you might encounter in life. Everything, and nothing, is sacred. Your life purpose? Fine. Need cat food? Great. If it has your attention, it contains gold to be mined. If it doesn't, don't waste your energy thinking about it.

GTD is also notable for its subtlety because, as simple as it is, it often touches into very delicate areas of your involvements and interests. Problems that involve some of your deeper emotions and elusive issues occasionally grab your attention and create distraction, and GTD provides an anchor for developing and grounding your own thinking and awareness about them. If, for instance, you are bold enough to "collect" an issue like "dad and hospice?" in your in-basket, mature enough to decide an outcome, and forthright enough to choose a next action to take toward that outcome, you will have applied GTD successfully and probably accessed levels in your consciousness that are almost unfathomable in their sensitivity and complexity.

So What, Really, Is GTD?

For those who may be unfamiliar with GTD, and as a comprehensive overview for those who have some experience with it already, it might be useful here to describe some of GTD's key principles.

Because so many individuals and even entire companies (particularly in the software arena) have, in the last few years, attributed a GTD influence in their products, services, and value propositions, in 2006 I wrote up a document for our Web site to describe, as best I could, what this methodology is about.

Sophisticated without being confining, the subtle effectiveness of GTD lies in its radically commonsense notion that with a complete and current inventory of all your commitments, organized and reviewed in a systematic way, you can focus clearly, view your world from optimal angles, and make trusted choices about what to do (and not do) at any moment. GTD embodies an easy, step-by-step, and highly efficient method for achieving this relaxed, productive state. It includes:

Capturing anything and everything that has your attention

Defining actionable things discretely into outcomes and concrete next steps

Organizing reminders and information in the most streamlined way, in appropriate categories, based on how and when you need to access them

Keeping current and "on your game" with appropriately frequent reviews of the six horizons of your commitments (purpose, vision, goals, areas of focus, projects, and actions)

Implementing GTD alleviates being overwhelmed, instills confidence, and releases a flood of creative energy. It provides structure without constraint, managing details with maximum flexibility. The system rigorously adheres to the core principles of productivity, while allowing tremendous freedom in the "how." The only "right" way to do GTD is getting meaningful things done with truly the least amount of invested attention and energy. Coaching thousands of people, where they work, about their work, has informed the GTD method with the best practices of how to work (and live), in that most efficient and productive way.

GTD's simplicity, flexibility, and immediacy are its attraction. Its ability to enliven, enlighten, and empower is its magic. What, indeed, is GTD? More than meets the eye . . .

GTD is no more or less complex than this; anything added or subtracted from it is probably off-purpose to what this whole methodology is about.

The Three GTD Models

The overarching approach that I describe above and that eventually became known as GTD is simply a compilation and coordination of three models that I recognized and synthesized over many years of consulting with and coaching a wide range of individuals and groups. I didn't encounter these formulas in a book or learn them in a traditional classroom (though they can and are now being communicated that way), but for the most part I discovered and tested them in very immediate, day-to-day situations with people who needed more clarity, direction, and forward motion.

These processes developed for me over the course of time as the most effective ways to understand and manage work flow, projects, and priorities. They also matured with me to some degree in that particular order, which I think is relevant because it is in that continuum—work flow, projects (situational management), and priorities—that they are most effectively understood and implemented.

What follows is a brief description of the three models; much of the remainder of this book will consider how and why these work, and how to work them, in detail.

MASTERING WORK FLOW

The Mastering Work Flow model consists of five stages:*

> Collect
> Process
> Organize
> Review
> Do

Basically this technique developed as the most effective way to gather, think about, organize, and manage the inventory of all the "stuff" that we feel we should, want, or need to do something about in our daily lives. It involves capturing all the raw input, making appropriate decisions about each item, organizing the results into appropriate categories, assessing the parts and the totality of the system as needed, and making trusted choices about what to do with it. This component, which reflects what I call the "horizontal" part of self-management, is the one most commonly associated with GTD because it is the most easily applied and is immediately productive. One element of this Work Flow model, which provides a set of recommended techniques for using lists to organize reminders, became the basis and key ingredient for scores of GTD software applications and blogs.

NATURAL PLANNING

One topic that the Work Flow model acknowledged but did not address was project planning and management. "Processing" what you "collect" (in e-mail, in-baskets, meeting notes, etc.) requires identifying projects as they emerge and deciding the very next actions required

---

* A more detailed outline is available in Appendix iv.

to move forward on them. For the majority of your commitments, that's sufficient to achieve a sense of control. However, there are many situations and desired outcomes that need thinking through in more detail, like your wedding, your new Web site, your book, and even your next vacation. For planning and executing those more complex projects, I formulated a straightforward and highly effective five-phase model.

In my early days of management consulting, "project planning" was always at least a peripheral interest for everyone who thought of himself as having projects they needed to oversee. (Actually anyone who is engaged in activities that require more than a single step is managing a project by my definition, but most people still don't think of projects as broadly as I do.) A common question I heard from this group was, "What's the best project-planning model, or software?" It seemed that everything available in that area was either too simplistic or too complex. In my rather elemental fashion, I accordingly began to notice how we all actually plan almost everything we do, naturally.

It was another one of those instances in which we think about things to get them done, and a majority of the time do so rather effectively, but we're not very conscious about precisely how we accomplish that. Merely leaving a room, going out to dinner, or planting a spring garden requires planning; it would be hard to get through a day without planning a course of action.

Our mind naturally advances through a five-stage process to take an intention into reality, no matter how large or small the event:[*]

Purpose and principles
Vision
Brainstorming
Organizing
Next actions

---

[*] See Appendices ii and iii.

We develop an intention, or purpose, and our thinking and behaviors toward it are shaped by our values. We next create a vision about what that purpose, fulfilled, would be like. Then, to relieve the pressure that the still-unreal vision creates vis-à-vis current reality, we automatically start generating potentially relevant ideas about how to achieve it (brainstorming). We'll then sort those ideas into components, sequences, and priorities (organizing), which then gives us a focus for what to actually do (next actions) to start to make them happen.

This Planning model (described in more detail in chapter 3 of *Getting Things Done*), though natural, is not standard procedure in more formalized or complex settings. The natural approach, though, can and has been used as a way to ensure appropriate focus, with the least amount of wasted energy and effort. It supplies the "vertical" dimension of thinking required for projects, situations, topics, and themes.

These work flow and planning processes, when actually implemented in real situations, fostered an amazing amount of improvement in any environment in which I introduced them. There remained, however, one more dynamic that needed to be addressed—setting priorities.

HORIZONS OF FOCUS

That one should think strategically and tactically about what to choose to do, at any point in time, has simply been a given to me—especially after many years of experience as a management consultant. "Management" by definition is the allocation of limited resources, which requires making good choices—in other words, prioritizing. But the way most of the time management and even strategic consulting models portrayed the prioritizing process seemed inappropriate or at least insufficiently developed to account for all the factors that truly influence the actions we take.

Much as I formulated the Planning model, I started from the basic premise that we naturally establish priorities and thus we might be able to learn from what we actually do as a matter of course. I identified the six Horizons of Focus and their usefulness by closely examining the factors that truly influence the choices we make.

Their development was triggered somewhat by chance. I had been asked to coach a senior Wall Street executive whose major presenting issue was "too many meetings." His assistant was being run ragged attempting to fend off people who wanted a spot on this guy's calendar, which was booked solid for months.

When I walked into his office, he closed the door and almost pleaded, "What on earth do I do about this schedule?" Having no prior clue about how to begin to address that situation with him, I decided to frame the question back to him in such a way that we could get perspective. I walked up to a whiteboard he had on the wall, and wrote a version of:

- Purpose and principles
- Vision
- Goals
- Areas of responsibility
- Projects
- Actions

I knew that each one of those levels had content that could have an impact on the conversation about too many meetings. Of course, no sooner had I completed the list than he turned to me and said, "Got it!"

"Got what?" I asked.

"It's not about meetings. It's about my kids!"

As it happened, he had allowed himself to be committed to all those meetings out of a belief that it would serve him politically to be seen to be working so hard. But in a flash he realized that he was missing quality time with his teenage sons because of it, and it just wasn't worth the price.

Now, this kind of realization was not unique, nor was the coaching that triggered it. I had merely found a rather simple way to frame perspective, in terms of our commitments to ourselves that, when used as a thinking and focusing tool, worked quickly and effectively.

Again, none of this is rocket science (unless you're a rocket scientist). We typically operate on all six of these levels, with various commitments pertaining to each one, even though for the most part, and for most people, they are only partially conscious. We have purposes and values. We are all moving ourselves toward visions (positive or negative). We have bigger things that we want to accomplish, to make the visions happen. We need to maintain several key areas of our work and our life at certain standards to enable us to achieve all of that. We all have projects that need to be finished to fulfill our agreements with ourselves on these various levels. And we all take actions based on some commitment on one or more of the five Horizons of Focus above it.

And the more direct the relationship between our actions and the most elevated horizon, the more it would be a priority—at least in substance. In other words, the more you know that the action you are taking is the best thing to be doing to fulfill your purpose, the higher its value to you will be.

Now, as I explained in *Getting Things Done* and will revisit in upcoming discussions about prioritizing, the Horizons of Focus are not the only factors you will consider when you decide to do what you do at 3:15 P.M. tomorrow afternoon: you will also take into account such practical matters as time, energy, and location. But this six-level framework nevertheless provides a solid and practical tool for thinking through your situation in a much more comprehensive and coherent way than a simple, monothematic "Set priorities" admonition.*

HOW THESE MODELS HAVE COME TOGETHER

In recent years I have realized that everything I have uncovered and taught touches on some aspect of increasing *control* and *perspective*—no matter where, with whom, or under what circumstances. I have reduced the GTD practices to those two dynamics, which is a more functional way to understand and work with what I had initially

---

* A condensed outline of the Horizons of Focus is included in Appendix vii.

called "horizontal" and "vertical." People can't relate to "out of horizontal" nearly as easily as they can to "out of control," and "I've lost perspective" is a more familiar concept than "out of vertical."

The art of mastering work flow, by collecting, processing, organizing, reviewing, and doing, provides the component of control. The Natural Planning Model and the Horizons of Focus both supply perspective.

You may have already noticed the similarity of these latter two models. The horizons actually represent the Planning model applied to a total scenario, such as your life, a company, or an endeavor—a hierarchical way of thinking that clarifies and aligns focus in an optimum manner. Why are we doing what we're doing? What would the successful outcome be? What are the components needed to manage and complete in order to get us there? What are the next actions to take?

IT'S ALL ABOUT FOCUS

As may be evident already, GTD is primarily about focus—eliminating the things that distract it and giving you tools that facilitate your ability to direct that focus toward what you need, on the way you need it, and on when you need to do it. If you're out of control, it will be almost impossible to focus, other than on the immediate emergencies at hand. Therefore, a key component of the method involves techniques for gaining that control.

Similarly, if you've lost track of your commitments at all the various horizons on which you operate, regaining those perspectives will be critical to have the most appropriate focus. Hence the second prime area for mastery: creating the right reflective activities for reviewing and renewing what has your attention at multiple horizons.

All of this comes together in physical action: what you decide to do at any given point in time. Physical actions are the end result of the five stages of gaining control, as well as the final operational expression of all the levels of life and work in which you are engaged. No matter how conscious you are of these stages and levels, you are nonetheless taking action all the time. The trick is to ensure not so much that what you are doing is, for you, the right thing, all the time (how, ultimately, could you know that for sure?) but that you are firmly in the driver's seat with a functioning process for discovering and engaging with your best choice.

GTD: The Mental Foundation

Interest has surfaced in the last few years in the concept of "emotional intelligence," which gave intellectual validity to the commonsense notion that the ability to monitor and manage feelings has a direct correlation to personal effectiveness and professional results. As communication, teamwork, collaboration, and well-managed relationships have become increasingly important factors in organizational life, this focus on the emotion component has been beneficial.

I will assert, however, that another kind of validation is in order, and actually way overdue—that of mental intelligence! We need to fully understand, manage, and enhance our thinking process. It's not that people don't have the capability to think; they just don't do so, or they don't think as effectively as they could, because their mental plumbing is clogged. If you refuse to think in an effective way about even an e-mail you've received or your notes from a phone call, it will have as negative an impact on your effectiveness as would over- or underreacting emotionally.

My experience, in fact, is that control of your thinking process will have *more* weight in such situations. How we feel certainly will affect how we think, but the opposite case is more often true. Defining "thinking" in its broadest sense to include any kind of focus and imagery held in the mind, in addition to the cognitive process of logic and rational judgment, means that your feelings will typically be more driven by the thoughts you hold than the other way around.

YOUR MIND DOESN'T HAVE ONE
It seems that the majority of people are for the most part letting their minds run the show in their heads. I'm making a distinction here

between thinking and the mind, of course, and I don't want to wade too far into philosophical or psychological deep water. But in my experience, thinking is what happens when intelligence marries intentions—I'm *using* my mind, as well as other intuitive resources, to make distinctions and decisions about and toward something. If you have ever *changed* your mind, there is obviously some part of you that transcends it and is capable of creative and consciously focused thinking. The mind is a great servant, but a terrible master.

Your mind will remind you of all kinds of things when you can do nothing about them, and merely thinking about your concerns does not at all equate to making any progress on them. More often than not, it seems that people are *having* thoughts, though not really *thinking* about what they're thinking about—at least not in an effective way that resolves, advances, or manages the content. But understanding how to work with this relatively reactive and mechanical part of our mental process holds a huge key to winning at this game.

WE'RE NOT BORN DOING THIS
None of us was born thinking, "What's true here? What are we trying to accomplish? What's the next action? Who's doing it?" If we had been, the propensity must have been programmed out of us from a very early age. I have met a few people who do tend to think and act that way as a matter of course—usually in isolated areas of their worlds. But even of that group, most don't seem to be very conscious of *how* they're implementing that thought process, nor do they transfer that behavior into other important aspects of their lives. A project manager in a software company may run great meetings and know how to keep a product launch on track, but he may be clueless about applying those techniques to his relationship with his mother or to his personal finances, though the same principles can and should be relevant.

When a senior executive who had run the highly respected executive development center for a major U.S. corporation ran across my material, he observed that I had "uncovered the heuristic" for the success his company valued in its culture but hadn't really known how to teach. It just modeled and expected those behaviors, such as not starting meetings without a clear objective, not allowing discussions to end without clarifying the next actions, who would be responsible for them, and so on. GTD simply made those practices conscious, understandable, and teachable as part of a coherent model.

These focusing questions are key to a productive engagement with our world—and are becoming more and more so as our realities and our commitments become ever more subtle and ambiguous in the increasingly complex lives we are leading. To make it all work, we need to think more about how we think and apply that awareness to much more of the content of our experience.

THE ATTENTION TO ATTENTION

How our minds focus attention and our abilities to manage that process have been the subject of much interest and research recently, but while the inability to focus appropriately can certainly reach severe levels, to a large degree most people I've met have some version of this condition. Though it is rarely intense enough to warrant professional help, it is prevalent in some form nonetheless.

This attention to the subject of attention has not surprisingly reached the world of organizational effectiveness. New technologies like e-mail, BlackBerrys, instant messaging, cell phones, and the like have brought to the fore the question of the potential costs of subclinical distractibility, and study after study has attempted to document the business downside to the lack of focus such phenomena foster. Their real economic costs are hard to measure, but inferences can be drawn from documented statistics about the decrease in average concentration time and increase in interruptions. Companies have consequently tried to institute such policies as "no-e-mail Fridays" and "quiet hours" not only to curb the inefficiencies that result from the psychic noise, but also to give sufficient breathing room for the reflective, creative process that some are savvy enough to recognize as strategically important for their knowledge workers.

Most of the studies of these issues and proposed remedies center on the external environment—too much e-mail, too many interruptions, too much or too little communication, too much change too fast, and so on. Solutions that focus only on decreasing the volume or speed of input will be temporary at best and artificially constricting and numbing at worst. We need to learn how to maneuver in the increasingly intermingled worlds of thinking and action, which will provide a lasting cure.

We're not born with the thinking process that we need to navigate our sophisticated world as it evolves along with our maturity. What we *are* all born with is a mind that wanders every chance it gets. And one of the places it wanders to most is the To-do lists of our life—at amazingly intricate levels of detail. While some of that wandering is healthy and useful, much of it is distracting and stress-producing, draining our energy and reducing our ability to stay focused, creative, and productive.

One of the great benefits of GTD is in providing guidance to discern the difference between creative thinking and ineffective concern, with the result that you can eliminate the negative aspect while opening the gates for greater access to the positive one and exploring what your mind is truly capable of. This process does not entail some esoteric scientific discipline or mystical epiphany (although people involved in both of those ends of the learning spectrum have latched on to GTD as something they could "finally" embrace). Understanding and fostering mental intelligence by putting the appropriate attention on what has your attention is as straightforward as cooking dinner. It happens when you do certain things, and it won't when you don't.

The Logic of GTD

Power is facilitated by access to clear space, a principle I experienced dramatically in martial arts training. Having a "mind like water"—an image taken from a karate metaphor used to describe a state of clarity and openness—has become a common theme associated with the GTD methods. Just as water responds perfectly and appropriately to whatever it interacts with, without stress, strain, or undue energy, when we are free of distraction we have a greater capacity to engage our world with the appropriate amount of energy, reaction, and investment. We are also able to detach cleanly from that engagement as soon as our focus needs to be directed elsewhere, and devote our full attention to the new task at hand. Flexibility and focus are the sources of power, and anything that diminishes either of those will hinder our productivity.

Interacting with your e-mails from your boss, processing the thought you just had, dealing with your kid's unusual silence, addressing the crisis in the department you just became aware of, are all situations that have an optimal response for you, depending on the countless factors that make up your universe at any given point in time. But if you focus too much on fruitless thoughts about them, rather than on the things you *do* need to think about to engage them effectively, you are not operating from a "mind like water," and they will demand more of your energy than they should. If you have ever taken thoughts and feelings from one meeting to the next, or brought home issues to work, or work problems home, it's neither productive nor fun. And frankly, if you have any thought more than once, in the same way about the same subject, you're probably involved in unnecessary work and exhausting your creative energy.

So, how does this whole thing work? What is the logic of this process?

Power = Concentration
Concentrated energy creates the most bang and has the biggest resulting impact. If you can't concentrate, it's impossible to maximize your effectiveness in any activity, whether it's playing the piano, breaking boards with your hands, trying to train your puppy, learning a language, or having an important conversation with your teenager.

Concentration = Elimination of Distraction
Have you ever had your focus derailed? What happened to your productivity?

Who distracts you more than anyone? I'm sure you've had days in which you were interrupted and put upon by hundreds of external events that diminished your ability to relax and get things done—loud noises, someone walking into your office unexpectedly, a crashing computer. But honestly, have you ever been in a quiet room, by yourself, and still gotten distracted? Sure. We can probably as easily let our own thoughts run down miscellaneous random pathways as have them knocked off course by others.

Distraction = Mismanaged Commitments

If you have found yourself wandering away from the content of this book while you were reading it, there's a good chance that where your focus went was to keep a commitment you have—something you feel you need or want to finish or handle. And there's also a good chance that whatever it is that yanked your chain has not been sufficiently managed. There are decisions unmade and/or reminders untracked about it. That's not intended as a negative judgment, but merely a description of what's true about the situation.

I'm not talking here about consciously directing your attention to something other than this book while it is in front of you. You may have decided to change your priorities for a moment, because something you read or saw reminded you of a trip you're taking soon to New York, and you decided to reflect on things you might want to do while you're in the city. Maybe you just want to shift your mental gears briefly and just let your mind wander and "graze" on whatever it wants to.

Genuinely disruptive distractions occur when your attention is *taken* by something, and usually something you'd rather not have to be thinking about at that particular moment. In truth, your mind somehow knows that the content of that distraction hasn't been appropriately managed yet, and it's simply trying to do that for you. Your "central processor" is working overtime with a program you have required it to run.

Your Mind Cannot Manage Commitments Well

In the previous section I stated that on its own the mind, as opposed to intelligent thinking, is not that bright. The problem is that it is severely limited in its ability to manage commitments. But, strangely, because it is such a good and devoted servant, when it realizes that the job is not being handled in a dependable way, it cannot let go of the job. Your commitments will be tracked and managed somewhere—and if they're not funneled into a system, they'll take root in your psyche.

But the psyche is truly handicapped in its ability to remember, to remind, and to automatically think and decide. If your mind had the capabilities that most people seem to believe it has, based on their trust of it instead of an external system, it would only remind you of things you needed to do, when you could actually do something about them.

For instance, right now, do you have at least one flashlight with dead batteries somewhere in your home? If so, where and when does your mind tend to remind you that you need new batteries? *When you encounter the dead ones, when the electricity goes out!* This is not smart. If your brain had any innate intelligence whatsoever, it would only bother you about batteries when you passed the right-sized live ones in a store! "Hey, guy, you need AAA batteries—right on the shelf there!" If your mind actually had a mind, you wouldn't need a system.

Since you woke up this morning, have you thought of anything you needed to do that you still haven't done? Have you had that thought more than once? Did the repeated thought lead to any more progress on the matter that was occupying you? Probably not. The net result is a total waste of time and a drain of your energy.

Your mind has limited space for this kind of recall. Studies have shown that short-term memory cannot handle even a dozen items before it loses track of and context for all of them. As you add more content for it to handle, it drops an equivalent amount off at the back end, in terms of conscious control.

The mind is also a terrible office. The most obvious priorities in your mental stacks tend to be whatever is latest (most recent input) and loudest (most emotionally charged content). There is a chance on a given afternoon that you will give as much mental real estate to "buy bread" as you will to "buy building." Probably more, because you're afraid of the consequences of forgetting to pick up the bread when you get home.

The part of our mind used for tracking commitments has no sense of past or future. That means that as soon as you begin to take account in your head of anything you need to do, some part of you keeps trying to be doing it all the time. Even a simple attempt to hold and manage two tasks creates some degree of internal stress and failure, because you can't do them both at the same time.

Until There's a Better System, the Mind Can't Let Go

In its normal operation your conscious mind lets go of everything but what you're focused on at the moment. The less-than-conscious part hangs on to everything that has not been recorded in some external system. You can fool others, but never your own head. It knows for certain whether or not you have written something down that you need to do, and whether you can be trusted to look at it at the right time. If either of those factors is missing, it will hang on tight. And unrecorded tasks have the tendency of bubbling to the surface at the strangest moments, such as when you're lying in bed at 1:00 A.M. *Oh, no . . . I've got to remember to tell Juanita I'm going to be in Singapore next week.*

The way most people seem to operate is by entrusting only their psyche to manage what's incomplete. But the mind then tries to keep all the agreements simultaneously, which is impossible. The result is the paradox that by continually attempting to relieve the stress of unfinished work, more stress is created.

So how do you break out of this cycle?

How to Relieve the Pressure of Broken Self-agreements

In order to relieve the pressure of broken self-agreements, you must know that:

- You have captured, clarified, and organized your commitments, at all horizons, and
- You will consciously engage with them as often as you need to.

Most of us are not distracted by the contents on our calendars. You're probably not feeling angst, for example, about where you're supposed to be at 10:00 A.M. a week from next Thursday. Why not? You trust your system. That assumes, of course, that you know you have all your calendar-specific reminders in there and that you have access to them and will review your calendar as often as you need, to ensure you'll see what you need to see, when you need to see it.

You haven't actually finished the appointments that are on your calendar, and may not particularly *like* what is facing you, but these future commitments are not creating a potential distraction of your focus right now. Similarly, you don't have to have completed any of them, nor even particularly find them attractive, to get them off your mind.

If you suddenly realized that you lost your calendar, what would happen then? All kinds of pressure would come to bear on your psyche, as it realized *it* now had the job of remembering and reminding, in lieu of your system. Executives who rely heavily on an assistant or secretary to be their system have the same sinking feeling when, unexpectedly, that person doesn't show up one day.

It's likely that you already have experienced the freedom in your mind from the risk of broken agreements, by virtue of the appropriate use of a trusted system, and the negative results that accrue if you don't have one. Is there any difference with respect to your agreements with yourself for all the other commitments in your life and work that are not calendared items? None at all.

It is possible to be as free from concern about virtually every one of your obligations, but it requires relying on the same elements that make your calendar work: you need to trust they're all in there, and that you'll pay attention to them when you should.

So why has almost everyone done the calendar thing, but almost no one has moved everything else in their life into a similar zone, by capturing it all and creating the habit of assessing it all appropriately?

Three reasons:

First, the data that is entered onto a calendar has already been thought through and determined; it's been translated down to the physical action level. You agreed to call Jim at noon on Monday: there is no more thinking required about what the appropriate action is, or where and when you're going to do it. Second, you know *where* those kinds of actions need to be parked (calendar), and it's a familiar and available tool. And third, if you lose track of calendar actions and commitments, you will encounter obvious and rapid negative feedback from people you consider important. If you make appointments with yourself and don't keep them, it's one thing; but if you neglect to pick up your kids, meet a prospective client, or show up at a meeting with your boss, you'll probably become aware of the oversight soon and feel some pain.

For the vast majority of the rest of the commitments people have, however, it's easy for one if not all of those three factors to be absent. The data to track is not clear; there is no familiar or standard system yet to track it; and the feedback from something slipping through the cracks is often not immediately obvious and painful. You know that summer's coming up and your kids' activities for those months are going to need to be planned, but you likely haven't yet framed that as a "project" to finish, nor have you decided what, specifically, you need to do next about setting it all up. If you decided that you needed to brainstorm with your spouse about some ideas for the family, you're probably not sure where to put that reminder. And, if you don't do that brainstorming, there's no instant negative result.

If all the "stuff" that grabs our attention came in neat packages, with the outcomes and actions already clear (no more thinking required), if we had set up and were implementing an obvious and easily usable tool to track and review them, and if we winced in emotional pain every time the slightest thing slipped through a crack in the system, then "mind like water" would be a lot more the rule than the exception.

When I get a chance to show people my own personal system, with the various lists of projects, actions, waiting-for's, and someday/maybe's, along with lists of my job responsibilities, goals, visions, and values, they often have a visceral reaction: they freak out. "You've got so many *lists*!" (and they're not saying that in a way that means they think it's a good thing). So one response I have is, "Okay, give me your calendar, let's just toss it." Most wouldn't think of doing that. To me, that's intellectual dishonesty. If one list works to facilitate a small portion of stress-free productivity, why not have as many as you need to cover all the bases?

Finish Your Thinking

The major component that has been missing to make this game playable across the entire spectrum of your life, however, is the training to finish your thinking. Calendars hold the result of completed mental work—they are the product of decisions about physical actions. They might not represent the best thinking (maybe you've scheduled the wrong meeting to discuss the wrong stuff), but within their own little sphere, they leave nothing else to be determined or decided.

Unless scheduling an appointment, though, most of the commitments people have still need decisions to be made about them. Mom's elder care, the upcoming vacation, the personal budget, the offer of a potential alliance, the problem with a key staff person—these have not yet advanced to the "runway" with real, physical, visible actions defined for them.

The problem with this kind of "stuff" is that when it pops into your mind, it may seem potentially so amorphous, complex, or ambiguous that you stop thinking about it right there. You're afraid that there's too much to consider, and you don't have the time or energy to do so at the moment. What most people don't realize is that you don't need to understand, solve, or completely plan these things to get them out of your head. "Finish your thinking" simply means to decide what the next physical thing to do is to move them forward from where they are. This is a prime example of not putting the appropriate attention on what has your attention. *You need to think about your stuff more than you think, but not as much as you're afraid you might.*

Once you have simply decided the very next actions to be taken on any and every thing on your mind, and parked reminders where you need them, then you're free to cut loose and just follow your own directions. And in my experience, 95 percent of the time, when I have the time and energy to *do,* I don't have the time and energy to *think* about what to do—that needs to *already be done.* If you happen to notice you're driving by a hardware store, you can't in that moment think through every home project you have that requires something at that location. You might have the time and energy to get the five items you need, but not to figure out what they are. If you have insufficiently decided what you need and where, you probably have major gaps in your ability to get things done.

That kind of unfinished use of your intelligence is one of the great hindrances to being able to see clearly and navigate the often murky and turbulent waters of life and work.

Perspective Is Your Most Valuable Asset

How you view the business of your life and the game of your work is the ultimate key to winning at them. You can be in what may appear to be the most dire straits and still be in confident control if you have the right perspective. And you can be living what seems to be the ideal, abundant life and still want to take your own life, with the inappropriate viewpoint. Perspective is key, but it is a very slippery commodity. It can be lost in an instant.

GTD principles and methods are designed to maximize your ability to maintain perspective and get it back when you lose it. We all need to manage the forest while we hug the trees. But it takes dependence on a concrete process about some often un-concrete "stuff" to disentangle our psyche from all the things that can get wrapped up around it from just three e-mails and two phone calls in twenty minutes. Since perspective is the most important mental framework you can develop, tools and techniques that support it are invaluable.

The Need for an Extended Mind

Recent research in the field of psychology has begun to establish a context within which the development of a system for capturing, clarifying, and appropriately organizing what has our attention is more valid, and even more necessary. Our mind can do certain kinds of things, in a highly creative way, that still surpass anything the most powerful computer can do. Its ability to integrate an almost infinite set of variables in any situation is uncanny. Give it a problem or a project on which to focus, and the amount of complexity it can absorb and creativity it can produce are extraordinary. Give it two problems to think about simultaneously, and it seems to blow a fuse.

If we can keep our focus to a single task, we're cool. The problem arises when there are not clear and clean edges between two or more problems we are trying to think about. It seems that when we make any commitment with ourselves at any level—small, big, personal, professional, sophisticated, mundane—that we don't complete in the moment, that "open loop" is tracked in our psyche, and some part of us is continually trying to move on it. It's as if we've hooked a fish that keeps pulling on the line until we reel it in or cut it loose. Instead of our thinking being free and targeted toward one object, it is trying to accommodate dozens if not hundreds of things simultaneously. We're operating in a continually short-circuited modality.

To manage this complexity you must have and use placeholders for your thinking, much as you probably already do with your calendar. Most people keep calendars in some system and not in their head. If they know that the calendar has all the data that represent meetings and appointments, and they trust they'll be looking at it when they need to, they're not walking around with their mind constantly wondering where they need to be when. When they do look at their calendar, their mind is free to be thinking creatively about what is needed relative to the appointments, in terms of logistics and the nature of the appointed activity itself. Reviewing the day or week can also then support creative thinking about an infinite number of associated things, drawn from a larger context. If you scanned your own calendar at this moment—both backward and forward in time—I will bet you will have thoughts triggered by that review that you wouldn't have had otherwise, especially if your main concern was just trying to maintain the accurate and complete memory of what time-based agreements you have.

The calendar is perhaps the most obvious demonstration of a self-developed system for extending the mind, but there are lots of other examples in which the world has allowed our thinking to relax—trusting that signs on the freeway will tell us where to get off, that our clocks and watches will tell us accurately what time it is, that the gauges on our car's dashboard will let us know when to get gas and if there is a mechanical problem. The key principle underlying all such systems is in play, accepted and assumed all around us.

The inventory of noncalendar items, though, that potentially have, and should have, your attention, is exponentially larger than the contents of your calendar, and the contents for the most part are not nearly as clear and specific as appointments or an indication that you need gas in your car. But the fundamental principle governing all of them still holds true—if you can decide what, specifically, something means to you and what you intend to do about it, if anything; if you can use a placeholder as a reminder of what you need to attend to; and if you can trust that you have the habit to engage with the system appropriately; there is no reason for any outstanding commitments to plague your consciousness.

Your insecurity about your personal finances or the problems that have emerged with your mother's health and living situation can certainly be more daunting to deal with, initially, than "Pick up Josie at 2:15 on Monday" or "US 101–2.0 mi." But if you face them armed with the appropriate set of techniques, they can be equally put to rest in your psyche.

That, of course, is easier said than done. Few people need lessons in how to make appointments and use a calendar, or how to read signs on a freeway. But people don't seem to be able to automatically figure out how to handle the many more ambiguous and complex data we must deal with in an efficient and effective fashion. That's why models for achieving control and perspective, as commonsense as they may seem on first encounter, need to be understood and practiced; and why, in a world of change-producing inputs growing in complexity, speed, and volume, GTD has created such a stir.

3 | Making It All Work—the Process

For a long time it had seemed to me that life was about to begin. . . .
But there was always some obstacle in the way, something to be gotten
through first, some unfinished business, time still to be served, a debt to
be paid. Then life would begin. At last it dawned on me that these
obstacles were my life.

—Alfred Souza

Chaos isn't the problem; how long it takes to find coherence is the real
game.

—Doc Childre and Bruce Crier

From time to time you will experience yourself either feeling out of
control or lacking direction—or both. If you didn't, you'd probably
be stale.

This could be true on a larger life scale, such as how you are experiencing your career, or, at a more mundane level, such as being disorganized in preparing a dinner for friends. This can (and will) happen
in and with your project in the garage, your family, your team, your
job, your company, your school committee, your life. Whatever the

impetus, you will realize you are somehow and to some degree "off"—and you need to get back "on."

But how do you get clarity, right now, about what you're doing? How do you get things unstuck and moving forward? How do you ensure that you're taking the steps that will lead forward?

Making It All Work is about how to get those answers—how to move, in the myriad situations in which you find yourself, from being at the mercy of the tempest to guiding your ship back on an even keel. It won't give you the specific answers, but it will give you a step-by-step guide to discovering them on your own.

The switch from being "off" to being "on" can occur in a few seconds or over a period of a few years, but the process to achieve that clarity and control will be the same. It does not happen at the whim of the fates, though it often seems that way. It is the result of an identifiable, understandable, and functional set of actions, primarily concerned with how we focus our consciousness about certain things in certain ways. Understanding and applying these relevant principles and procedures are the core lesson of this book.

The symptoms of lack of control and perspective show up in the range of experiences and conditions that at the very least could be called "suboptimal" in terms of self-management. The vast majority of people with whom I have interacted within the last two decades, when asked why they have been attracted to or interested in my work on productivity, have expressed a very similar set of goals:

- Reduction of stress
- Cessation of procrastination
- More balance
- More energy, vitality, motivation
- Fulfillment of more potential
- Greater focus
- Better project, time, and people management
- More access and expression of creativity
- More freedom

These personal aspirations and improvement opportunities also have organizational equivalents, where much of this material has been tested and honed. Those involved in evaluating their own companies and cultures often define their corporate aims in these similar terms:

- More productive individuals, teams, cultures
- Better communications
- Reduced stress
- Improved work/life balance
- Improved execution
- Aligned focus
- Clearer priorities
- Effective time management
- Innovation and creativity

In the simplest terms, there are only two things you or your team or company needs to do to achieve positive and productive engagement with the commitments you face and to achieve all of the desired results above: get organized and get focused. And doing those in either order is fine—you can get things together and then decide what's important, or set your priorities and get organized toward that. This dual process—getting things under control and appropriately focused—is equally functional for your life and for a task as straightforward as cooking dinner.

Still, reaching and maintaining that balance is a lot easier said than done. How, exactly, do you get organized? And how, exactly, do you determine your priorities? The complexities of our multilayered life and work and the speed with which new events and input are occurring have far outpaced our abilities to find balance by following such an elementary formula. The simple has become too simplistic and therefore ultimately dysfunctional.

In truth the concept of needing to "get organized" should be reconceived to "get control," for which getting organized is only a part of the solution—and not the first one, at that. Likewise, "set priorities" needs to be amplified to "clarify our objectives at the appropriate horizon," which will entail much more thought than simply formulating a strategic plan.

A number of immensely complex systems and tools have in fact emerged to provide relief and clarity across a broad learning and development spectrum, including time management, personal organizing, and management consulting. Because most of these proffered solutions were suited only to limited kinds of circumstances, however, or were simply too cumbersome to accommodate rapidly shifting realities for most people, few of those models and tools have had a very long shelf life.

Often, too, such models addressed only part of the situation—they offered either ways to get control or to achieve perspective, but not both. As it happens, these two aspects require different procedures, but one without the other won't stand up to reality. Control without perspective is micromanagement, and perspective without control is crazy-making.

The Core Process

There is a middle way. It's not a one-shot silver bullet, but rather a set of behaviors—mainly a sequential way of focusing thinking—that works. Wonderfully. Every time. Without fail. It's simple, but not superficial. It can be learned and practiced by children, yet can catalyze and contain infinite sophistication and complexity for the most senior executive in a global corporation.

Over many years of working with this kind of material, I've been driven to find the simplest formulas that would work universally—no matter what the context. *Making It All Work* is the result of that research and focus. As far as I can tell, the method can't get any simpler than what you will read here. Chances are likely, if it does, it won't work. And if it's more complex, it's probably overkill, and will also fail. There is a balancing point at which a system has just enough structure to facilitate expansion and freedom but not too much to constrain it. Although my model is not overly complex, knowing which part of it to use, when, and how to work it optimally, can take quite a bit of practice over time, to develop both the awareness and a facility with implementing the right part of it at the right time. It is my intention to inspire you to recognize its potential and make it as easy as possible for you to experience the satisfaction that comes from taking advantage of it—even the smallest parts.

There are actually five stages of activity to really get things under control and six horizons that must be scanned and assessed to most effectively set priorities. If you skip any one of them, you won't reach the apex of productive engagement of which this system is capable. You'll need to capture, clarify, and organize literally everything that has your attention, with a subsequent appropriate review and engagement process of the total inventory. And your actions will need to support projects within areas of focus and responsibility, toward whatever goals you have defined that will move you toward your vision, all guided by your purposes and values.

That's quite a bit of verbiage, but in actuality it describes very specific things to think about and do. And when you have done so, they will provide you with trusted choices about your course of action—in your life, and for the dinner you're preparing for your friends.

Making It All Work will describe all the parts of this model in some detail, help you to recognize when you need to utilize which parts, and give you some very practical ways to implement them. It will provide some great tips about working with your kids, your projects, your teams, and of course yourself. Much of what I will be sharing with you will be self-evident common sense. But there's a very good chance that you will be glad to be reminded about the sort of common sense that probably should be more common than it is!

The Road Map for Life and Work

I love maps. I use them regularly. If I'm not using or needing or wanting a map, five things are true:

1. I know where I am.
2. I know where I want to go.
3. I know how to get from where I am to where I want to go.
4. I haven't run into a detour or unforeseen change in the route.
5. I'm aware of all the possible interesting, cool, creative options available on my route.

Anytime at least one of those factors is absent, I want to get my hands on a map. I may know I'm in Los Angeles, but I'm not quite sure where Sonoma is. I need a map. Or, I know I want to get to the Eiffel Tower, but I'm not sure where in Paris we are right now. Hand me that map. Or, I'm in Los Angeles again, I see where Sonoma is, but what's the quickest route to take to get there? Let me take a look. Or, I'm traveling up Highway 101 and hear on the radio that there's a big fire that has created a major detour—what are my other options? Or, I see where I am in L.A., I see that Sonoma is in northern California, and I determine the best interstate highway to take. But what else might be reasonably accessible en route that might be fun to visit? Give me the map.

Wouldn't it be nice if you had a map for life and work that served the same functions? Have you ever not known exactly where you were, what was true, or everything that was going on that you should have been aware of? Ever been unclear about where you wanted to go? Ever had a goal but not a plan or path to achieve it? Ever wondered what opportunities you might be missing outside your predefined structures? If so, you are in an ideal position to take advantage of the models I will be sharing with you here.

Making It All Work will give you a road map for life. Or for throwing your kid a birthday party. Or for arranging your home office. Or for hiring a VP of marketing. It will provide whatever you might need to get more in control or more appropriately focused.

Feeling lost is a consistent knowledge-worker phenomenon. When you have to think and constantly *rethink* precisely to know what to do, given the slippery changing nature of work today, it is incredibly easy to lose your way. Ever find yourself wrapped around an unexpected e-mail for forty-five minutes and then wonder what happened, and what the heck to do now about all the other stuff you thought you needed to tackle, whose status has now changed, but you're not sure exactly how to go about doing so? Ever get a spontaneous intuitive hunch that you should phone someone, and that call turned into a deep and fertile conversation that generated tons of new ideas and things to decide about and deal with?

Loss of control and perspective is the natural price you will pay for being creative and productive. The trick is not how to prevent this happening, but how to shorten the time you stay in an unsettled state.

And this rapidly shifting mass of what we could call our "work" is not just limited to the traditional office contexts. It's as true now for your twelve-year-old, your pastor, and any working single parent as it is for your director of marketing. Ask any of them if they are 100 percent sure that what they're doing right now is exactly what they should be doing, given the range of their involvements and interests. They need a map as much as anyone.

And, just as I have never visited everywhere that's on a given map, you may not need or want to do anything at this point in your life with respect to some of the areas I'll be describing here. I will discuss, for instance, "thirty-thousand-feet" thinking, which refers to goals and objectives that you may have for the next three to twenty-four months. You may already be clear about what those are, or frankly have little interest in doing anything new or different about that particular horizon for yourself. Although you may not need to pay attention to that part of the road map at the present, there is a good chance that at some point you *will* want to focus at that level, and it may serve you then to have my map at hand to give you some quick guidance about how to navigate it.

However, if there is any part of you that at this moment has any question or hesitation about whether you have fully integrated every single factor, commitment, and interest pulling or pushing on you into your current focus and activity, then there's bound to be some part of this map that will be highly useful to you—now.

If you do believe that you have achieved that balance-point state of clarity, freedom, and direction, that's terrific. But if you were to fine-tune your conscious reflection across the spectrum of the six Horizons of Focus I delineate, you might be surprised to discover subtle areas that are actually ringing some internal warning bell. You just may not be aware of them because louder and more insistent sounds are monopolizing your attention.

For instance, many executives I've worked with have said to me, after several hours of gathering the inventory of their projects and commitments, "That's it, can't think of anything else, we've got it all." When I've asked them to delineate the areas of responsibility of their job (what we'll be calling a "twenty-thousand-feet" item, they've remembered an item like "grow staff" as one of their duties. Or someone will, on deeper reflection, realize that he has an issue with a brother about how they're relating to their parents (a "fifty-thousand-feet" issue) and they acknowledge it's been a problem they know they need to do something about. Or even a matter as seemingly insignificant as "You know, it's been in the back of my mind that I might want to take dance lessons" can hold the germ of something rather profound as you go through your life experience.

WHAT ARE WE MAKING WORK?

The potential double meaning of "making it all work" is also a clue to the message of this book. What if we considered everything we did as "work" instead of restricting that term to what we do for money or to what we do that's hard? What if relaxing while on the beach was viewed as much as "work" as digging a posthole or drafting a proposal?

The definition of *work* I will use in this book is quite universal: anything you want to get done that's not done yet. From that perspective arranging for your kids' summer activities or getting a tan is as much "work" as hiring a new head of marketing or responding to your boss's e-mail.

It is interesting that the word *work* often has a pejorative spin, as in "That's not fun, that's *work*." Yet, at the same time we are thrilled when we actually get something to *work*.

Do *you* work?

Not to get too lost in semantics, but the challenge that we are dealing with in all this is getting to the state in which we can trust that what we're doing at any point in time is what we think we *should* be doing. Actually, we want to get even beyond that to simply *doing* what we're doing, with our full attention and energy, and operating from a sense of clarity and self-trust. Then we are really working, in both senses of the word.

But your life and your job seldom tell you exactly what needs to be done, and when. Indeed, there are circumstances in which either the nature of your job or the situation makes it quite obvious what the immediate task is. If you are hired to operate a machine with a predefined set of procedures for doing so, and you have everything at hand to do so, your work will be obvious. Or if a stack of documents needs to be stapled immediately for the meeting you're running to, the task at hand is pretty clear. If your two-year-old just knocked over a glass that broke into a hundred pieces on the floor, knowing what to do about it is self-evident.

But how much of your life *does* involve such clear choices? How often do you face a range of conflicting alternatives? Most of us live in a world in which we're not even sure what all our options are, much less which one would serve us best. As the late Peter Drucker cautioned all who venture into the world of "knowledge work," the toughest task is actually defining what your work is. Taking into account everything that should be considered within the range of "work" is quite a task in and of itself; creating and maintaining an appropriately clear environment within which to make those choices is equally challenging. If you assume, as I do, that "knowledge work" means you have to think or at least focus intuitively to know what to do, then the task of defining your work is as true for parenting as it is for publishing, painting, or putting.

Making It All Work is about the work you have to do to know the work you have to do when the work you have to do doesn't tell you the work you have to do. The work you really have to do is not self-evident—it's up to you to figure that out.

THE HOAX OF "LIFE/WORK BALANCE"

The popularity of the concept of balancing life and work is understandable because, indeed, many people seem to allow the pressures of what they're doing professionally to encroach inappropriately on other priorities. Coming home from work and dealing with family responsibilities and then staying up late answering e-mail may be preventing sufficient rest and creating unhealthy stress.

But to my thinking there is an inherent fallacy in affirming that "life" and "work" are mutually exclusive spheres. The truth is, when you are "in your zone"—when time has disappeared and you're simply "on" with whatever you're doing—there is no distinction in your psyche at that moment between "work" and "personal." It is equally possible to be in a positive, productive state when you are writing a proposal as it is playing with your dog. Nor is there any sense of overwhelm or lingering doubt about what you're doing. The concept of "balance" is irrelevant. You're usually only aware of balance when you don't have it.

When you're in that productive state, you are probably not dutifully calculating how much time you are being "personal" and how much time you're being "professional"—you're merely experiencing, "What am I doing?" and "What's next?" I have met many people for whom a lifestyle that involves 95 percent work is in balance. If they backed off so strong a focus on their job, they would feel uncomfortable because for them such time in their life is what positive engagement entails. They would get bored at home. That same person, two years later, may need to take a three-month sabbatical and explore the Andes, with no computer or phone, in order to stay in balance. The key is attaining balance, not trying to juggle life versus work. The key issue will be how to eliminate distraction, whatever its source, and to have focused alignment in whatever you're doing.

4 | The Fundamentals of Self-Management

If you lack the iron and the fizz to take control of your own life, then the gods will repay your weakness by having a grin or two at your expense. Should you fail to pilot your own ship, don't be surprised at what inappropriate port you find yourself docked.

—Tom Robbins

The two keys ingredients for making it all work are:

Control
Perspective

If you can maintain a sufficient level going of each of these factors in yourself or in your organization, you will probably find not much room for improvement. Your world will be in order and you'll be focused exactly as you should be. Only when one or both of them slip away from optimal should you be concerned that something is amiss, something needs righting, something needs to happen differently.

Control and perspective are closely intertwined dynamics, but achieving each one involves different approaches, whether the matter at hand is your teenager doing homework, your soccer team's practice, your next vacation, or your product launch. If your kitchen is a mess, for example, cleaning it up and placing all the tools and equipment where they belong will be a very different exercise from deciding what to cook and how to present it. But the two activities remain very connected, in that without an organized kitchen, it will be very challenging to stay focused on the dinner itself; likewise, an insufficient focus on the recipes, the various components of the dinner event itself, and the plan for deploying them will allow the situation to quickly get out of control again.

There are five stages to achieving control and six Horizons of Focus that lead to the gaining of perspective. Knowing what those are and how to employ them appropriately is the master formula for effectively managing any endeavor and navigating any environment. Each of these eleven elements has its own set of tools and behaviors that will enable it to be used optimally, and integrating all of them in a balanced way creates the most positive experience. Because they are so interdependent, your productivity will only be as good as the weakest link in that chain.

The Matrix of Self-Management

A matrix constructed on the axes of control and perspective can be useful, both as a map for assessing your own standing with respect to these elements (or that of another person or a particular situation) and as a guide for improvement.

The four quadrants described by these axes identify, in very general terms, the syndromes that are typically experienced with the varying combinations of low and high control, and low and high perspective.

The obvious optimal state would be elevated levels of both—the sector that is labeled "Captain and Commander."* Finding oneself in

---

* Originally I used the term *Master and Commander* because of its lovely linguistic connotations, as well as the heroism celebrated by both the book and movie of that name. Researching it, however, I discovered that the Master and Commander is a junior officer—not entirely appropriate for my model! The nautical context fits so well, though, that I'm using the best hybrid title I could muster.

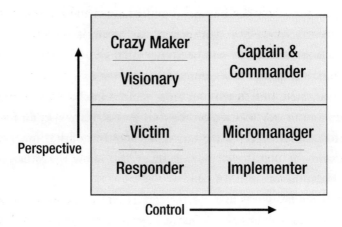

any of the other three quadrants, though, is not necessarily a bad thing. Just as any high-performance vehicle frequently gets off course, the best of us often fall away from the high-control, high-perspective state. It's the nature of human experience, which is always in some form of motion, to veer off course—sometimes in major, but consistently in minor, ways.

If, however, you tend to spend too much time in one of the less-than-optimal quadrants, you'll probably deserve the negative labels that are attached to them—Victim, Micromanager, or Crazy Maker. But these labels are best used as warnings for a course correction, much like the lane control bumps on a highway, when you drift as a result of your exploration and forward motion. In such cases a positive aspect will more aptly describe the syndromes—Responder, Implementer, and Visionary.

VICTIM/RESPONDER

The bottom left area of the diagram describes a person (or a situation) who has little control and little perspective. In its most negative expression, it characterizes a Victim—someone who is helpless, at the mercy of outside forces. If you are in that quadrant, you are effectively in a storm—somewhere between a mild squall and a major hurricane—operating in a crisis mode. In a self-management context, this means that you are simply dealing with only the latest and loudest. You are likely doing "emergency scanning" of voice mails and e-mails, letting the not-yet-critical stuff mount up in heaps, dealing exclusively with the tasks you have to do in the moment. Of course, the bigger the pile of unprocessed stuff, the more difficult it will be to navigate clearly and efficiently through it, and the more likely something will turn into a crisis from neglect. You're not able to hold the world back long enough to do the catching up that would be required to keep the next crisis from happening.

In this quadrant you're just trying to keep the ship afloat. Directions and goals won't mean much until you can ensure you're not sinking to the bottom. It will likely feel difficult to make any progress because you can never seem to get enough breathing room to plan, organize, and elevate your focus.

When events transpire that cause the seriousness of this situation to be revealed in an obvious and dramatic way, it can create enormous stress, if not downright panic. When in the course of preparing a nice dinner for friends you burn the sauce, notice you forgot a key ingredient, can't find the special pan, cut your finger, and suddenly realize your guests are going to show up before you have time to shower, your suddenly feeling like a victim of circumstances would be putting it mildly. If you start a new job and unexpectedly discover how many key projects and processes your predecessor screwed up that you're now going to have to fix, throwing in the towel might seem like a preferable option.

In its milder and perhaps more insidious form, and when experienced over an extended period of time, this diminished sense of control and perspective can give rise to a kind of numbness, out of sheer emotional self-protection. Most people I have encountered in the professional world have been in some version of this reactive state so consistently, and for so many years, that they're not even aware they're in it! Only when some relief begins to appear do they begin to realize how much pressure they have been under. It is much like gravity, in that you hardly have any idea how much weight it places on the body until it is absent.

On the Positive Side

Being out of control and out of focus is not inherently a bad thing. In fact, we all very likely find ourselves being in this quadrant many times a day in the natural course of getting things done. Much of our life and work is actually involved with responding to situations that have been put in motion, by ourselves and by others. We naturally play a defensive game one must play when we chase a "stretch" goal, navigate a major change, or respond to a simple but productive inter-action. Of course bigger objectives and risky moves into new and uncomfortable areas are even more likely to lead to a certain amount of running like crazy to play catch-up.

Entrepreneurs in the early stages of a new venture, which typically includes equal amounts of surprising successes and daunting setbacks, would often give anything for some consistent sense of control and perspective. They've jumped on a wild horse and are just trying to hold on for dear life. Even a single conversation with a key person over lunch can generate unexpected opportunities or issues that now must be dealt with, totally destroying the best-laid plans for the afternoon.

No matter how much your life and work are up to par, you will have to face at least momentary "leaks" in systems that will have to be reengineered to allow you to return to an even keel. And the more energetic and creative your endeavors are, the more likely that a larger portion of your time and energies will be invested in doing catch-up. Much of the energy in propelling a rocket is spent in course correction— it is, in a way, always veering out of control and off target. It achieves its goal precisely because it has a responsive feedback mechanism that prevents it from wavering too far off its designated path.

Also, we may be in one quadrant about some issue and in a totally different one for others. As I write this, my e-mail is quite under control, but I am feeling somewhat disquieted by a very interesting opportunity and project that presented itself in a meeting this morning with a major corporate client. I'm not entirely sure yet what this proposal might mean to us, how to best take advantage of it, and how it fits within the larger scope of significant projects we already have in the works. So my momentary workaday in-basket is on positive cruise control, but I am definitely leaning toward feeling out of control with respect to the murky perspective at some of my longer horizons. Whether I face this challenge as Victim or Responder will depend on whether I'm actively engaged in getting myself back to my zone, having integrated the new input and recalibrated my psyche accordingly.

MICROMANAGER/IMPLEMENTER

If as a rule you operate with a high control factor but lack perspective (in the situation described in the lower right-hand quadrant), you will likely place an inordinate emphasis on structure, process, and system—the characteristic traits of a Micromanager. You will have a tendency to overorganize, trying to maintain more control than is really necessary to get where you're going. Form, in other words, will overtake function.

This is the natural domain of the proverbial bean-counter, the financial guy who, if he wields too much power, strangles a company by cutting off investment in innovation, design, and research. At some point there will be no more beans to count. Publicly traded companies always risk long-term growth and survival when they are too focused on controlling their stock price by managing only toward the next quarterly earnings report. Another typical example of this sort of thinking is the person who, instead of having nothing well organized, has *nothing*, well organized! He typically spends a large portion of his day building systems for replenishing paper clips at the expense of the bigger game he should be playing.

This perspective often creates the ironic situation of being too controlled actually meaning being *out* of control. If your grip is too tight on a golf club, you will lose control of your swing. If your rules are too strict for your kids, they will rebel. A boxer or karate master will attempt to coax his opponent to fear losing control, which causes the opponent to tense up and overreact. (The tactic is called a "fake.") If your policies and procedures are draconian, you will wind up only stifling creativity, flexibility, and momentum in your environment.

Though there are many people who are chronically overstructured, we all slip into this arena regularly. How often have you avoided some particularly distasteful task at your desk by "getting more prepared," that is, rearranging your notes, changing your font style, filling your printer with paper, and then playing a quick game (or two) of solitaire as a break from your intense preparations?

How much is "enough" structure is a tricky question. Most of the time-management formats that have been designed and promoted in the last half century simply overdid a good thing. The original Day-Timer featured dated pages with fifteen-minute increments because it was designed by an attorney who needed a good way to track fifteen-minute chunks of billable time. The "ABC" priority-coding system became popular as a way to train a workforce that was being introduced to discretionary time. Daily To-do lists made sense when the world moved slowly enough to ensure that they could remain valid all day, and your environment was quiet enough for people to be able to pay attention to them.

Even the raft of sophisticated software designers who have attempted to create the "latest and greatest" GTD implementation applications have often overshot the bounds of real-life functionality. Most of them missed the mark by requiring too much mental effort to make life fit into their supplied forms.

On the Positive Side

We do have to have some degree of structure, and we must constantly be able to "fill in the blanks," that is, execute. And in fact, to get anything done, we must ultimately "complete the form" by arranging physical assets as needed. The very process of taking actions requires some predetermination and design. We organize ourselves to fulfill our directives, whether that's simply talking or creating a whole corporation. Realistically, a majority of our days are actually spent doing things that either we or someone else has laid out for us to accomplish.

There are also times when your energies should *primarily* be focused on processes and systems—on upgrading structures to handle what you have put in motion.

When you're in the structure and fulfillment mode, you can't also be in the visioning and outcome-thinking frame of mind. It is impossible to focus consciously on your life purpose and thread a needle at the same time. If you really operate professionally at the most sophisticated level, you may be able to quickly refer to your company's values in your mind while you're chatting with a problem employee. And if you're really tuned in and lined up with your life, you may manage to keep your long-term vision for a retirement lifestyle in mind while you're fixing the coffee grinder. But in either of those circumstances it would be nigh impossible to also be thinking about all sixty-five of your other projects, along with your strategic plan. You can switch between any of these horizons rapidly, but they can't occupy the same space simultaneously in the psyche. So in reality we all lose some degree of perspective every time we act or engage ourselves in anything, at any level. When you focus in, you filter out: that is the very nature of our consciousness.

The key here is maintaining the capability to unhook from and/or change the form or structure that's guiding you, as soon as it has served its purpose. Knowing when to refocus from another viewpoint, and when to sacrifice a system that has begun to constrain expansion and expression, is a sign of mastership.

CRAZY MAKER/VISIONARY

People who have a high component of perspective but a low control factor fall into the quadrant of the Crazy Maker: they have too many ideas in proportion to the amount getting done, they take on too many commitments vis-à-vis available resources, and they make everyone around them nuts by random and uncontrolled directives. Their systems and behaviors are not functioning to capture and contain all of their creative output.

In its extreme form this is the totally self-distracted state, with an inability to hold a focus for any appropriate length of time—the condition that is commonly referred to (rightly or wrongly) as attention deficit. In its milder form it is expressed as overcommitment: your psychic bank account is overdrawn, and you have made more agreements with yourself and others than you have the ability to keep. This can range from promising too much to too many people to simply allowing yourself to collect far more to read on your coffee table (and all over your house) than you could ever possibly finish.

I refer to this as the "bright bauble" syndrome, and it's one I myself fall into rather easily. I am prone to getting distracted by and attracted to the most glittering and glamorous thing in front of me, especially if it's "warm and fresh"—whether doughnuts, e-mails, or ideas. I can resist anything but temptation, and all that's required for something to qualify as a temptation is for it to show up in my visual or conscious field. I need and use GTD myself so much because I often have to have blinders, just like a horse, to stay on course.

On the Positive Side

Of course we can never really stop visioning. By our very nature we are always imaging outcomes and goals. As soon as we decide to leave a room, we have made a commitment that is unfulfilled, which creates a cognitive dissonance that generates the juice necessary to get up and moving. Looking out on a horizon, being attracted to something that we want to experience or accomplish, is core to expressing and expanding ourselves, whether it's a matter of putting on a hat or creating a conference.

Many executives we have coached fall into this quadrant. They are successful because their visioning capacities give them the ability to create and lead into new territories, and they are sharp enough to establish and cooperate with other people and structures that make up for their lack of order.

There are also times when, in order to stay on course for yourself, you will simply need to unhook from organization and execution and get a little crazy, that is, stretch into new places and spaces that will bring some valuable disturbance into, if not totally blow up, your comfortable, well-worn patterns.

CAPTAIN AND COMMANDER

The ideal of the model I'm proposing here incorporates an appropriate mix of perspective and structure, with your energies and focus directed by an internal rather than an external source. This is the state of flow, of being in your zone, of being "on." You are guiding your ship through the waves, wind, and water with a light touch on the helm and a keen eye on the horizon. You are committed to a course and prepared to make the slightest corrections that may be required.

When you achieve this state, there is no sense of overwhelm, no distinction between personal and professional, no dilemma of a life/work balance. You are doing in a state of being, and can simply *be* in an active and dynamic way. It is possible to have this experience while building a garden shed, playing with your cat, just sitting and thinking, or working through a challenging meeting with your boss or your board. This state doesn't seem to be dependent on the content or substance of what you are doing, nor even if you particularly *like* doing it. That doesn't mean you can gain access to this positive experience by just doing *anything* (wouldn't that be nice?); if you could, you would never fall out of this quadrant. The secret lies not so much in what you're doing, but in how you are *engaged* with what you're doing. And the optimal way to be engaged is to learn to walk the thin line between function and form, vision and implementation, stretch and structure.

Many Visionary/Crazy Maker types are deathly afraid of and resistant to any form of "getting organized" because they equate it with their opposite quadrant—the Micromanager. They are averse (and rightly so) to the "anally retentive" constraints that can stifle risk-taking and momentum. Implementer/Micromanager types are likewise repelled by any invitation to "make it up" and create their ideal scenarios, without sufficient evidence to support the possibility of actually achieving it. They're afraid they'll be thrown into the maelstrom of the Crazy Maker, endangering the stability of everything and everyone around them.

This is not, however, a zero-sum or either-or situation, though many people act as if it is. There is no freedom without discipline, no vision without a form, no structure without a function. If there were no lines painted on the road, you wouldn't be free to let your mind wander and be creative while you drive. You'd be too busy hoping no one hits you. But if there were too many lanes and restrictions and rules, you'd have traffic moving much slower than it should, as everyone was trying to pay attention to the right place to be. As precarious as walking the critical line might be, there is an optimal relationship of control and perspective. And when that is achieved, all is very well, indeed.

On the Negative Side

It would appear that there's no downside to being in this quadrant, for there's nowhere further to go in terms of managing yourself. That would be true, if this were a simple, one-dimensional model. But it's not, for as you'll see, these quadrants can be highly situation-dependent as well as multilayered. Being on "cruise control" is great, until the road takes a sharp and unexpected turn, or traffic suddenly screeches to a halt because of an accident. In other words, you can get into a rhythm and pattern that's working, and potentially be ignoring something you should be doing to keep it going that way. What future crisis do you need to be preventing? What new vision should you be developing and evaluating to keep you fresh? What new structures and processes might you be researching now to handle the increased flow that will result from your success?

Theoretically, if you are Captain and Commander, you'll also be paying attention to those preventive maintenance and development responsibilities . . . and on at least a subtle level you can't really be fully in your zone if some part of you is aware of those needs and they're not being addressed. But the point is, we can often *seem* to be in a state of fully integrated flow, let ourselves get lax, and be thrown out of it because of some negligence. The relief and contentment of having your current situation in proper control and perspective can easily seduce you into believing that you don't need to be thinking about the future.

The Matrix Is Relative, Situational, and Fluid

As mentioned earlier, how particular individuals experience these quadrants of control and perspective are not cast in stone. You may, because of the nature of your temperament and personality, find yourself more frequently in one pattern than another. But you can easily move into a different quadrant depending on what you're doing and the level at which you are doing it.

For instance, you may have certain areas and projects under control, but not others. You may have a clear perspective on your finances but you're not sure where you're going in a relationship. Your desk is organized but your gym locker is a mess. Your personal life could be humming along nicely, but your professional situation could be in turmoil.

Your profile could also vary by horizon. You might have a clear set of goals for the following year and still have ambiguity about your job description. Your daily calendar and action lists could all be in order, and yet you are not sure if the job you have is the right one for where you'd ultimately like to be in your career. You're clear about your life purpose but uncertain about all the projects that you have commitments to complete in the near future. You could have a fulfilling set of personal affirmations and aspirations and still have three thousand unprocessed e-mails yelling at you in your computer.

Not only can you be a Crazy Maker in your garden and a Micromanager in your golf game, but you can also move from one quadrant to another very quickly within one particular universe. You get on top of your workload and your job (Captain and Commander) and get so inspired that you wreak havoc by taking on a huge and ambiguous new project (Crazy Maker). So you run around playing whack-a-mole to patch up the cracks (Micromanager) and then fall down exhausted, feeling like you've gone backward instead of forward (Victim). The next morning you get a grip (Responder), focus on where you're going again (Visionary), integrate your project's plan and actions into your total work inventory (Implementer), and take your partner to dinner because life is good and you're on track again (Captain and Commander).

So what? Our lives are full of an almost infinite number of situations and moments in which we could get more control or get a better viewpoint, or both. The first step in improving what's going on is acceptance of what *is* going on. If you try to resist or refuse to recognize current reality, you'll never find the handlebars. If you seriously try to make things work, it will be very useful to have an awareness of your own position in this matrix. If you want to advance to the level of Captain and Commander, or ensure that you stay there, it is important to understand that there will be different strategies to adopt, depending on the situation in which you find yourself and your relationship to it. You may need more control, or more perspective, or both. And to achieve either of those, you may need to focus on different components of the prescriptive models.

The secret to accomplishing all of this will be to notice what is most noticeable to you.

Paying Attention to What Has Your Attention

To most effectively utilize the fundamentals of self-management, it helps to have a reference point about where to start. You won't have to look far, because what usually most needs your attention is what most *has* your attention.

Things are on your mind because you are consciously putting your focus on them or because your attention is being grabbed. In the latter case your thinking is being pulled toward something that in some way needs your engagement, and it more than likely is something that needs greater control or perspective to release its hold on your psyche.

Many important things for you are not on your mind because they don't need to be—they are on "cruise control." What, then, does that say about the affairs that *are* grabbing your attention? There's something about them that has not been captured, clarified, decided, or handled sufficiently. That inventory of items that are on your mind because they must still be managed appropriately is the grist for the mill for winning at your game.

Identifying what's on your mind is the core practice in the first of the five stages of getting control—clearing—which I will describe in more detail in the next chapter. You may have already been thinking that making a To-do list is all that I'm referring to, and in a way that's true. But what most people put on those kinds of lists is but a minority of what they should, to really gain maximum control and perspective. If anything is still on your mind, in the sense of holding your attention hostage, you can still improve your clarity and focus by paying appropriate attention to it.

If you don't pay attention to what has your attention, it will take more of your attention than it deserves. The accumulated amount of mental, psychic, and emotional energy that will be expended on whatever the thought is, over any length of time, will be far greater than would be necessary to either deal with the situation that triggered it or decide not to.

What it takes to truly release the hold on your mind of any of these kinds of potential distractions is not to consider them distractions but rather to handle them as a ringing phone—a call coming from a situation. If it goes unanswered, it will continue to call. If you do pick it up, however, and then deal with the incoming message sufficiently, it doesn't need to call again. But if you don't pick up the line for the less-than-critical things, the circuit will stay busy and not allow the rest of your inputs to have adequate space.

All of this is to affirm the somewhat counterintuitive notion that, in one respect, everything is equally important. Everything, that is, that grabs your attention. If what you need to be able to manage your life and work is full access to your focus, any time and all the time, then whatever diminishes that capability should be eliminated. Ignoring it is an option, but not a good one. If it will go away in time, put it away now. If it won't, get it into your system like the rest of your world that you can manage with minimal effort, because it's in a trusted system. The good news is that the process of dealing with these blips, to get them off your screen, is identical for the small and the large ones. But if you don't accept what's there to begin with, you're undermining your effectiveness.

The unique power of the principles in this book can only be accessed to their fullest when they are applied across the total spectrum of your reality. In other words, you will be prevented from moving into Captain and Commander mode whenever you *don't* pay attention to what has your attention. It doesn't mean that everything hooking your focus is equal in substance and potential meaning. Hardly. It does mean that you must responsibly unload and identify all the vectors that *are* pulling on the situation and the psyche in order to be able to address substance and meaning most effectively.

If you are attempting to "set priorities" for yourself, and subliminally know that there are at least forty-three things impinging on you, such as "get cat food," not yet tracked and managed, you'll resist the whole process and feel even guiltier than you did to begin with. If in the staff meeting you are attempting to inspire your team with the new vision and mission statement of the company, but everyone in the room knows (but no one is saying) that a third of them are getting laid off next week, that unacknowledged elephant in the room will put such a cloud over the meeting that not only will your attempt at motivation be ineffective, you will lose major equity in terms of trust and leadership.

So, if you're not sure where to start, start with what *is*. Get it on the table. I have been in countless situations as a consultant, counselor, or coach where I didn't have the foggiest idea what I should or could do to assist the client or the team. And over the years I learned that, without fail, one technique always pulled it out, always yanked victory from the jaws of defeat. I just asked, in some form, appropriate to the situation, "Okay, so what's true right now?"

That's also why the GTD model is so consistently successful. As opposed to putting forward a starting point at some idealized place of "priorities" or "strategy" or "values," which from one point of view would be where you "should" start, we suggest that you begin with where you are. Very few people, when we ask them to capture what's on their mind, start off with, "Fulfill my destiny on the planet." Most begin with something like "Fix printer" or "Get babysitter for the weekend." If your destiny, or your strategic vision, or your ideal outcome for your mom's elder-care situation is the first thing on your mind, fabulous. Grab it. If it's not, and you really want to effectively identify and incorporate those higher-horizon commitments, you must start with what's taking up the space in front of them. More often than not that's twenty-two e-mails you've been avoiding, the sitter you need to arrange for your kids for tomorrow night, and cat food. If you don't deal with those effectively, they will undermine your recognition of the bigger stuff or at least diminish your ability to focus on them clearly.

The next chapter will explore in greater detail this critical first step in making it all work—clearing the deck.

5 | Getting Control: Capturing

				Purpose/Principles	P
				Vision	E
					R
				Goals	S
					P
				Areas of Focus	E
					C
				Projects	T
					I
Capturing	Clarifying	Organizing	Reflecting	Engaging/Actions	V
					E

CONTROL

We want our minds to be clear—not so we can think clearly, but so we can be open in our perceptions.

—Mary Caroline Richards

Before you try to change something, increase your awareness of it.

—Tim Gallwey

When people will not weed their own minds, they are apt to be over-run with nettles.

—Horace Walpole

Capturing is the first of the phases of gaining control and creating a sense of positive engagement with your world. I have used various words to describe this initial stage, and it could as easily be called "collect," "clear," or "corral." The fundamental principle is identifying what's true, now—the information that is potentially relevant in the context in which you're focused. It describes the real parameters of the playing field, so you can engage in the game on a firm footing, without wondering where all the edges are.

This process involves isolating in some conscious, objective way what has the attention of a person, a group, or a situation. It's not about where to *put* attention—that comes later; but about acknowledging what is pulling or pushing on it. This initial step can provide huge benefits, immediately—some of which can be quite profound.

For every given person or situation there are myriad things that do not cause any distraction or pressure—all the items that we could describe as being "on cruise control." When the lights are working, the front office is taking care of business, your kids are doing fine in school, your parents seem like they're managing well, and your own blood is pumping properly, such issues will likely not even occur to you as you move through your day.

It's when something emerges as a blip, big or little, on your internal radar that there is potential for dissonance or imbalance. The room is too cold, you're thirsty, you receive an irritating e-mail from your sister, the printer can't deal with the new font you installed, someone mentioned a job opportunity that interests you. It could be that your company just received some bad press, or some really good press that has the phone ringing off the hook.

Most of these kinds of interruptions are just part of the normal way we experience our world, minute to minute—scratching whatever itches, taking care of the everyday business of life. If we don't deal with them in some constructive and appropriate way, however, they don't usually go away but more often than not hold at least a tiny part of the consciousness hostage.

The reality is that everything I categorize as important to collect already has been—it's just been gathered up into some place in the psyche instead of being kept available for objective review and analysis against every other issue of a similar nature. It is, for our purposes, as good as "lost" if it is roaming loose in the morass of the subliminal mind.

The first thing to do, when you are feeling in any way out of sorts, is to clear the air by grabbing hold of whatever is pulling on your focus. If there is a lack of clarity, it is necessary to identify anything that might be the source of that discord.

In other words, if it's on your mind, write it down or record it somehow in a concrete way. You can jot it on paper, type it, write it on a whiteboard, or even talk it into an audio recorder (though that method does have the drawback of leaving it in your conscious awareness until you play it back or transcribe it). You can add it to a list, or write each item on a separate sheet of paper and collect them in your in-tray. It doesn't matter how you capture these thoughts, as long as you get them out of your head and have them all in some way easily accessible for review.

The same process should be adopted by teams and other relevant groups of people, though the data will need to be collected in a form that can be shared by all members. Having the group just "download" in a free-form fashion, with someone playing scribe on a whiteboard or on a shared computer screen, does the job nicely.

The Personal Mind Sweep

Over the years that I have been teaching about and coaching stress-free productivity, this initial stage of gaining control has taken numerous forms, for both individuals and group situations. The most basic and thorough version is something I call a "mind sweep."

One of the first exercises that we lead people through when we work with them one-on-one in our company's Work Flow Coaching program is an overall scan and capture of anything and everything that has their attention. This process is described in *Getting Things Done* in some detail, but the essence of it is rather simple: you identify anything in life or work that you think might need to be different or considered for whatever reason and create at least a crude placeholder for it in one delimited location. An in-basket is perfect for this, though compiling a list can also serve the same function.

We start this process with a client by merely surveying his physical environment—what's on, in, under, and around their desk? What's on the shelves, in the cabinets, in the drawers, in the files, in the closets? What's in his briefcase? What's on the walls and bulletin boards and whiteboards? Anything that isn't supplies, decoration, reference material, or equipment is an item they need to address, as it is effectively staking a claim on the client's attention. The broken printer in the corner, the print on the wall he's been meaning to change, the tennis racket in the corner that needs restringing—not to mention all the stacks of documents, magazines, mail, and folders scattered in various places, none of which is where it belongs permanently. We don't editorialize at all about what we find, but simply ask the client, "Do you have any attention on this?" and let him make that call. Of course many people initially insist that "it's fine there," but once they relax into the process, they come around to acknowledging that they've been meaning to do something about it but they don't know exactly what that is.

All of that incomplete material is gathered into the in-basket (or, in most cases, because of its volume, in an expanded section around it). Then we ask if there is anything else the client can possibly think of that has his attention, that hasn't yet found its way into that stack. Invariably there is—the context of the inventory he's been packing in psychic RAM. We suggest that whatever shows up be written on separate pieces of paper, and likewise tossed into the in-basket. That will allow it to be processed later more easily, because people are much more capable of focusing clearly on a single item and making a decision about it than attempting to work off a long running list on a sheet (though that can still work, if needed).

To facilitate this capture we also provide an Incompletion Trigger list, a checklist of most of the common things that claim people's attention personally and professionally. There are multiple levels of awareness involved with what has attention, and it's very challenging to range around in the mind and find them all, in one sitting, without some help. A good reminder list helps jog the psyche and uncover some things stored deeper in the attic. (If you're interested in trying it for yourself, you can refer to the trigger list in Appendix i.)

The mind sweep and the whole gathering process in our coaching can take anywhere from part of an hour to several hours, depending on the volume of material to be assessed. In general, the more senior and sophisticated the client, added to the length of time he's been in the same location, the greater the volume. It becomes easier for attention-grabbing things to accumulate when someone takes on bigger and more ambiguous projects and responsibilities. Also, the longer he has remained in that one location, the bigger the pile. Unless someone conscientiously undertakes regular and pristine purges and recalibrations of everything in their environment, the "stuff" of life and work can take up permanent residence almost anywhere and be extremely hard to dislodge.

THE EVEN MORE SUBTLE STUFF

While there is usually a large volume of incomplete commitments in the more obvious areas of your physical life, such as projects and situations around your office and around your house and with people you are interacting with on a day-to-day basis, there are often more qualitatively weighty things on your mind that are not quite as evident and lay hidden behind the more visible ones.

To find these, you could use the Horizons of Focus also as a checklist, which contain the six levels of commitments we all have, to some degree, but which are more refined and elusive. While the higher-altitude agreements with ourselves are sometimes tricky to get hold of, the ability and willingness to pay attention to what has your attention at those levels will become the source of inspiration and intuitive judgment.

Actually, the more subtle and elusive the matters are that have a hold on your mind, the more important they can prove to be.

TEN THOUSAND FEET—PROJECTS

Many projects are self-evident, and if you did a mind sweep, you probably identified many of them immediately: buy a new car, hire an assistant, install the new printer in your office, repair the lawn mower, and so on. But there are in fact usually many more topics on someone's mind at this level than he would normally capture when he thought about "projects," literally, but which are nonetheless extremely important to identify, clarify, and organize along with everything else in the "extended-mind" system.

For instance, many people are still trying to finish moving into a new residence or office. They're not aware of "finalize move-in" as a matter that still compels their attention as a project, but it does. Typical examples of projects that people often don't recognize as such, but that are definitely on their radar:

- Next holiday
- Dealing with elder care for one or more parent
- Setting up summer programs for kids.

The biggest culprits that elude objective capture at this level are the subjects that you consider "problems," which you have yet to recognize as projects. As a parent you may have concerns about your son's math grades. There may be an uncomfortable situation between two of your employees that's bothering you. The content could be something as minor as your getting increasingly irritated by how fast your laptop battery is draining, or as serious as your discovering that a family member has a major illness. Few people are ready and willing initially to acknowledge all of those kinds of distractions and identify them as situations to complete or resolve.

TWENTY THOUSAND FEET—AREAS OF FOCUS AND RESPONSIBILITY

This next horizon usually contains numerous concerns that are lurking in the psyche somewhere, but aren't immediately obvious enough when you try to pinpoint what has your attention. For example, if you think about your job description at a high level, you'll probably come up with several "hats" you wear—you're probably responsible for several areas, not just one. Are any of those not up to par? If you're responsible for staff development, is that all fine for now? If you're expected to maintain operational plans in your department, are they all functioning optimally?

In our Work Flow Coaching program, we recommend that each client review his job description to trigger anything that might be on his mind about it. Without exception, people find at least two or three significant issues that have been tugging at them to address, think about, or grapple with.

Expanding that view across your entire life, you can isolate areas of interest and responsibility that you have some commitment to maintain at least implicitly at some internalized level or standard—finances, health, recreation, relationships, self-development, self-expression, household, family, spiritual life, and so on. Most of these areas are functioning at a comfortable equilibrium, but there are undoubtedly a few of them that are niggling at the back of your mind.

For instance, your pants may be getting tighter and tighter, and it's bothering you more and more (health, energy). You keep wondering if your retirement account portfolio is up to date (finances). You're more and more curious about what it would take to learn to play the piano (self-expression). And you know you ought to be doing something for your sister's fiftieth birthday coming up in a couple of months (family).

Getting all of those kinds of subtle attention-grabbing situations out of your head and into the funnel for your systematic process of clarification and organization gives a tremendous boost to your sense of control.

THIRTY THOUSAND FEET—GOALS AND OBJECTIVES

This horizon is the first "jump into the future" focus. Though they are yet to come, you might have things pulling or pushing on you right now that you will have to face at a longer horizon.

Up at this level there may be things bouncing around in your mind about what you need or want to be accomplishing in the future. If you have a strategic plan clearly laid out with the appropriate goals, objectives, and projects identified and in place with the right people in your organization, it's probably not dragging on your attention. If you're missing some parts, or even the whole plan, and you know you ought to be addressing the problem, it's a significant issue to capture. Many times, even if you have plans or a set of goals formulated, a review of them will often reveal areas that you recognize you've been concerned about.

Personally, there might be some things that really need to happen by a certain deadline in the next few months or within a couple of years, and those often don't show up in your mind until you focus on the particular topic they concern. You know you need to pass a licensing examination by the end of next year. Or you need to have saved a certain amount of money by the following spring to take an anniversary cruise. Or you need to get your extra bedroom completed in time for a new baby.

Concerns that have your attention at this level are not always previous commitments that you need to take stock of. They may involve such matters as aspirations and inspirations that you may have not paid a lot of mind to, because of so many other distractions in your daily life. They're all still there—just a bit hidden under the more obvious demands. You may also have areas in your life about which you have been thinking you *should* set some goals—like improving your financial situation, or learning a language, or running a marathon. Even if such goals haven't been clearly articulated, the question of *setting* them already has a piece of your psyche attached. That's something to capture.

FORTY THOUSAND FEET—VISION

On the next plateau of your engagement with the world—the level of vision or images of long-term success—things to grab out of your head can range from major and obvious issues and opportunities to those of a much more nuanced nature. The apparent ones would include topics like a phone call from someone offering you a career opportunity that would represent a sea change in your professional life. Or your life partner might have received that kind of offer but it would require you to change jobs and cities if he or she took advantage of it. Or you may sense that there is a potential downsizing coming in your company, and you know you should be thinking through the contingencies in case you wind up being part of the group that is let go. You may have a nagging feeling that the straitlaced corporate life you're living is not really allowing you the expression you think you're capable of or that your free-form "creative" lifestyle is not providing you the resources you need to be able to experience some of the more influential things you want to be able to do as you get older.

FIFTY THOUSAND FEET—PURPOSE AND PRINCIPLES

This is the arena of major, defining matters of your life experience. If you have a solid sense that you are fulfilling your purpose and that what you value as truly important has its appropriate place in your life, there's nothing you need to collect from or attend to about this horizon, other than what you're already doing. But if there is a matter that is not clear or aligned, it will be difficult for you to attain the "mind like water" state, pervading throughout your consciousness.

For instance, if you are bothered by the fact that your key talents and gifts are not really being recognized and utilized—by yourself and by others—that concern will gnaw at some part of your mind until and unless you create an appropriate set of actions to explore or create opportunities for greater expression. Or, if some disruption in your world is causing you discomfort because it is disturbing to your principles, you won't be able to have a totally clear head until that is addressed. The major reason people change jobs, for example, is their boss. It's not just a question of antipathy (you can work constructively with people you don't necessarily care for personally)—it's that the boss is behaving in ways that are outside your core values.

People are seldom comfortable acknowledging and objectifying these kinds of dissonant factors at the higher altitudes of their commitments. But the more sensitive and deeply rooted these areas are, the more powerful and positive the payoff will be if they are captured and dealt with in the same systematic manner as "buy cat food." That involves an outcome to identify, with a relevant action to be determined, organized, and carried out.

I had a surprising experience in this regard. During the first break of a seminar in which I was delivering this material, after I had the group do a small version of a "mind sweep" for themselves, I was approached by a participant who said, "David, what do I do with this?" He showed me the first thing he had written on his list, the first subject that had been on his mind—"God." He was wearing a clerical collar. Now, here was an interesting turn of the tables—he was asking *me* what to do about *that*! After a momentary panic about what I could possibly say to him, my inner GTD coach came out and said, "Well, what exactly does that mean to you? Did you write it just as an affirmation and inspiration focus point, or is there something you think you need to do that's not done yet?" He thought for a second and then seemed quite enthused about whatever the "aha!" that emerged then was. (I didn't feel comfortable questioning him about what he had actually discovered.)

Many people are resistant to capturing and dealing with these more in-depth areas because they tend to want to have the answers before they're willing to acknowledge that they have the questions. In other words, they want to know their life purpose before they recognize that they don't know precisely what it is. That's even a stickler for identifying projects as well—they want to know how to achieve or finish something before they admit that there's something to achieve or finish. The key is simply to become familiar and comfortable with the idea that it's not necessary to know anything in its fullness in order to get control of it. What's important is knowing the next step to take to make progress toward that clarity. Identifying the issue or content of the distraction and getting it into the system is most often the best way to begin to take charge of it.

Many times my projects involve "looking into" something. I don't know what I'll find out, or whether I'll decide to do anything with it once I do obtain more information, but I am now engaging, and it must be in my system in order to get it off my mind. Goals like "identify life purpose" or "revisit company purpose and principles" often turn into practical process-type projects, like "research life coaches" and "finalize off-site meeting for organization alignment assessment."

This is not to say that you must know what your life purpose is, or even that you should necessarily have one. You can still feel absolutely clear in your head without such an agenda ever occurring to you—as long as that no-thoughts-or-cares-about-it judgment is a genuine one. For the purposes of getting on top of your game, however, if you do ponder those kinds of questions or concerns, they are grist for the mill. When in doubt, write it down. Put it in your in-basket. Trust that there is going to be great value in moving this kind of content into your systematic processing. You can always dismiss it later, having decided you're really going to let it go because it's not a matter you can do anything about; or at least put the question or thought on hold until at some point in the future you can revisit it properly. All fine.

As a friend of mine once said, a man who was raised on a farm and who's found GTD to be a great boon to his life and work, it's as if everything now is just thrown in front of the tractor—it gathers it, processes it, plants seeds in the row, and all sorts of great things sprout. It's immaterial to the tractor what it takes in—it simply captures what's in front of it. So should you.

As the highly productive habit of collecting commitments in discrete external locations that invite you to manage them later is crucial, there are many other forms of capturing current realities that can also have huge benefit in enhancing your positive engagement with your life.

Journaling

A wonderful way to begin to experience an increase in control during this first phase of capturing is to journal. Often the incomplete energies and loose edges of our lives are manifested only when we are willing to drop back into a more reflective mode and take note of what seems to want to express itself only through a more stream-of-consciousness modality.

Over the years I have gravitated toward two types of journal writing for myself. One is a kind of ad hoc running diary of events to record various aspects of my current situation in my workaday world; the other is more inner and spiritually focused. I started out with only a single journal, but discovered over time that it seemed more appropriate to recognize two kinds of capturing platforms. The more mundane journaling I use for much the same purpose as I do "unloading" to my wife at the end of the day, recounting the events— usually the good stuff and the challenging stuff—that are still in some way on my mind. The journal is just a way I can do that by myself. I use my laptop computer and a running word-processing document for that kind of writing, a format that seems to suit both the energy and the content. On the other hand, for my more reflective writing I use a fountain pen and an elegant leather-bound personal journal. I don't know exactly why, but for me that approach helps me dig a little deeper and encourages me to be a little more self-disclosing.

Much has been written about journaling and its therapeutic effects. A common theme through many spiritual teachings is the power of pure observation—that the simple act of noticing what's going on, with as much neutrality and objectivity as possible, is the first key to inner freedom.

Though a more indirect process than the other capturing activities, writing in a journal or diary is a great example of this first and critical stage of getting back "on" in case things have slipped.

Brainstorming

If your focus on any project or situation seems scattered and disjointed, and every time you bring the topic to mind your brain goes slightly on tilt, bouncing around like a pinball, the ideal solution to get your thinking under control is to brainstorm.

Now, we're all generally brainstorming much of the time—we're pointing our focus at some object and generating all kinds of associated ideas about and around it. What I'm referring to here is the specific technique of recording random thoughts about something outside the mind in a concrete, viewable fashion. Brainstorming can take the form of simple jotted notes on a paper napkin, mind maps drawn with pen or generated in software designed for that purpose, a gathering of ideas written on a whiteboard or easel pad, or lists created collaboratively by a virtual team on the Internet. Essentially, brainstorming is mind-sweeping on a particular theme, grabbing everything that you notice has your attention when you focus your thinking in that particular area. You need to plan a wedding, so you start by just jotting thoughts as they pop into your head. You need to create an agenda for the staff meeting, so you start picking off topics that start rolling through your mind that might be relevant.

Brainstorming by capturing your thinking in a place other than your mind transforms the process considerably. If you have a useful idea, leaving it in your head causes a part of your internal computer to try to keep track of it. That then diminishes to some degree your mind's ability to process other thoughts because it's expending energy trying not to lose the first one.

On the other hand, if you write down the idea, a part of you knows that your brain no longer has to keep hold of it, so it's free to range and roam into new territory. If your goal is to have the best ideas that you can about anything, you want to be able to draw on as many possibilities as you can come up with, which gives you the widest range of choices. Providing fleeting thoughts with an external parking place keeps the flow of creative thinking going. Having a place for ideas, whenever and wherever you might have them, combined with the habit of free-form recording of those ideas, guarantees a great deal of valuable thinking that wouldn't otherwise occur.

Cleaning Up

Another of the ways to achieve immediate payoffs from this confront-what's-true phase is to clean up.

You never know how much of your attention is being held captive by a physical space until you do a thorough job of purging it and notice how different you then feel. I have a saying—"When in doubt, clean a drawer"—a sentiment that is also true for your car, your golf bag, your clothes closet, your toolshed, your desk drawers, your garden—whatever. Though the sense of losing control in this area can be rather unobtrusive and creep up on you only slowly over time, a clean-up is one of the more obvious ways that you can feel a quick surge of the Captain and Commander energy.

There is no universal standard of "clean," despite the fact that many people have tried to establish a standard. To you what's spotless with everything in its place may still seem an out-of-control mess to someone else. What's important here is that you do have some standard, no matter what it is, so that when things begin to sneak in that don't really belong where they are, the way they are, or the dust grows a little too thick, you'll have a way of assessing the situation. Instead of maneuvering in an environment with freedom and clarity, when disorder takes over you start to avoid it. You don't want to look in the glove compartment of your car. You won't open the center drawer of your desk past the pencils, if you open it at all. You dare not examine your old computer files. These spaces are now controlling you, since what you resist sticks to you.

A main reason that such distracters emerge so stealthily is that we accumulate all kinds of things that are functional when we obtain them, but they lose that functionality over time. When they reach that state, though, they don't throw themselves away. Crap self-generates but it doesn't self-destruct. Your center desk drawer was the perfect place to keep ballpoint pen refills, as long as you had that pen, but you haven't had that pen for two years. While a part of you is aware that those refills don't belong there, and you've told yourself you need to do something about them, the intention does not remain in your conscious mind. It's as if that part of your mind went numb, to relieve the irritation. Clean your drawer, throw away the pen refills, and then that part wakes up, leaving you feeling like taking someone to lunch.

Group Capturing

Mind-sweeping, brainstorming, and cleaning up all can easily be applied in collaborative situations. Teams, couples, departments, families—any context in which two or more people would find it useful to gain a greater sense of order, balance, and control in relationship with one another—can use this primary stage to great advantage.

I've noticed an interesting phenomenon in this regard. My wife and I have often found it useful to do a brainstorming and mind-sweep about all the issues that have our combined attention. The resulting content and how we experience it is different from what it would have been had we simply combined our individual captures. There is apparently a "collaborative psychic RAM" space, which, when emptied, provides a general sense of clarity and freedom within an entire group.

Certainly in professional situations—project or management teams, committees, boards, and so on—it is particularly critical to bring the group into present time and space together by allowing the members to download what has their attention, at least within the context of a particular meeting or of the group's responsibilities. That does not mean, however, that everything on anyone's mind at that moment is or should be considered strategic or relevant to the agenda. It does mean that if anyone in the group has distractions relative to the topic at hand, or to their participation in it, an acknowledgment of those will be important to facilitate cooperation and constructive communication going forward. If there's an "elephant in the room" that no one is willing to acknowledge—some data that any of the participants has that they know could impact on the subject but they are not disclosing or admitting it—it will short-circuit optimal collaboration.

It's a great idea, when starting meetings that are held regularly, whether in a department or a family, to have everyone contribute what primarily has their attention at the moment. You wouldn't necessarily need to write those descriptions down (though sometimes that could be useful, if someone raises a topic that might need to be addressed then or later). In my many years of consulting with teams and groups, I learned that trying to move things forward without at least a nod to the issues pulling on everyone's psyche is an exercise in futility.

Cleaning and purging as a team or group can be exhilarating, and much easier to do when others around you are engaged in the same activity. Bringing the range of everyone's information and involvements to the surface, recognizing and tossing out what is no longer relevant, has a healing effect that seems to be magnified when two or more are involved together in that clearing process. You have probably had the experience of cleaning a garage with your kids, a closet with your spouse, or a filing cabinet with your boss or assistant, and it feels terrific.

I don't know fully yet why and how this principle works in a group setting as effectively as it does—I just know it works. There is apparently something about information sharing in that format that enhances clarity and cooperation. Perhaps we all are more attuned to one another than we realize, and if someone is disconnected from the mutual intention of the occasion because of unacknowledged issues, they just won't participate fully in the game, which will mitigate the group's cohesion and positive energy.

Getting the Capture Habit

Capturing and objectifying what's true, especially when it involves an issue that is affecting your thinking in any way as a matter that needs tending to, is a simple but often profound technique to acquire and practice. If you ignore those potential distractions, as slight as they might seem, or try merely to store them on some shelf in your mind, you do so at the peril of losing some measure of control of your world.

I know that viewed in the light of the many more "important" things going on in the daily lives of most people, an activity like getting rid of, or simply organizing, old electronic accessories into a box so labeled may seem like the last thing in the world that should ever be a priority. How much difference could that possibly make, in the larger scheme of things? You may think that those minor infringements of clear space are not generating significant stress. But my point is, if it feels so gratifying when you actually do bring up the rear guard by capturing those subtle tugs on your psyche, what were you feeling before? Maybe good, but just not as good as you could.

I understand that this sort of organizational thinking could be construed as obsessive, and the line indeed between keeping things optimally clear and in present time and being inappropriately distracted by incompletion may be a subtle one. As I mentioned in describing the Micromanager quadrant, you can start to lose control if you try to maintain too much control. Keeping things clean and organized becomes a disorder only when it prevents you from paying attention to more serious incompletions and distractions. Usually that sort of out-of-balance syndrome is an overcompensation for the lack of control in more significant areas.

The fact is, because you will probably never have everything captured, defined, and categorized completely, you will need to pick your battles. My garden shed seems to have a vortex of energy that attracts not-quite-finished stuff. I only turn my attention to getting it back to a state of equilibrium when the number of important tools or supplies that I can't find causes my frustration level to rise to a certain critical point. I do a reasonably good job of creating some systems in the shed that make it easier for me to keep things replaced properly while I'm focused on a project in the garden, but it's almost never totally pristine. The same is true of one of my desk drawers that has become the repository for various small electronic and digital accessories— earphones for Skype calls, adapters, power cords, and so on. I've learned to use plastic bags and my labeler to corral these runaway parts, but it's hardly ever completely current.

My objective here is not to judge the failure to capture things that have part of our psyche as either right or wrong—it's simply to point out that those distractions do affect our energy. And the recognition of how that process operates can be very useful tactically when you are navigating the complexities of your world. There are times when the capturing function can be the most important tool to utilize to get you on top of your game.

People experience great relief, individually and in a group context, in simply knowing that all the puzzle pieces are on the table. I remember, growing up, when I used to work jigsaw puzzles, that if we ever discovered that even a single piece was lost or missing from the box, we would have to throw the entire puzzle away. It was tough enough just to find some of the right pieces from the pile, especially as we were only starting to put it together. If you realized that the piece you were struggling to track down might actually be missing, it undermined the winability of the activity and therefore the fun of the game.

Over the years this one initial major component for making it all work—capturing whatever commitments and ideas that might have meaning and value for you—has been one of the most powerful incentives in creating converts to the GTD method, even when that's all they were motivated to do. I guarantee that if you only increase the amount of things you write down (and don't lose) consistently by 10 percent, it will change your life for the better.

A TV sitcom writer told me that reading *Getting Things Done* had been a transformative experience for him, solely because it gave him the idea and motivation to do a total mind sweep. In only one sitting he captured every single thing he could possibly churn up from his psyche that he thought he would, could, should, or might do. He swore that once he'd accomplished that, it was the first time in his life that he realized he didn't have to do them all at once, that he could only do one thing at a time, and that he could actually permit himself to *not* do anything on that list if, in the moment, it wasn't appropriate.

He admitted that he didn't do anything else that I suggested in my book, but insisted that that one experience was life-changing. (He confessed that he even lost the list!) Now every time he starts to feel that his world is bigger than he is, and the internal pressure gets too high, he just sits down and makes another list, and he's fine again.

A Weapon Against Interruptions

One of the most significant advantages of acquiring the capture habit is the help it provides in dealing with interruptions. If I ask a roomful of people what gets in their way of being as productive as they could be, "interruptions" always ranks high on the list. Because the ability to focus and concentrate is the key to maximum performance, it is understandable that having that focus derailed by unexpected input would be bothersome at the least. A majority of the organizational environments I have seen have the interrupt-itis disease, which tends to go along with meeting-itis, an equally deadly malady. The best practices for controlling your world that I am putting forward here, however, go a long way toward mitigating the negative results of those syndromes.

I've noticed that one of the main reasons people are so bothered by interruptions is that they lack good capturing skills and tools. Say you're the victim of a "corporate drive-by"—Melissa pops into your office wanting some information about XYZ project she is working on. If you're not used to writing such requests down, throwing them into your in-basket, and trusting that you'll get to them sometime in the next few hours, you'll tend to take immediately the five or ten minutes required to find and gather the information Melissa needs. You know you'll have to do so eventually out of courtesy and/or because of your responsibilities, but you know it's not the most important thing you should be doing right at that moment, which makes you feel irritated. It could very well be that handling Melissa's request is the wisest choice right then, but without the appropriate habits for the use of pen, paper, and in-basket, you won't really have an alternative.

Doing tasks when they turn up can be an effective way to be productive, if they are the most important thing to do at the moment or if they can be completed in two minutes or less, as affirmed by the two-minute rule (see chapter 9). But because most people don't have enough trust in their abilities to capture these kinds of inputs into their work flow funnel, to be clarified and organized in a timely manner, they find themselves running down lots of those "rabbit trails" when they could easily be dealt with later.

The Value of Bookmarking

Taking notes while you're engaged in tasks can serve a tremendously valuable function in enabling you to keep track of where you leave off. In the hectic world of work you will often have many plates spinning at the same time, and as you go from one kind of interaction to the next it will serve you well to take notes that you can toss into your in-basket and consult later to pick up the threads appropriately. Often you will find yourself without the time to fully clarify and organize those interactions as they're taking place, and it's great to trust that you have a trigger to recall them when things slow down a bit.

For instance, when you are on the phone, have pen in hand and jot notes about the call. You may simply throw the notes away when you hang up because nothing came out of the conversation you need to act upon. But if there was a germane topic discussed, you'll want to process those notes to determine actions, reference material, and so on. Often, though, you'll be moving so quickly through the morning that you won't have time that very second to deal with them. If they're tossed into your in-tray, however, you can trust that you'll be reminded appropriately before too long (assuming you deal with your in-basket appropriately, as will be described in the next chapter).

I often take notes in my mind-mapping software while I'm on a conference call, with a fresh map for each client or topic. At the end of the call, if I have to get busy with other things, I'll print this map out and throw it into my in-basket. Later I'll separate out any necessary actions, record whatever data I want to keep, and file the printed map in a folder for the project. It's a great way to keep tabs on many things going on simultaneously.

As another example, if you are keeping separate lists of agendas for your next conversations and meetings with someone on your computer, print them out and take notes during each one on the printout itself. When you come back from the meeting, toss those notes into your in-basket, so that when you later process them, all the open items will be dealt with appropriately.

Some Best Practices for Capturing

If you accept the idea that externalizing what has your attention is a worthwhile pursuit, then it's constructive to ensure that you have the right gear and some good procedures to best take advantage of the principle. We don't seem to be born wanting to write things down, and keeping them in the mind is such an ingrained habit that we need all the help we can get to switch that pattern. Our minds have a seductive way of convincing us that what we're thinking about, while we're thinking it, is so clear and obvious that we'll never forget it and will have easy access to it exactly when we need it. Of course, two minutes later, when we're thinking about the next obvious thing we're sure we won't forget, we've forgotten the first one! It would be bad enough, of course, if you actually did completely forget the first thought; but it's now probably stored in psychic RAM and has already started to eat away at your ability to stay maximally focused.

Again, you need to apply "mental intelligence," realizing that you are actually much smarter than your mind, and so you must manage what it is accepting and creating. It's actually the mature part of you that recognizes the mind's limitations and leads you to utilize the equipment you need to accept and work within them.

TOOLS

Obviously, if you're not going to finish a task when it first appears, and you're not going to keep it parked in your mind, you'll need good tools for grabbing and steering these placeholders until you can get around to the more executive function of clarifying and sorting the results.

Collection tools are likely different from those you would use to organize. Whereas action reminders, like people to call or errands to run, are best structured into lists you can access easily, when you are grabbing thoughts on the fly you don't want to be constrained by structure. Anything will work to catch input, as long as it's instantly at hand and you don't lose track of the contents. You can write things down, throw reminders in an in-tray, speak into an audio recorder, call your own answering machine, or even send yourself an e-mail. Today there are many different capturing devices and systems using new technologies. For example, you can call a number, speak, and have the transcription e-mailed back to you within a few minutes.

THE POWER OF PEN AND PAPER

As nifty as many of these technologically advanced tools seem, there is still nothing that works better the majority of the time than pen and paper. Sure, if you're driving in a car, recording something through your phone or audio device might be safer and easier than trying to write it down. But notepads, sticky notes, spiral notebooks, journals . . . even the backs of envelopes will serve you best if you want to stay squeaky clean in the head. Ideas show up at the strangest places and times, and the more closely at hand the tools are to grab them as they come in, the better.

It is not a mark of senility, but rather of sophistication, that the older you get, the more often the good ideas you get don't happen where they will ultimately be used. You'll be buying bread at the store when you think of something that you need to bring up at the staff meeting; when you're in a staff meeting, you'll remember that you need bread. If you want the task to buy bread to happen, you'd better capture the thought about it while you're in the staff meeting. And if you want the potentially useful agenda for the staff meeting to occur, you'd better grab it while you're in the store.

Likewise, the more senior you are in your job, the more your good ideas about your work won't actually happen at work. You will not likely, in the heat of battle of day-to-day activities, have the capability to be open to the creative, out-of-the-box thinking that can occur on a beach or a golf course.

So, the more constantly available your capturing device, the more it will get used, the greater the flow of thoughts and ideas you will allow yourself, and the easier it will be to create value whenever and wherever you happen to be. One of the two most useful tools in my own life is the wallet I carry with a paper pad and small pen attached, which goes with me everywhere I take my driver's license and credit cards. The other tool is my laptop computer. One of those devices collects the thoughts that might have meaning and value, and the other serves as my "extended mind" to manage what I have captured. Because I have set up my own personal systems and habits to ensure that all my random inputs will have a home, often all I need to stay clear when I'm out and about is my pocket notepad. If I discover that I need some data from my other systems, or need to do something with or in that system that's not with me, I simply make a note to deal with it when I'm back where it's possible.

It's a good idea to keep notepads and pens wherever you have a telephone, and wherever you're likely to need to remind yourself about anything, such as in your workshop, on your boat, or in your car (while you're waiting, not driving!). Anytime I find myself situated somewhere for longer than fifteen minutes, and there's a flat writing surface available, I will take out a legal pad and pen. I've discovered that if I feel any resistance to writing something down, simply because I just don't have the tools handy, I won't do it. Better to make capturing as easy as possible, before you need it.

WHITEBOARDS

Another great tool is a whiteboard. I guarantee that when one is around, (as long as it's accompanied by fresh, wet markers!), I will get more good ideas than if nothing to record them was available.

Obviously whiteboards are great tools to have in meeting rooms, for group brainstorms and planning sessions. They are also terrific to have in your own office, at home or at work, for thinking out loud with yourself, as well as with others. Many kitchens have small whiteboards that can serve a similar function.

A useful technique is to have a digital camera handy, so that at the end of a good data-collection or organizing session, someone can take a picture of the board and e-mail it to the group for archiving and triggering follow-up, if needed.

There are now many computer and Web-based versions of whiteboards that serve the same kind of function for individuals and virtual teams across a shared platform. Mind-mapping software is another one of my most valuable tools. Since I love creating and thinking at my computer, having a capturing device like this sort of free-form application has boosted my productivity tremendously. It somehow gives me an elegant excuse to just have ideas and validate the process with a sophisticated piece of technology.

SUCCESS FACTORS FOR CAPTURING

Not only do you need the right tools to be able to maintain clear mental space, but you also need to ensure that you don't undermine the capturing process with some inappropriate constraints. You also should realize the potential future value created by effective capturing behaviors.

Some rules and best practices you should keep in mind for capturing:

No Bad Ideas

Too often people are hesitant to express themselves due to their fear of judgment or punishment for having an idea that is "wrong," stupid, or inappropriate. If your business promotes that kind of right/wrong thinking and a hierarchical value chain of intelligence and perception, your staff won't be invested, no matter what. On the personal side, if you resist acknowledging and capturing incomplete and unhandled items of your own because of your own self-judgments, you'll remain in a somewhat psychically constipated state. You must be willing to admit what you don't yet feel is under control before you can deal with it positively.

Overcapture

There's more than you think in what you think. If you are willing to step into the very unfamiliar space (for most people) of identifying and looking at virtually *everything* that is on your mind, by writing it down somewhere that you (and potentially others) can see, you'll be amazed and inspired by what that process triggers. You'll take the conversation to a deeper level, and will see details and creative additions to the topic you won't have seen before.

Stream of Consciousness

In the vein of the previous point, there's no end to the value that can be generated by permission granted to the psyche to express itself, and range freely, ad infinitum. I defy anyone to take a specific project, bring everyone into the room who may be involved in any way with the production or the outcome of the event, give everyone free reign to express what might be on his or her mind about it through the close of the meeting, and not come up with a stunningly well thought out, planned, and organized event. Significant components will also be created that would never even have been considered, were there not a forum set up for that kind of thinking.

No Commitment

The recognition that idea generation is not the same as making decisions about goals and plans is a critical element in the overall objective of achieving and maintaining control. Personally, before you're willing to stretch out and express thoughts in areas that are still unformed and unfamiliar, you must be able to trust that you will not suffer a negative consequence for having a bad idea. You must feel confident that you have a context that gives you the freedom to ramble, spout out about, express concerns about, and explore ideas, without a responsibility to commit to or defend them. A great phrase to add to your organizational and personal vocabulary is, "Well, another way to look at this is . . ." You want to know that you have considered all the options.

Capturing as a Lifestyle Factor

Writing things down takes intention and some effort, so it has to become a routine that is followed consistently. For some people this activity has a connotation of lower-level professional behavior. Many executives like to think of themselves as above such menial tasks as taking notes, which makes it relatively easy to slip into the "I don't need to write it down" mode. Certainly, you don't need to write everything down—on many occasions you will simply be listening and touring in your mind. But recognizing when something might have meaning for you in the future and getting used to scribbling it on a piece of paper, to be thought about and dealt with later, is a highly productive habit.

Thinking *About* Your Stuff, Not *of* It

Remember that your mind is for having ideas, not for holding them. Once your head is freed from the noise that keeping things in it produces, you will notice that you are more likely to be focusing on your life and work in new ways. You should be thinking *about* your stuff, not *of* it.

It's an interesting paradox that people seem to want to keep things in their head as a way to *maintain* control of them, not realizing that such behavior only creates the opposite result. When you experience anything out of whack or off center, instead of trying to clamp down harder on it in your mind, apply free-form externalizing of whatever details you can identify. Again, remember that your mind is not designed to be simultaneously focusing on more than one topic, and that happens when the input is kept internal.

One of the most graphic representations of this principle came from a parent who wrote to me about his experience with his very young son, whom he was trying to train to clean up his own room. The dad was having no success at all, until one day he thought he'd try something that keyed off his experience in my GTD seminar. He and his son got a big box, put it in the middle of the room, and made a game out of going around the room, gathering everything that wasn't in its proper place, and putting it in the box. His son would then pull out one toy or piece of clothing at a time, which he put away with enthusiasm! Trying to grasp simultaneously all the factors inherent in "clean your room" simply blew his son's psychic fuses and threw him out of control. When the task was broken down into one item at a time, it automatically triggered positive engagement with what had previously been an amorphous source of stress and procrastination. This methodology can be as effective for an executive team as it was for a three-year-old.

As you build an awareness and a set of practices that support this first and very critical part of gaining control—recognizing, acknowledging, accepting, and externally objectifying what has the attention of yourself and others—you will come into possession of a master key for reducing stress and increasing creative, intelligent thinking.

Many people I have worked with over the years reach this first stage, find it extremely rewarding, and begin to write all kinds of things down that they never used to capture before. Unfortunately many of them stop there, and their world begins to fill up with lists, Post-it notes, notebooks, and miscellaneous paper and computer files that still need something done with them. Once the raw materials are corralled, the next stage, clarifying, must be applied to keep that sense of control developing.

6 | Getting Control: Clarifying

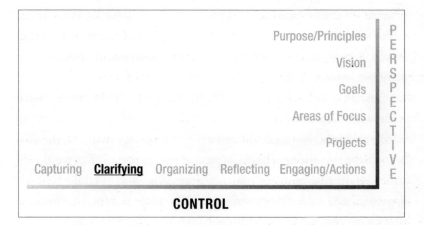

If you aren't yet at the point of clarity, then make that your first goal.
It's a big waste of time to go through life being unclear about what you
want. Most people wallow way too long in the state of "I don't know
what to do." They wait for some external force to provide them with
clarity, never realizing that clarity is self-created. The universe is waiting on you, not the other way around, and it's going to keep waiting
until you finally make up your mind. Waiting for clarity is like being
a sculptor starting at a piece of marble, waiting for the statue within
to cast off the unneeded pieces. Do not wait for clarity to spontaneously
materialize—grab a chisel and get busy!

—Steve Pavlina

This second stage in gaining the upper hand on life and work is the one most associated with "knowledge work athletics"—a phrase given to me by an Australian consultant who read *Getting Things Done* and suggested that what I had done was describe the actual moves of the thinking process required to define what our work actually is. In the Clarifying stage, you get the opportunity to focus your attention on what has your attention, so it will stop expending energy inappropriately. This is why GTD is fundamentally much more about mind management than about time management. Without this crucial stage of thinking and decision-making, making trusted choices about what to do at any moment in time is nigh impossible. In the original GTD workflow model, I referred to this stage as "processing," but in its broadest application "clarify" is a more encompassing word for the principle at work here.

The behavior in this phase—the thinking required to decide what to do with something when it's not obvious or self-evident—is one in which we are all engaged. But, as with much of my material, the goal is to make conscious what is typically instinctive. What we do instinctively is for the most part not done as well as it could be if we approached it with more awareness. When the productive thinking process is applied with focus and intention, it creates much more value. It is also a behavior that you can practice, acquire as a habit, and then do with great facility.

Although many people may have gained the constructive habit of capturing on the front end, they still seem to resist this all-important decision-making stage of processing what they have collected. By doing so they are avoiding the determination of meaning. I'm not referring here to the Ultimate Meaning—that's a philosophical/spiritual analysis outside the scope of this book. "Meaning" in this context refers to the relative meaning of the things we engage with. Is it a subject you care about, and if so, how exactly do you frame your relationship to it?

The chairman of a successful investment advisory company was thrilled with his newly acquired GTD habit of writing ideas on Post-it notes while he was in meetings with his senior team. The problem was that he now had hundreds of yellow sticky notes all over his desk, drawers, and notebooks. He hadn't yet adopted the equally critical habit of getting all those inputs into one bucket, from which they could then file themselves back to the front of his consciousness, one at a time, forcing the appropriate decisions to be made about each of those ideas. He was resisting the exercise of determining meaning.

The Organizer as Therapist?

In recent years the whole arena of "personal organizing" has experienced quite a heyday. One article in the U.S. national press focused on the phenomenon of the "organizer as therapist," citing anecdotal evidence of how people had begun to express their vulnerabilities and core life issues when confronted with how to deal with the things that they had accumulated around them. Salespeople in the stores catering to the organizing bug were dealing with customers breaking into tears as they asked them helpful questions about what they needed to organize.

There is a logical explanation for this phenomenon. Usually things remain disorganized when people don't confront their meaning. To actually decide what you're going to do with or about something demands that you deal with how you relate to its content, your agreements about it, and how it fits into the rest of your world. What do you do with old pictures of family? To answer that question some part of you will have to visit (or revisit) the question of how important visual reminders of people who have played a role in your life are to you. As simple as making those kinds of determinations is for most people, the process can surface quite a plethora of unfinished internal business.

You are as likely to avoid deciding about an e-mail invitation to an event you're not sure about going to as you are to avoid deciding about whether you need to intervene now in your dad's health and elder-care situation. A project team is as likely to avoid deciding whether it should get the financial data someone suggested it access as its members are making a determination about whether they should renegotiate their committed timelines with the head of the division.

The Nature and Volume of "Stuff"

I have referred in my writings to the phenomenon of "stuff"—those things that have landed in your world physically and psychologically that don't belong there forever but about which you've yet to determine what you're going to do. It is the inventory of things impinging on our awareness that are still, to some degree, out of focus.

Most of the contents of a mind sweep or a data-gathering in the capture phase will still be of this nature, as are many of the items piled on your desk or in one of its drawers. You might have merely written "mom" on a list as you were capturing what had your attention, and there's obviously more to clarify about "mom" before it will actually be released from your head. While it's great to have collected that thought to begin with, the main reason for gathering such subjects into one place is to make them more obvious and you more motivated to deal with them, one at a time.

Have you received a letter—at home or at work—that you've opened and read, and it's still lying around somewhere? If so, why didn't you throw it away? It's been read, right?

"But, David, it's a letter!"

"Understood. But what are you going to *do* with the letter?"

"Do??? . . . It's a *nice* letter."

"But what are you going to *do* with the nice letter—write the sender back? Put her new address into your address book? Share the information with your partner? File it as reference, under 'Nostalgia—Letters—Misc.'? Get a warm feeling again by putting it in a tickler file and having it resurface in five days to give you a nice surprise?"

The letter is a classical example of "stuff." As it is, it owns a piece of your brain. Every time you walk by it, it lies there, pleading with you, "Decide about me, process me, clarify me!" Because you can't stand that whining static, you go numb to the letter. It no longer "bothers" you—you're just partially unconscious regarding it.

Notes still residing on note-taking pads are of a similar nature, as are scraps of paper often pinned on bulletin boards. The majority of contents of most To-do lists are still in this amorphous state of suspense, as are situations that have emerged in a company that the senior team knows are going on, but has yet to decide what to commit to do about them.

"Stuff" takes the form of collected business cards, miscellaneous notes in planners and calendars, broken items laid aside on your worktable, and the bottom layers of coffee-table piles. It's as obvious as the contents of that office cabinet left by the previous tenant and as subtle as the internal feelings of a staff person triggered by his boss's angry response to the report in the last meeting.

Basically, "stuff" is everything in the giant in-basket of your work and life, only a tiny fraction of which most people have actually funneled into their working capture lists or trays. Most is floating around the house, office, and psyche, still uncollected, much less clarified. As I mentioned earlier, it is easy for the more subtle commitments we have at the higher horizons of our life to fade into the background and continue to gnaw at us. Problems that haven't been turned into projects and actions; dreams and inspirations that haven't been acknowledged as consciously as they should be; changing situations in life and work that haven't yet been consciously identified—these represent "stuff" in its more elusive forms.

Assuming you have taken the previous chapter about "capturing" to heart, you will have made tremendous progress in simply identifying all of those kinds of attention-grabbing agendas and items, and putting some reminder of them in front of you, to be dealt with.

Dealing with "Stuff"

If you avoid the clarifying stage and do not deal with your "stuff," it will continue to pull on and exhaust your consciousness. What does "deal with" really signify, in this context?

It is a matter of determining the specific meaning of a particular item for you, and then moving it to the appropriate place for things that share that meaning (a subject that is covered in the next chapter on the third phase of control, organizing). In the first phase of capturing, a best practice is to *avoid* doing analysis and decision-making, so you don't constrain the gathering process. But the second phase is where you put on your self-consulting hat and determine how to relate to what you've identified. Thoughts are usually on your mind for a reason, though in the moment we may not stop to determine exactly what that purpose is, nor what to do about it.

THE VISION VERSUS EXECUTION DYNAMIC

The difference between the first two stages of gaining control—capture and clarify—is significant, and any failure to make that distinction can be a block to your effectiveness. I described the two polar-opposite quadrants in the matrix of self-management—the Micromanager (Implementer) and the Crazy Maker (Visionary). That antithesis comes into play here as well, though the polarity is now embodied within your own self: there's the part that has ideas and the part that decides what to do about them. They are very different types of behaviors that operate from very different perspectives, using different tools.

The Visionary part of you operates best with few constraints—it likes to have all sorts of ideas, thoughts, and inspirations wherever and whenever it can. When you're in this mode you can read a single issue of a magazine and generate at least a dozen things to do—restaurants to try out, cool new travel accessories to buy, six ideas that might improve the next staff meeting. The in-basket, as a capturing function, is the perfect tool for this part of your personality. Grab that idea on a notepad, tear out that article that could be useful, and so on. Don't hold back—there's potential gold in there somewhere! Having a trusted capture tool or bucket at hand serves this function wonderfully, inviting you to have even more thoughts, and giving you more things to explore and do. Don't worry—someone else will deal with it!

In fact, that "someone else" who will take the handoffs is a very different person—namely *you*, in operation mode! It's your job to take each newly generated and collected item and make the hard-nosed executive decisions about it: What is this? Is this really worth doing? How does it fit with all the other things I have to do? This is the role of the clarifier—evaluating the raw inputs against all sorts of constraints and criteria.

The stumbling block shows up when you force the Visionary to make considered decisions and choices or when you demand that the Implementer expand his thinking and be creative. Both modalities will short-circuit when faced with those relatively unnatural acts. This, again, is one of the major reasons that traditional time-management and organizational formats have been rather unsuccessful in being adopted: they have insisted on compressing antithetical approaches into a single all-purpose directive—get organized! To really gain control, an individual must have an unfettered ability to maintain a flow of creative thinking and then have a trusted way to assess and manage the resultant inputs and outputs. Most people make a list, trying to do both at the same time, and it just doesn't work. That approach is neither fully capturing nor fully clarifying. Making one list in an attempt to get focused and organized will certainly be more effective than keeping everything in your head. But using it to combine two functions is extremely limiting to the psyche.

The distinction between capture and clarification is more evident, and therefore typically handled more skillfully, in team and group settings, simply because brainstorming has become such an accepted practice for planning and decision-making sessions. One of the key principles of good brainstorming is "the more the merrier" in terms of the free flow and capture of ideas. Good brainstorming is stifled by any attempt to analyze and evaluate the meaning and merit of those ideas too soon. Every possibly relevant thought should be expressed, and in front of everyone, and then the focus can shift into the modality of determining which ideas are more important and more useful. If you try to do that all at once, you'll undermine the event.

The Key to an Empty In-basket

This second stage of control features the critical component of cleaning out your in-basket, including voice mails, e-mails, and any paper-based or physical things you have collected. If you want to attain what many call the "holy grail of GTD"—having all your in-basket zones at zero—you must become adept at this part of the model.

I have referred to this stage as "processing" because it involves the all-important sorting and sifting that must be done with the hundreds of inputs you must deal with daily. But as a universal principle, it has implications far beyond just cleaning up the in-basket.

After we accept the information about what's going on (capture), we then create a relationship with it. What does this mean to me or to us? We can accept what we experience in the world, and must, to freely move beyond it; but closely tied to the acknowledgment of what we experience is the need to define our relationship to it.

Relative to the game of work and business of life, this is the essential thinking that has to be applied to the physical inputs we allow, plus the random ideas, thoughts, and perspectives that show up when we approach a problem, project, or situation. Some of those inputs and thoughts will be more useful than others, some will need to be reassessed later, and some will be irrelevant after all.

We tend to automatically notice things in our world that some part of our psyche has programmed us to regard as meaningful. Not everything is information that attracts our attention. The mail delivered to someone on the next street does not have significance to us, but our own does. This sort of prefiltering enables us to deal with the practicalities of our daily life. Once a potentially meaningful item gets into our world, however, it is seldom as clear on first encounter as it needs to be, to create closure with it internally. We must devote conscious energy and focus to it. There are three further critical stages still remaining to be applied in order to relieve the pressure that is created by the bombardment of recognized "stuff"—clarifying, orga-nizing, and reviewing it.

The problem is that most people want to move on to "organize" before they extract exactly what needs to be organized. They seem to be treading water without ever making any real progress, rearranging incomplete piles of still-unclear stuff.

But once you actually make the necessary decisions to clarify what particular things mean to you, organizing becomes rather simple and organic. You can structure your system to fit the nature of the contents.

"David, what do I do with this piece of paper?"

"What is it? What do you think you should do with it?"

As obvious and commonsense as that last question probably sounds to you, you might be surprised how much unclarified stuff like this is lying around the desks, homes, and minds of some of the most sophis-ticated people and companies in the world.

If you try to skip this stage of thinking, you will never see any light at the end of the tunnel, and you'll be continually compensating by trying out the latest gadgets that still somehow don't provide what you need, the way you need it. Once you really integrate this clarification process into your life- and work style, you will find yourself comfort-able with a wide range of tools that can genuinely work for you. If you haven't applied this process, nothing will seem to serve you very well.

The Critical Questions to Be Answered

All this discussion about the importance of this phase of achieving control and the almost universal avoidance of it might give the im-pression I'm talking about a very complex formula or model. On the contrary, to really get the things you have captured off your mind, there are only a few very straightforward but critically important questions that must be answered about each one. It's a process you know how to do—in fact, you're doing it all the time. The practice simply needs to be applied more consciously, more consistently, and sooner than it typically is.

In brief, you just need to decide whether something is actionable or not, and then determine the outcomes and actions required for those things you've committed to move on; for those that don't have an action tied to them, decide what's trash, what's to be reviewed later, and what's to be classified as reference.

The tactical version of this procedure, applied to managing your own work flow and clearing your in-basket, was illustrated in *Getting Things Done,* in the "work flow diagram" that became well-known in the GTD community around the world (see Appendix vi). But, as with all the principles that I introduced in the first book, there is much more to the dynamics of this applied thought process than may have seemed evident on first glance.

As I go into greater detail about these clarifying questions, it will be helpful to bring to mind something that you may have captured on a Mind Sweep list, or anything that happens to be on your mind right now, and notice how you might answer them.

IS IT ACTIONABLE?

This is the first distinction that must be made about anything that presents itself in your world—is there some action that needs to be taken about or because of it?

There are two possible answers here—"yes" and "no." "Maybe" is actually "no, but the item might require action later," with the assumption that you are clarifying meaning *at this moment in time* to you.

People often avoid making this distinction and allow rather large quantities of things to accumulate in blended stacks. Whenever actionable and nonactionable items are parked in the same location, a numbness develops in the psyche regarding the whole lot. If you scan your personal universe, notice (if you can) areas that you are resistant to examining in detail; they will probably reflect an inventory of both actionable and nonactionable things. When your mind focuses on the pile, it will automatically attempt to sort it into what the various items within it mean; and if those meanings are different, the discrepancy is just too overwhelming to tolerate. Soon you won't pay much attention to the stack, other than perhaps to recall it with a mild annoyance. The problem is that we don't seem to go numb to just that pile—it affects our total energy and clarity.

E-mails that require a response or an action are held in the same file as those that need only to be referenced or deleted. Magazines to be read lie in the same pile as those that should be thrown away. Notes on a whiteboard are often a blend of valuable projects and irrelevant asides. Bulletin boards are special culprits in this regard, easily becoming home to an incoherent combination of phone numbers, reminders, schedules, inspirations, and cartoons. Shared project management thinking, especially in Web- and software-enabled collaborative versions, can easily become subject to this numbing dynamic. The two areas in which this primary lack of clarification manifests itself are (a) the accumulation of unprocessed inputs, and (b) groups of two or more that allow meetings to end without responsibly identifying action items and commitments that may have been generated and who owns them.

This is one point on the road map for gaining control and perspective that I have seen change how people live and work as well as impact entire corporate cultures. When someone begins to sensitize herself to the pressure of indecisions about things lurking on her desk or in her mind, and when a company begins to model and expect responsible closure on its interactions, in terms of what now needs to be moved on by whom, it can mark the onset of a brave new world. Ambiguity is a monster that can still take up residence and lurk in the sharpest, most productive places and among the most sophisticated people. Embedding the habit of forcing this one decision—is it actionable or not?—can be the catalyst for shifting a person or a culture from Victim to Captain and Commander modality.

If you were willing to be honest in the first capturing phase, and aware enough to write down "my company's stock price" and "my nephew's drug problem" and "Dad's health situation" and "the declining real estate market" and "my boss's personality" and everything else of an important but still-ambiguous attention-grabbing nature, and if you were willing to ask and answer the basic question about whether there was something that could possibly be done about that situation, you'll own a master key to winning at the game of work and business of life. This is another prime example of being dependent for your positive experience not on the world's circumstances, but on how you are *engaged* with those circumstances. Believe it or not, it's all in how you think about it, which defines how you approach it.

THE FUNDAMENTAL THOUGHT PROCESS FOR GETTING THINGS DONE

Once you have determined that an item is actionable, you must then apply a critical thought process to it—one that represents a real secret for productive work and life. It is the essential clarifying activity for a vast majority of what grabs everyone's attention, and it comes down to the two questions:

- *What's my desired outcome?* What am I committed to accomplishing or finishing about this?
- *What's the next action?* What's the next thing I need to do to move toward that goal?

These two questions, which I recognized years ago and put forward as the key determiners of the "work" that needs to be managed, remain at the core of the thought processes of the Getting Things Done models. What does "done" mean? What does "doing" look like, and where does it happen? These questions are almost never both answered completely when we encounter "stuff" that we know we ought to do something about. We have to apply intentional thinking and decision-making to get them clear.

This is the primary junction at which you transform vague "stuff" into real projects you can actually manage. "Mom" is not a subject about which you can do anything; "Give mom a great sixtieth birthday party" is a concrete goal that can give you a clear direction and focus. "Draft list of possible invitees to Mom's party" is a very specific task you know you could accomplish, quickly and easily, at your computer. It's not a great distance to get from "Mom" to a clear self-instruction that gets you going physically toward an inspiring finish line. But it can be a light-year of psychological space if you have yet to define clearly your end point and what action, exactly, will start you toward it.

THE TACTICAL VALUE OF OUTCOME FOCUSING

A critical ingredient for high-performance positive engagement is having and holding an intention toward what you desire, or what you want to become true. Many books could be filled (and are) with the multitude of ways available to understand the power and utility of outcome thinking. Goals, objectives, quality, mission, purpose, direction, intention—these are all concepts that have been wrapped around the central idea that you need to know where you're going in order to get there most effectively. While reiterating that somewhat obvious truth might seem redundant here, it does have a very tactical application, that is *not* so self-evident—namely, in its relationship to dealing with how to get a handle on the confusion and overwhelm of the day-to-day.

As I've explained earlier, many of the things that pull and push on your attention are still in the nature of "stuff"—items you're aware that need to be dealt with, but that still exist in a rather amorphous state. Training yourself to overcome the need to "have it all together" before you define what you're really seeking to finish or accomplish has a profound impact on your ability to get things done in a sustainable, relaxed way.

Before you try to figure out how to solve a problem like an issue with an employee, it's wise to put a stake in the ground for yourself, like writing "Resolve situation with Carolyn Jones" on a list of your projects. It's common to resist making that commitment clarification until you actually decide whether you are going to fire her or not. The truth is, at that moment, your desired outcome is to have the situation reach its optimal closure, either way. More often than not, if you haven't decided exactly how you're going to handle the problem, you'll be procrastinating about the whole thing. If, however, you've trained yourself to identify a definite outcome like "Resolve XYZ" and use that as a trigger for your mind to formulate next actions toward achieving it, it's likely to get you unstuck and acting before you normally would, and in a more effective and relaxed manner.

If your consciousness can focus simply on moving toward resolution rather than having a situation all figured out, you'll tend to point your thinking toward specifics—"Oh, yeah, it's occurred to me that I should check in with Steven, Carolyn's peer in the department, for his perspectives on this situation. I'll have John set a time for Steven and me to meet." It is much easier to progress when such steps have been determined.

One of the surprises to me over all these years of working with thousands of relatively sophisticated people is how challenging it has been for most to grasp this very operational application of outcome thinking. Is summer approaching with you still having lots of things to decide and set up for your kids' activities over those months? Have you had "Get the summer set up for the kids" on some sort of Project list, from the moment it occurred to you that you needed to start thinking about it?

Have you identified all the ideas you've told yourself to "look into" as research projects, which you are managing as concretely as any of your others? Most people tend to wait until they've already done enough research to make a decision, before they're willing even to admit they've been engaged in a project. The truth is, the project exists as soon as you have a commitment to make the decision. Typically a good 10 percent of my own active projects start with "R & D," which is my shorthand for "Look into." The topic could be a new cell phone I heard about that I might want to buy, a potential strategic partnership, or the next vacation my wife and I are starting to think about taking, though we're not sure exactly when, where, or for how long ("R & D spring holiday with Kathryn").

Another common outcome set that people are prone to resist is what I consider "process" projects—the outcomes of having a procedure or system in place to handle whatever negative event keeps occurring. It is common for our clients, when doing a mind sweep, to write down things like "pay bills," "exercise," "more time with Jonathan," and "sales strategy." It's understandable that such concerns would be on someone's mind. Now it's possible that each one of these items could be considered an "area of focus"—what I identify as the twenty-thousand-feet horizon, which includes all the parts of your life and work that must be maintained at some standard, to maintain a balanced whole. "Bills" is about maintaining finances in order, "exercise" would refer to health and vitality, "time with Jonathan" might be family relationships, and "sales strategy" could simply be a reminder about the responsibility for growing sales.

But we usually don't have to press too hard on the people who have identified such projects, to discover that what's really got their attention is a more ambitious scheme they'd like to set up or accomplish *about* these areas, apart from just having a reminder to maintain them. For instance, "pay bills" often clarifies as "set up my electronic bill-paying system" or "establish our personal finance processes." "Exercise" becomes "Set up an exercise routine." "More time with Jonathan" can often be interpreted as "Implement a program of quality time with kids." And "sales strategy" might actually mean "Ensure sales plan is operational." The difference in each case here is subtle but significant.

The first words and ideas were important to capture, but still fuzzy in terms of the actual game to be playing. The real projects at hand, more discretely and accurately described, offer quite a different and much more highly effective focus for achieving success.

It's almost impossible to motivate yourself or anyone else to play a game in which you're not aware of a concrete goal line. That goal can be a very big and long-range one or a very short-term one, and as long as you can measure where you stand in relationship to it (it's there and you're here), you have the game defined. That knowledge leaves you much clearer about how much energy and how many resources you need to win. When the end result is vague, it's hard to maneuver to get wind in your sails.

There are many different types of positive futures and images that we all occasionally will need to work with to define a course and stay on it. Later chapters will offer more detail about the various horizons of outcomes that give us perspective. Being good at working with one of these levels, however, does not necessarily make you proficient at another. I have coached many senior professionals who are comfortable with identifying long-term goals and objectives, but have a heck of a time focusing themselves on the kind of project-level outcomes I've given here as examples. No matter how sophisticated we think we might be, there always seem to be one or more areas in our life and work that we tend to allow to remain unclear, causing us angst and distracting our focus. Learning to capture and face all of those little demons equally, applying the bulletproof formula of defining specific and complete-able outcomes for the items we deem actionable, is a fundamental success behavior for making it all work.

THE REALITY CHECK OF THE NEXT ACTION FOCUS

The other equally important component for getting and maintaining clarity and control is defining your relationship to the world in terms of concrete physical actions to take. I will expand on this later in chapter 9, on the final control stage of engaging, but there is a significant reason to touch on it now, relative to this discussion on how to eliminate confusion and fuzzy thinking about whatever has your attention. Half of the secret to achieving clarity in any situation is asking, "What are we trying to do here?" The other half, and at least as critical, is, "What's the next action?" It's relatively easy to fulfill the first part, set a goal. And everyone involved can sneak away with at least short-term impunity about who's actually responsible for reaching that goal and establishing how it fits into the whole mix of available resources and other goals. Having to grapple with defining the next action, however, means plugging into concrete reality and requires a specific investment of time and energy and a reallocation of resources, bringing all kinds of previously unseen and unspoken thoughts, issues, agendas, and concerns to the surface.

People can easily believe that they're clear about a project, but you often won't find out that they're not until you force the thinking and decision-making required to answer that straightforward little question about what next physical step should be taken. I have observed many a project management meeting, trying to move to closure on their inspirational and seemingly concrete decisions, goals, and plans, but instead revealing a major lack of clarity by simply trying to get consensus on the next actions that should be taken after the meeting.

If there is one litmus test to determine the degree of control, perspective, and clarity in any situation, whatever the number of people, it would be this: Is everyone involved in agreement about the subsequent actions that need to be taken, and who's going to be responsible for them? If that consensus exists, there is no need for further capturing, clarifying, organizing, or reviewing; there is no need to discuss or examine desired outcomes. You're on. That's not to imply that the resulting actions will inevitably be the right ones—it just means that positive engagement has been maximized in this particular situation, for all involved. Whoever is playing will be in the optimal position to direct his focus to the job at hand and to learn and course-correct while moving forward.

As all roads lead to Rome, all success comes back to action. It is the final of the five stages of gaining control, and the ultimate expression of all six horizons of maintaining perspective. If you simply took every item that has your attention, on any level, and forced yourself to determine the very next step to be taken on each of them, moving it toward some closure, you would be amazed at the clarity you would achieve.

IF IT'S NOT ACTIONABLE, THEN . . .

In addition to all the stuff you interact with that you need to address, there are many other things that show up in your world that, while needing no further action or commitment on your part, do require you to make a determination about which of the following three sub-categories each one of them falls into:

It's Meaningless

An obvious set of items that have a discrete meaning would be those that actually have no meaning at all: things you no longer need, or didn't need in the first place—junk mail to toss, e-mails that have no interest or relevance to you, absurd telemarketing messages on your answering machine. This category includes anything in your environment that has no reason to be there, or to exist at all. Think of it as fodder for the Delete key on your computer, your wastebasket, recycle bin, Dumpster, shredder, or local charity.

Trash, once it is determined to be so, is usually not a problem, unless your garbage collection service in on strike, your kitchen disposal is broken, or you're just too lazy to pull out the dead rose from the garden. The biggest problem is deciding whether it's trash or not to begin with. As the previous section explained, if you can't really deal with ascertaining whether something should be moved on, accepted as is, or simply eliminated, you'll find yourself in psychic quicksand.

I estimate that 95 percent of the clients with whom we work individually have surrounded themselves with stuff that consists of at least 10 percent trash. And 50 percent of them could eliminate at least 25 percent of what's lying around them. That's not by my standards, but by *theirs*. They've simply been avoiding making the decision about what their stuff means to them, and/or are not willing to move the stuff to its proper place. Unless an active reclarification process is applied continually to the "stuff," it tends to expand and even self-propagate. In turn a general psychological haze grows in proportion to the amount of trash that's accumulated and been unacknowledged.

As mundane as this particular category may seem, it can often touch many deeper and more sensitive issues. In order to not be controlled by a box in the closet, full of mementos of an ex–life partner, you must decide whether they are still meaningful or not, that is, is there still a reason to keep them? There is no right or wrong answer to that question—only *an* answer. If you avoid making a decision, they will have *you*, not you them. Again, this is why professional organizers often step into a counseling role. When faced with the choice of clarity or familiarity, most people default to the latter; being put into the position to have to decide the real meaning of something, in present time, will often surface uncomfortable issues.

Our staff is well trained to avoid editorializing about whether our clients should keep stuff or not. If they want it, they keep it. Throwing something away that still has genuine meaning can create its own distraction. The relevant issues in that case may be finding the space to hold it and the ease of finding it in that space.

I do have to say that, after many years of working this process with all kinds of people, those who have learned to say "no" more easily to the various things that present themselves into their world seem to have a much more comfortable time making all kinds of decisions that are important for winning at the game of work and business of life. Recognizing and acknowledging this category of things to eliminate is critical, if only to make the conscious clarification of *everything* a universal habit.

It's to Hold On, Until a Later Time

Of course, it's fine to decide not to decide. That will be the fate of quite a number of things that show up in your world, things that you have yet to decide are actionable or not. It actually is okay to remain in that state for the moment.

One of the most interesting, subtle, and underutilized distinctions is whether a possible action or project is one that should be moved on—now, if possible—or whether it can simply be started at a later date, or perhaps not moved on at all. This delineates a set of items I have referred to as "someday/maybe" types of commitments. You might want to take a class in ballroom dancing, but not now. You would like to be able to hire a full-time webmaster, but not yet. You'd like to be able to know how to write and run macros within Excel, but . . . well, no way at this point in time.

My personal Someday/Maybe list is quite a bit longer than my active list of projects. It includes some ideas on one end of that spectrum that I would consider in the "fantasy" category—like taking a canoe trip down the Mississippi River. On the more "realistic" side, it contains projects like scanning my old photos for digital storage and rewriting a segment of our Web site. Nothing in this category has a specific next action attached to it—that's a defining characteristic. Active projects all have specific next actions determined that I would actually move on if I had the time and opportunity. None of the someday/maybe's include any commitment to moving forward at this point in time.

Becoming aware of the power of this clarified okay-to-not-decide-to-move-on category was a major epiphany for one of the most sophisticated people I know. As a senior partner for a large global consulting firm, he was continually coming up with new, creative ideas that might add value to his clients' projects. The problem was, on a not-very-conscious level, he thought that if he had an idea, he ought to be moving on it. Because he had to turn down his idea-generating engine to prevent overwhelm, he felt stale. As soon as he realized that he could give himself permission to have a parking lot for *possible* projects to pursue, without having to allocate resources to them (i.e, he created a Someday/Maybe list just for those kinds of thoughts), his brain jumped into high gear again and he tapped back into a wealth of productive thinking, from which he could later pick the ideas that seemed appropriate for the time and resources available. As simple and obvious as that lesson may seem, it's another example of the many basic GTD concepts that, when applied to real-life circumstances, can generate huge, unexpected value.

Another important reason to identify and acknowledge this category is the propensity for most people in our culture to seriously overcommit, at least in their mind. Because few individuals are willing to capture and objectively lay out the full inventory of their commitments, they can temporarily get away with holding an unrealistic set of agreements with themselves without having to confront their full implications.

When, however, people begin to recognize the value of acknowledging the extent of that workload to themselves, their next big hurdle to surmount is a list of hundreds of action items, and not freaking out at the sight of it. Many of the clients we have coached over the years have run into a major snag in the implementation of GTD, when they get to the point of responsibly tracking their projects and actions, and the feeling of shame or exhaustion or defeat at having so many "incompletions" in their life and work is more than they can handle emotionally. Their response is to go numb to the lists, to avoid looking consciously at the contents objectively, and to neglect to keep them current. Their extended mind has retreated to its former state—pretty much driven by the latest and loudest.

At this stage our coaches have discovered that a major key to progress is in reminding folks that the someday/maybe category needs to be established or refreshed, and utilized. They need to get to a new level of forthrightness with themselves, reviewing each item on their lists more consciously, and making responsible decisions about whether there is really any chance at all that they can get to those actions soon. If not, the projects should be moved to a holding tank, so the clients can constrain their focus to a more manageable set of possibilities. Of course, the main reason they are hesitant to do *that* is because they don't feel confident that they'll deal responsibly with what's been deposited in the tank.

This is another good example of the holistic nature of the model for control—these stages can't really manifest optimally in isolation, but must work together. You won't allow yourself to relax about a commitment unless you know you'll be reviewing and engaging with it appropriately. And if you're afraid of moving it off a list of active to-dos because you're aware that it needs to be available for consideration with some frequency and the active To-do list is the only one you really pay attention to, you'll keep that "maybe" commitment on that list with all the others. Lacking a trusted organization system you review thoroughly and regularly, including a separate list of what you have "on hold," forces you to leave everything on active lists, which then become so overwhelming that you don't really pay attention to their contents anyway. And you're back to square one.

It's Reference

The final category that is decisive for clarity is one that does not involve action, but has value as information—now or in the future. This is the big area of reference, which takes the form of archived data, and support and collateral material for projects and topics of interest. Typical material can be as granular as someone's phone number, and as immense as the World Wide Web.

Deciding what to keep within accessible distance as reference will always be a judgment call—an infinite amount of information could potentially be relevant to virtually any topic. The key for clarity in this category is again simply to *make* that judgment call: Should I hang on to this or not? I have two recommendations: (a) when in doubt, throw it out, and (b) when in doubt, keep it.

People often complain about their files—both paper-based and digital—insisting that they have too much or that it is simply unusable because of its disorganization and volume. Those could be valid issues, certainly, but in my experience most of the pain in this area is again a function of the lack of clarity of meaning. If you are keeping stuff on your desk or in your briefcase or in the bottom kitchen drawer simply because you won't decide the meaning of it, you'll be controlled by it. As soon as you do determine what's reference, what's trash, what you need to move on, and what's actually okay to not yet decide about, you can collect as much as you care to, and it won't be disturbing to your clarity of focus. It's not about volume—it's about coherence in your relationship to what it is.

The Power of the Fundamental Thinking Process

If you haven't yet applied the principles I'm describing as a conscious process in your universe, the pure conceptual model I'm laying out may seem absurdly simple, basic, and not of particular import. That's understandable, because there is nothing inherent in this methodology that requires deep intellectual rigor to comprehend. Nor are any of these behaviors unfamiliar to most people. I don't think there is anything that I have uncovered in all these best practices that an average twelve-year-old couldn't grasp, recognize, and utilize, in some fashion, to his or her benefit.

A characteristic of these practices is that we hardly need to think about them when things are obvious and easy. We carry out these practices automatically and rather unconsciously when things are flowing and relatively habitual and simple. But when the world throws us for a loop, and when the familiar flow of habitual engagement is disturbed, even such simple procedures as capturing and clarifying not only come to a halt but are often resisted and ignored. The Captain and Commander mode demands that these patterns be consciously applied to whatever has thrown you out of control and blurred your focus. You need to learn what you do well when it's easy to do well, and apply the behaviors discussed in this chapter when you respond to the things that pressure you.

To bring this back to a practical example:

Suppose I have received a letter or e-mail asking me to speak at an upcoming conference. I open it, read it, and then I have some choices.

I may decide it's trash—it's a form letter, not worthy of any further attention. It's out of here.

I could determine that it's not something I want to do, nor do I need to respond to it, but it might be useful later on to know about this group, so I file it as a piece of reference material.

I might think it's possible that I could accept the invitation, but the dates they are requesting are being held tentatively for another client. I won't know for another week if I'm available. So I decide to table the question for ten days, putting the letter in my tickler file, which will deliver it back to me to reassess at that later date.

I may decide that I'm potentially interested, but I want to find out more about the engagement. I now have a project, "Research XYZ conference participation," which I place on my list of projects. I decide the next step is to task my assistant to research the company and brief me about it, which I do by a quick e-mail.

I could add it to a "hunhhh" stack of stuff on the side of my desk.

Which option undermines clarity, control, and perspective? I know this is a tough quiz. But I offer this challenge: What's still of a "hunhhh" nature in your own world right now? How much more completely could you get it captured and clarified?

Appropriate focus creates momentum and decision-making criteria. But that focus does not always happen on its own. The more you have trained yourself to integrate that kind of meaning-clarifying thought process into your life and work, such that you routinely bring it to bear on the more challenging inputs you face, the more you will experience being on the winning side of this equation.

Do your kids know how to think this way? Does your staff? Are any of them allowing things to impinge on their focus and energy, without knowing how they could more productively identify the source of their distraction and how to deal with it? I see schoolchildren carrying huge weights of information and materials in their backpacks and satchels, and I ask myself—why? Are they still simply being given lots of "stuff" and not being taught how to process it appropriately? Almost everyone in the school system who has become familiar with my material—students, parents, teachers, administrators—has expressed his exasperation with the paucity of this kind of training within the education system. There's a lot of information, but not a lot of instruction about how to think about it.

Capturing and clarifying what has your attention is a pivotal step to getting things under control. Without the next phase, however, what you accomplish can all slip away pretty quickly. If your mind doesn't trust that meaningful things are accessible, as they might be needed, it will undermine the whole game by taking everything back into its murky attic. It has to be confident that things are organized.

7 | Getting Control: Organizing

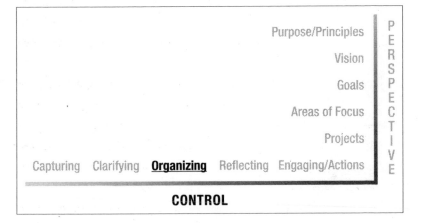

For the first twenty-five years of my life, I wanted freedom. For the next twenty-five years, I wanted order. For the next twenty-five years, I realized that order is freedom.

—Winston Churchill

Wherever we find orderly, stable systems in Nature, we find that they are hierarchically structured, for the simple reason that without such structuring of complex systems into sub-assemblies, there could be no order and stability—except the order of a dead universe filled with a uniformly distributed gas.

—Arthur Koestler

Everyone accepts on some level that being organized is a good thing, or at least recognizes that being disorganized will work against you in some way. There will always be a rebellious contingent that swears by the value of chaos as a source of creativity and spontaneity. But if you actually walked into any one of those people's day-to-day lives, you'd see they'd established some level of order on almost everything that is meaningful to them. Pots and pans are probably in (or near) the kitchen, toothpaste is likely close by to where they brush their teeth, and the keys to their car are likely kept in a contained number of places. If someone was "totally disorganized," he probably couldn't get out of bed. In fact, he probably wouldn't even *be* in his bed—he wouldn't have enough structure to find it or get into it, let alone own one.

Given the vast changes in speed, volume, and ambiguity of what grabs our attention these days, we face an increasing need to have an "extended mind" that can truly relieve the pressure from our psyche and free it up for more valuable work. Enabling such an expansion requires understanding, setting up, and utilizing a more rigorous organizational structure than our brain is capable of.

Inefficient systems drain energy—that's a principle of pure electrical mechanics. A short in the wire, or circuitry, that is not hooked up right, will prevent the maximum flow of power.

If you could return phone calls while you were waiting for someone to show up for a meeting, but you didn't have a list of all the calls you needed to make or the phone numbers themselves, you'd likely be inefficient, that is, you could have used those fifteen minutes productively if you had had what you needed in order to take those actions. If you happened to be "out and about" in your car, and didn't bring a list of all the errands you needed to run in order to move things forward and maintain the details of your life, you'd be likely to miss opportunities to complete those tasks with less investment of your time and focus. Not that you should necessarily do so—at that moment you might have higher priorities, given where you are and what you're up to. But without being organized, you wouldn't even have those options.

The ongoing cultural dialogue about organization seems to reflect or even foster a mystique about the whole topic that gets in the way of its ability to produce effectiveness. I've come to realize that a key mistake that has been almost universally made is the belief that "getting organized" is one event. As I mentioned in an earlier chapter, when the subject of addressing the experience of a lack of control is condensed to "getting organized" as a single practice, it misses the mark and likely produces even more stress than it was intended to relieve. If you're expected to know what to do with something before you give yourself permission to capture it, you'll resist the whole game. If you are supposed to sort things before you have determined their specific meaning, you're operating contrary to how your brain functions. And if you have to set priorities and make decisions, without taking into consideration the context of everything that has your attention, you'll be stepping onto a slippery slope. The inherent artificiality and incompleteness of the required data sets and contexts of most organizational systems won't produce the desired result of adequate control and perspective.

What "Organized" Really Means

What, actually, does "being organized" really signify? Is there some universal standard against which you can hold your husband, your boss, your daughter, or anyone else (including yourself!) who may be driving you up the wall with his or her "disorganization"?

Well, take heart—there actually is a valid definition. Being organized simply means that where things are suits what they mean to you. If reference material isn't where reference material typically goes in your house or office, you're disorganized. If trash is lying somewhere that is not where that kind of trash belongs, you are disorganized. If you have a phone call to make, noted on a sticky note that is not in a location you will access when you want to make calls, you are disorganized. This is not a judgment—it's a simple description of reality. If you want to manage what you need to manage with maximum efficiency and least expenditure of effort, then everything that means something to you should be in its proper place.

The bad (or good) news is that "organized" is a totally self-defined concept, with stable and rigorous definition for each individual. No one else can determine meaning for anyone else, even about so simple a subject as whether he still wants to read a particular magazine. Again, as strange as it may sound, if someone has a big pile of stuff in the corner of his office that he himself has defined as "stuff I don't want to deal with until some undetermined time in the future," and that's exactly where he's decided that kind of material belongs, he's organized.

Although they are often used interchangeably, "neat" and "organized" are not necessarily the same thing. You can be very neat and still not have what you really need to be reminded of in a place that you will be able to see and evaluate when you know you ought to. Likewise some "messy" people have habitually placed all the things that have a specific meaning to them in one identifiable (to them) location.

Often in my seminars I have people do a fun little exercise to highlight this point. I invite them to look in what they've brought with them, especially in wallets, purses, pocketbooks, planners, packs, and briefcases, to see if they can find anything that does not belong there permanently that has been there longer than a few hours, besides money. Of course most people unearth several such items—old receipts, tickets, dead batteries, miscellaneous slips of paper with scribbled notes, and so on. (You wouldn't believe some of the bizarre discoveries people have made, in their own personal accessories.) I point out to them that if they turned up detritus like that, they have identified at least one minor but unnecessary source of irritation in their life that is subtly yelling at them, "Throw me away!" Quite a few find something that does belong somewhere, but not where it has landed—such as reference and support material that isn't serving any function in its current location, but rather is communicating, "File me! Store me!" And a number find items that actually do need to have action taken, but because they have hardly been in the appropriate place to trigger any such action, most people have gone numb to them.

The point here is that matching the concept of meaning to location is a simple one, but it creates an ongoing challenge to keep your world in order. What makes it an especially tricky matter to stay on top of is that the meaning of things changes over time. Today's newspaper is tomorrow's recycle content or fire-starter, but if it's not moved to its newly appropriate locations by tomorrow, you have become to some degree disorganized simply because of the passage of time. The ballpoint pen refills stored in the center drawer of your desk probably did belong there, *when you had that ballpoint pen*. But since you lost it six months ago, its refills are now merely dross and residue creating drag on your systems.

This sort of effort may seem like nit-picking—a messy purse or a crowded desk drawer is hardly the source of great turbulence in your life or work. And no matter how organized, in the truest sense, you might get, there will always be some portion of your universe that is out of synch with changing realities. Indeed, it may never be a high enough priority for you to achieve the perfect state of efficiency in your own systems. My point, however, is that to the degree that you can match up the proper category of item to the appropriately designated location, you will experience a greater ease, flow, and efficiency.

Racing sailboats are kept "shipshape" for a reason. Good sailors ensure that all the sailing gear is cleaned and organized because more surprises can occur at the most awkward times on a sailboat than in most places, so disorganization can have a high price tag. My briefcase (as opposed to my garden shed) is kept closely monitored to verify that everything is exactly where it needs to go. Because I live a relatively mobile lifestyle—I am as likely to be doing productive work between planes in an airline club or while waiting in my dentist's foyer as on a weekday morning in my office—having my virtual desk (briefcase) pristinely in order is a necessity. If I have receipts from previous trips kept in miscellaneous pockets, meeting notes stuffed between folders, and expired cell phone batteries rattling around loose at the bottom, it doesn't make for ease of use when I'm on the run and don't have time or energy to be distracted. You will have to decide for yourself to what degree that experience of frictionless functioning is worth the invested effort needed to achieve it.

Can you be too organized? Not in the pristine sense of how I define the word. If things aren't where they should be, and accessible as you need them, you're simply not organized enough. If you have created structural systems that are unduly complicated and that cause you to have difficulty in accessing what's required, when it's required, you are also disorganized.

This definition of organization also applies to projects, events, and enterprises, though "proper location" in these cases may be more conceptual and contextual than physical. In other words, if you're trying to organize a meeting, all the miscellaneous potentially relevant topics and logistical details should be captured and processed first. Based on the resulting clarified outcome and actions required, the components of the agenda, sequential steps, and relative priorities should be sorted and placed in their proper positions in the plan, allocated to the right people. If a dumb idea winds up being treated as an important component, or if a detail about the food service is misplaced, then the meeting is of course not as organized as it could be.

Meaning Precedes Organization

If you try to get organized before you have defined meaning sufficiently, you will be frustrated in the effort. Though that may seem self-evident, it is not reflected in most people's common behaviors.

A good example would be meeting notes. I have been asked countless times, "David, what do I do with my meeting notes?" My retort is, "What's the relevance of your meeting notes?" It's more than likely multiple meanings will be embodied in a single set of notes. New projects and actions may need to be extracted. Information may simply need to be filed in case it will be useful reference at some later date. Other data may have to be assessed two weeks later after other events have transpired. And irrelevant materials may just need to be discarded. If all those conditions hold true for a set of meeting notes, there is not one thing to organize but several, with each designated for its appropriate spot, depending on what it means to you.

Meeting notes per se usually still fall under the rubric of "stuff," as merely having taken notes does not mean that you are organized. They're a necessary first step, but hardly adequate to attain maximum control and focus. I have encountered many professionals who keep running diaries of meeting notes in spiral-bound notebooks, stowing away their growing archives in a storage drawer or on a shelf. Though there may be some value in being able to review such a detailed chronology of events and input, for the most part those notes are serving as little more than a safety net. Their owners don't trust that they have gathered and organized the information and action items in appropriate places, so they continue to hang on to the raw source material, just in case. Such systems are dangerous because of the potential land mines that might be lurking there, or at least inconvenient because the information is not easily accessible by topic or category—only by date of input.

Most To-do lists, organizing trays and boxes, and even "action" file folders I have seen in use reflect a similar lack of clear categorical distinctions. Although they were introduced with all the best intentions for "getting organized," they are functioning as little more than receptacles for rearranging incomplete piles of unclear stuff.

The steady growth of the organizational gear industry only reflects the hunger for gaining control of the huge volume of miscellany that people are collecting in their lives. All the plastic, wire, and wood boxes; all the trays, holders, notebooks, folders, and desk accessories at least provide defining boundaries that help contain and separate stuff. But without a good underlying model for how and why to contain and separate *what* stuff, and for what *purpose,* shoppers still wander glassy-eyed down the aisles of the office supply and organizing stores, rather clueless as to what they really need. Much like software sitting on your shelf or on your hard drive that seemed like a good idea at the time but now lies fallow, simply taking up space, too much lower-tech gear, however nice looking, remains unused and in the way.

Sophisticated Systems for Mundane Details

Another interesting phenomenon about this stage of control is that the more mundane the level you're trying to organize, the more complex your system must be to manage it well. As you'll see, keeping track of your commitments at the higher elevations is relatively straightforward and simple, as they involve much less content and input, less frequently, and they require less frequent review and access. Your strategic plan or lifestyle vision can be expressed in a few images, goals, and outlines. But keeping up with all the specific details on your projects and all the actions that support all your other commitments can be quite a challenge.

Many people seem to assume that because items like phone calls, errands, and tasks for their assistant are so simple, obvious, and relatively mundane, they only need an equally simple and mundane system to manage them. On the contrary, because of the associated volume of commitments at the action level and the speed with which they change, the tools required to keep up with them all demand a bit more sophistication than simply a calendar and a To-do list. Your organizing processes and tools can't be too enormously complicated, or you wouldn't use them. But they do have to be sufficiently complex to allow for a total inventory and for the ability to view discrete portions appropriately. For that reason, people have often referred to the GTD model as a "sophisticated approach for sophisticated people about very mundane stuff."

The Organizing Categories

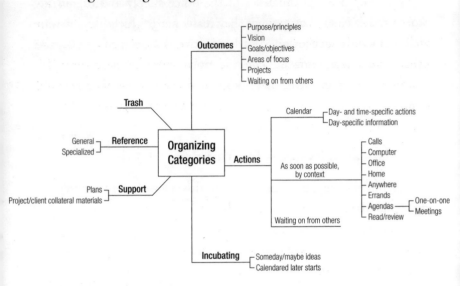

There is obviously a close correlation between the previous chapter, on clarifying, and this one, on organizing. Much like function and form are two sides of the same coin, thinking and tracking the results of that thinking are fundamentally related. As we have discussed, any attempt to be "organized" involves first determining what things mean to you, and then parking those items in a category where those things belong. This principle holds true for everything from arranging your own personal information and reminder system to organizing an event or an entire enterprise.

The key distinction to be made about anything that has potential meaning, system-wise, in your world is to determine whether it falls under the heading of outcomes, actions, things incubating, support material, reference, or trash. There are certainly other meaningful categories of details of your life—for example people around you, physical structures, decoration, and equipment—but all of those, in a way, belong where they are, the way they are. They don't, in other words, require systems per se. Even though people in an organization have to be managed, it's actually their *actions* that need a system of management. You very likely will have to define outcomes and actions about people, equipment, your house, and paintings on your wall, but assuming they're fine as is, they demand little organization other than making sure you can find them when you need them. It's the more ambiguous stuff that needs a good systematic approach and clean categories within which to park appropriate contents.

OUTCOMES

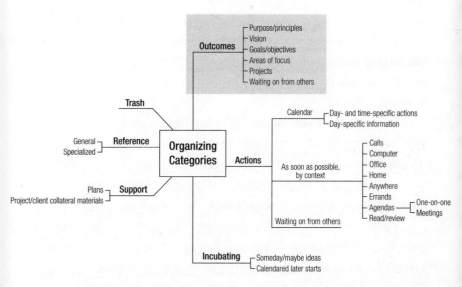

From time to time you will need a broad set of reminders to keep you focused at various horizons. It can be very handy to have lists and other representations of their contents that you can view and review to maintain a steady and specific direction, keep motivated, and maintain appropriate standards. Often simple documents can serve this function.

In this section I will identify the typically effective subcategories of outcomes that you will probably want to track. Whether you wish or need to subdivide these further will be up to you to determine. For instance, many people prefer to separate "personal" projects from "professional" ones. Others like to distinguish between the goals of their company and their personal ones. Some sales-oriented professionals opt to keep their "client projects" separate from all their others.

As with many aspects of maintaining control, you will have to find the right balance between making too few distinctions in your system and too many. Certainly, with a computer and enough data properly gathered, you could ideally separate your sixty projects into personal versus professional; those that deal with your internal processes versus those that are externally facing; those that require lots of resources versus those that are easy and quick; and so on. But even if you did have a system that could track and sort all of that data easily, on the run, someone would still have to select among all those possible sorting criteria when the project was entered, and it may require more time, effort, and thought just to populate the system than is worth the effort.

Once they get a taste of the GTD model and are motivated to get effectively organized, people tend to want to overcategorize their lists. The main reason for that impulse is that they don't really trust themselves to engage with the contents of their system as regularly and conscientiously as they should. Once they begin to have the confidence that they will be looking at *everything* in their system and on their lists as often as needed in an appropriately reflective mode, they usually let go of the angst of having to have everything so rigorously "automated."

Let's examine the "Outcomes" category from top down:

Purpose

Once you're clear about the purpose of your life or your company, even though it is self-evident to you, it might be useful to have a written version that you can review on some regular basis. If you're like me, you can often stray in your thinking from a solid alignment with your purpose, and it's handy to have a document at hand as a reaffirmation of your core inner directive. An organization's purpose or mission statement can provide a similar benefit, and can be especially useful when major changes, challenges, and opportunities are afoot.

Where do you keep statements of purpose? Wherever you'd like. On the wall, in your notebook . . . anywhere that you'd like to be able to access it easily when it deserves a revisit. I keep my personal statement on a mind map in my computer dedicated to my "fifty-thousand-foot" horizon.

Principles

Company principles and values are most often maintained as a list, which is featured on wall plaques, posters, Web pages, or anywhere else that provides sufficient visibility to interested people. We keep a list of our company principles on our Web site, as well as in an executive-level database, framed as "We are at our best when . . ." A simple, numbered list of our twenty-plus standards of best behavior works fine.

On the individual level, a list of personal affirmations or a written personal "credo" would be ideal. How you organize the list may depend on how you want to be reminded of the contents—for years I maintained a set of 3×5-inch index cards, each with its own affirmation, held together by a rubber band. I could carry the batch with me and reaffirm the statements whenever I wanted to be inspired or had a moment to work on my own self-programming. Now I simply keep a list on my computer, synchronized to my PDA.

Vision

Where and in what form would it be wise to keep track of long-term success images and goals? Again, a simple list is often all you will need, kept in a document or database. If you prefer visual representations, you could try representing them with "treasure maps" or collages of pictures and text. I keep both lists and pictorial maps, most of which are linked on another mind map I maintain for my forty-thousand-feet thinking.

Goals and Objectives

As you drop to this more operational horizon, your structure may need a little more detail, though even a dozen or more objectives could still be rather easily maintained as a list in a document. Where do you keep your own performance goals now, if you have them? Where is the plan for the company maintained? As long as these are appropriately accessible, then there's probably nothing more elaborate needed.

Keep in mind that I'm not talking here about the behaviors of creating, reviewing, and engaging productively *with* these lists—that's a very important topic for a later chapter. For purposes of this discussion I'm just describing the boundaries of the category and what tools are needed to keep it distinct.

Areas of Focus

This area of outcomes represents the aspects of our work and life that could be considered the contents of a "high-level maintenance" checklist. As such, those aspects can easily be recorded on a list or two— perhaps one for your job and one for your life. If you have a current job description for yourself now, where is it kept? Do you have a list of all the areas of your life that you need to check in on regularly, to make sure you're not missing anything you need to be addressing or thinking about?

As there are usually fewer than twenty items to be reminded about at this level, a simple document identifying them is sufficient.

Projects

As we descend into the more day-to-day operational aspects of your work and life, the structure that you need to maintain this particular inventory is going to have to be capable of accommodating a greater quantity of data. At any given time most people have between thirty and a hundred projects to keep track of (given my definition of multiple-step outcomes you're committed to finishing within a year). Even as many as eighty-five projects can still be maintained on a list. I'm not referring here to all the plans, details, and collateral material— these fall into another organizational category, which I refer to as "support material." For the purposes of this discussion I'm merely suggesting a list functioning as an index of all your projects—much like looking at the titles of all your file folders, if each project had its own folder.

Because projects should be reviewed at least weekly, the purpose of managing this ten-thousand-feet horizon of outcomes on a single list is simply to give you a convenient overview of all of your commitments, such that you can easily identify gaps in action or momentum for any of them.

Outcomes You're Waiting On from Others

At times you may find yourself waiting for other people to finish something you care about. Though this category is primarily useful for tracking the most mundane level of actions, there are situations in which it might be functional to maintain a "key things I'm expecting others to be doing" list. This would be particularly true in the case of a senior executive who has several key direct reporting staff to whom major projects have been delegated. The executive is not involved on a day-to-day operational basis with any of the projects, but is merely interested in keeping general track of such high-level tasks.

ACTIONS

Now we're down to where the "rubber hits the road"—the physical actions you need to keep track of, with its three associated subcategories: calendared actions, those to do as soon as you can, and the actions you're waiting for other people to take. These also contain several subcategories that you may find highly functional. Because most people actually have over 150 items at this horizon, it's simpler to keep track of them in more discrete subsets than in one big To-do list.

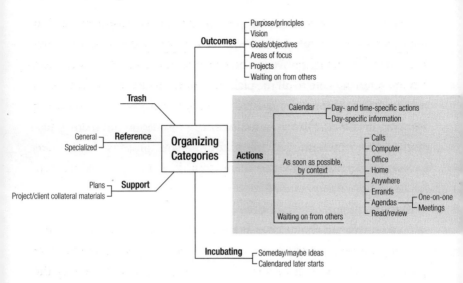

The action area has received the most attention by GTD fans around the world because it represents the biggest departure from the previous traditional time management and personal organization models and because it deals with the multiple events that happen day to day and minute to minute in everyone's life. It's easy to feel out of control in this space because of the speed and volume of items that need to be tracked. It's also where you can get a tremendous sense of relief and positive flow once you get the chaos tamed.

A core aspect of successful GTD implementation is having a total-life action list as the foundation of hour-by-hour decision-making, instead of a simple daily To-do list that often reflects only the latest and loudest demands. There is nothing at all wrong with deciding the most important actions to take for yourself, if you have time. But life changes quickly, with new and random inputs forcing you to rethink your priorities constantly, and very often you will be in a situation with constraints of context, time, and energy. Even in this mode you can still be highly productive if you have all your options for actions easily accessible to you. To be able to work that effectively, though, you need to have a good system for tracking and reviewing discrete action reminders.

It can be intimidating enough to go through the clarification stage, which necessitates deciding all the next actions on all the moving parts of your projects and current commitments. But when you become aware of how many such reminders you have to keep tabs on, it can easily seem a daunting organizational task. The following subcategories have proven themselves to be the most universally effective ways to sort them, allowing you to focus only on what you need to see, when you most need or want to see it.

Calendar

The calendar is the most basic focusing tool on the runway. It charts your next actions specific to particular days and times, and therefore provides critical pinpoints around which you'll manage most of the rest of your work. While you're probably already using your calendar for appointments, we have discovered that it holds a lot more power than most people realize.

The calendar should represent what I refer to as the "hard landscape" for your day—the mostly stationary events and information around which you must negotiate everything else. It's what I pay attention to first, as I start and then proceed through the day; and it is usually open and available to me for most of that time.

The calendar is the best place for three things—appointments, day-specific things to do, and information I need or want to be aware of on that day. The contents of my calendar mean, specifically, "everything I definitely need to know and do today."

Appointments are self-evident, like a 3:30 P.M. teleconference with your sales team. Day-specific tasks are also firm reminders, but they are relevant for an entire day, not a particular time—for instance, if you need to call a client on Friday to confirm that she received your FedEx package due to arrive that day. Or, if you realize that you need to call someone before the end of the day to set up a meeting tomorrow, but can't do it immediately, you'd note a reminder to do so on the calendar, without its being tied to a particular time. If you are using a software calendar system, you may find that its "all-day event" space, usually at the top of the screen, is the best place to put day-specific reminders.

These two types of activities—appointments and other to-dos that have to be handled that day—should be the first things you take note of each morning to let you know how much discretionary time you have for other things, if any.

The third type of entry on your calendar should be any information that you might need or want to be aware of on that day—notices of events taking place that might be meaningful, due dates or start dates, support data for appointments, and so forth. On digital calendars, use the all-day event spaces for this information as well, or attach notes to the appointments.

Your calendar should contain *only* those three items—appointments, day-specific actions, and information. If it is used for any more or any less, it won't be totally trusted for its designed purpose. If you add entries such as what you'd *like* to get done on a given day, you'll have to keep rethinking your schedule, wondering what's real and what's not. If you include less than the three key elements, your mind will constantly be trying to fill in the gaps. If you are surprised by an unexpected request or demand on your time, you need to be able, at a single glance at your calendar, to have a trusted sense about what you can and can't afford to do, at that moment.

Actions to Do as Soon as Possible

The vast majority of the actions you have to take don't actually have to be done on one specific day. They should be done as soon as you can get to them. That doesn't mean they don't involve some sort of time sensitivity, but, because more "wiggle room" is available for most of these, making a commitment to complete them on a specifically calendared day will more than likely be artificial, given how often circumstances change. Work from these next-action lists whenever your calendar lets you know you have some discretionary time. This category of action is sorted based on the context needed to complete the action.

CALLS

A Call list is a frequently used list by many people these days. It contains all the telephone calls that you need to make, which can be done from any phone, anywhere.

COMPUTER

This list holds all the actions that require a computer to accomplish: e-mails, documents to draft, Web surfing, and so on.

OFFICE

This is the list of any actions that require being physically in your office to perform, such as reorganizing files and printing and reviewing a large document.

HOME

This list contains actions you need to do at or around your home—fix a light switch, organize your tool area, prune your apple tree, and so on.

ANYWHERE

This list contains actions that can be done anywhere, such as reviewing a large document that you've been carrying around in your briefcase until it's finished.

ERRANDS

This category tracks the actions to be taken when you are "out and about"—picking up dry cleaning, taking a dress to the tailor, buying a new stapler, and so on.

AGENDAS

This section contains further subsets of actions that required being in real-time conversation with one or more people, such as keeping track of what to go over with your assistant, what to bring up at the next staff meeting, what to talk over with your spouse or partner. Many people have several of these lists, one dedicated to each of the key individuals with whom they interact and one for each upcoming meeting.

READ/REVIEW

It is useful to gather things you need to read in one location, to remind you of outstanding commitments in this area as well as to provide an easily accessible inventory of this material when time becomes available for skimming and scanning information, such as while you're waiting for meetings to start or your computer to reboot.

WAITING FOR . . .

This grand little subcategory has probably relieved as much pressure as any one single aspect of GTD. It holds reminders of anything and everything that you are waiting for from another source, which includes all the projects you've delegated to others, anything you've ordered that hasn't arrived, any lent items, anything you're waiting to have confirmed by your boss or prospective clients. Often the next action on an item committed to finish is actually not yours to do—it's in someone else's court. Your responsibility is to track who's got it, confirm when they got it, and check its status as appropriate.

CUSTOMIZING THESE CATEGORIES

Having coached many thousands of people in the use of these kinds of organizational formats, I can assure you that the way they are defined and described here can provide a highly workable system for anyone from a high school student up to a senior executive overseeing multiple projects across many platforms in a global corporation. They have stood the test of time with the best and brightest as well as with people with relatively stable and simple lifestyles.

That said, once you grasp the principle of setting up categories based on what things mean to you, you should feel free to introduce your own variations to these themes. As a matter of fact, the inspiration for me to begin to research this context-specific way of organizing action reminders came early in the 1980s when I was teaching these methods using a paper-based loose-leaf planner. By that time I had already discovered the value of a Next Action list, not written on my calendar but accessible constantly on a dedicated list next to the calendar. Mobile phones had just appeared. I often found myself in a situation in which the only work I could do was to make calls, so it started to make sense to create a second auxiliary list just containing calls, separate from all my other next actions. Whenever I was in an airport with a half hour of free time before my plane took off, it was a lot easier to simply review my Calls list than to try to search out the calls I had on a much larger list of actions. A good friend of mine, a semiretired executive, began to implement my methods, and he soon came back to me with his own inspiration to create an "At sailboat" Action list. He had quite a number of tasks he wanted to keep track of and remind himself about, but they were things he could only do when he was on his catamaran in Maine. That "aha" started the whole process that led to my sorting actions in this context-specific way. As computerized list management began to emerge in the 1990s, it became even easier to sort actions by category.

So, understand that these action categories (or any others) are not "necessary" per se or set in stone in some inflexible methodology. They exist only to reflect the most efficient, systematic way to structure the components of whatever you need to manage. Based on what a given item means to you, determine how and where you can best park the placeholder for it.

For instance, my chief technology officer uses a category of actions he calls "Brain-dead." There are times when his mental functioning is not firing on all cylinders, and yet he'd like to stay productive and engaged. The best thing for him in those periods is to have specific tasks easily at hand that require minimal mental horsepower. When he's toast, he can pick from among those. That's an ultrasmart strategy, because when you have little access to intelligence, you probably don't have the wherewithal to remember what you need to do that doesn't require much energy!

If you work out of two offices, you might find it useful to have both an "At office A" and "At office B" list. If you're like me and fly at lot, you can try separating your "At computer" group from your "At broadband access" group. The former requires simply a laptop, connected or not; the latter needs a good Web connection. (Many of my own actions require a quick Web surf, which I can't do easily in the air.)

You might also find it helpful to compress some of these lists into fewer ones, especially if you find the use of so many categories unfamiliar and confusing. If you work at home and don't move around with your computer much, you could easily combine "home," "office," and "computer" into a single list, for instance.

INCUBATING

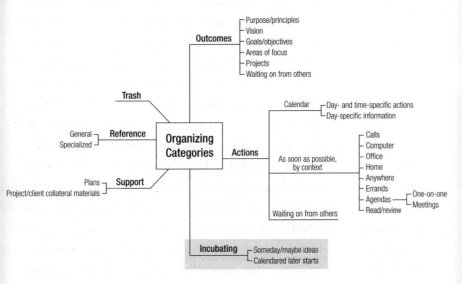

You may decide that among the many things that have crossed your mind and landed in your in-basket, there are actions, projects, and ideas that you don't actually want to move on or even decide about immediately. They need to be put on a "back burner" for some designated period, to be considered again later.

This unique category is comprised of two subcategories: items that you need to review with some regularity and those that need to surface only on a specific day in the future. You need two different structures to handle those distinct functions.

Items for Regular Review

The first category—things you want to reassess regularly—should be put into some list or bucket that you review as frequently as necessary. If, for instance, you've told yourself that you think you want to start learning Spanish sometime soon (though not this week), you'd probably want to be reconsidering that commitment with some frequency.

A Someday/Maybe list is an ideal place to hold these kinds of reminders—especially if you are reviewing that list on a regular basis. If you have developed the habit of conducting my recommended "weekly review," in which you scan *all* of your potentially relevant lists once a week, you can include this incubating category appropriately.

This Someday/Maybe list can include a wide range of projects and topics. If you're like me, you'll have a significant number of things that fall under the heading "long-range fantasy." This could include a "Would be cool to do before I die" list, with entries like visit a space station, or just random whimsy like "take a hot-air balloon ride" (which you might actually get an invitation for next weekend). On the more practical end of the spectrum would be projects that may have been on your active Projects list for a number of weeks, like "research a potential boat trip for our staff meeting," but which, given what's happened in the last ten days, you're now convinced need to be tabled until some later time.

Most people have quite a few subcategories under the someday/maybe heading—books they might like to read, dishes they'd like to cook, restaurants they want to try, places they'd like to visit, classes they'd like to take. If you are comfortable with a good list-management tool, drawing up this type of list can be a source of fun and creative explorations. At various times I have had lists like "Next Time in . . ." for interesting things I hear about that I might want to experience when I'm in a particular region or city and "Topics I Might Want to Write About."

Many people have come up with some interesting ways to distinguish these subcategories. One person I know created three distinctions among these someday/maybes: a "not now but soon" list, a "not now but later" one, and a "never now" group. I understand what drives this kind of discrimination—there are so many possibilities that constitute the range of "not now but still of interest," and so many other very immediate and actionable things that have to be considered regularly, that it's easy to go numb when confronted with one big list of nonactionable projects. As I mentioned previously, if you don't trust that you'll really be rigorous with yourself in reviewing every item on these lists with regularity, you'll wind up keeping so many tasks on your active lists that you'll find you're overwhelmed.

These are admittedly subtle distinctions, which most people will probably find way too granular to pay a lot of attention to. But given what I've experienced and understand about where our culture is headed, having a well-oiled, refined personal system that can capture and feed back tasks that have different levels of meaning will become more and more critical for balance and control in an increasingly complex and ambiguous world.

Calendared Later Starts

There is another set of items that we clarify as demanding no current action but that we want to rethink or start at a particular time in the future. This category would require different tools than those used for a regular review. For this group you would park information on a calendar or use a tickler (or suspense, or bring-forward) file to bring it back in front of you on a particular date. You could also enlist the help of someone like an assistant to route you reminders at a later date.

Some possible actions need time and space for reflection, until you feel comfortable making a decision about them. Your intuition or simply the state of your current data informs you that you don't yet have enough context, understanding, or confidence to make a judgment call.

Topics under this heading can range from products you see in a catalog that you're on the fence about buying, to an offer to partner with another company in a particular area of your business, a collaboration that might be of benefit to you but about which you need more data to make an informed decision.

You should determine precisely when you want to be reminded of these projects again, and set up triggers accordingly in your system. If I see something intriguing in a catalog, but can't decide if it's worth getting, I usually park it in my tickler file to show up for me again two weeks in the future, as that's about how long my impulse-buy energy lasts. If a major opportunity is presented to me that I'm ambivalent about, I determine when I should reexamine my judgment and put some appropriate reminder in the system. It could be two weeks or two months—I just need to make a decision and park the trigger so I can relax about keeping my agreement with myself about what it means to me.

Whether you use a calendar, a tickler file, or an assistant (in person or computerized) to rattle your cage at a designated time is simply up to what works best and is easiest for you. As long as you trust the process to deliver the reminder when it's due, you're set.

SUPPORT MATERIAL

For many people there is a large volume of data that falls into the category of support material—information that is relevant to projects, themes, and topics that you will want to have available when it comes time to take action on or think about them.

For projects, this would include any project plans and details about them. It could encompass collateral material that might be relevant—articles, brochures, or links to related topics. It could involve histories of client interactions and archives of documents.

Though this category can take in a great mass of material, it is

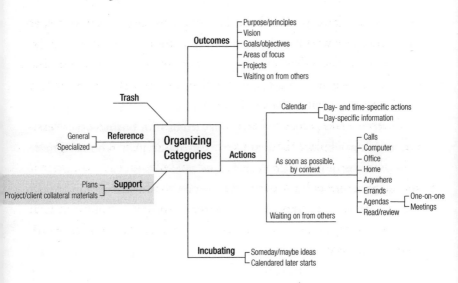

rather straightforward to delineate organizationally. Information simply needs to be sorted by the theme, topic, or project, in files, folders, boxes, or notebooks so it can be accessed handily when needed for review.

What contributes to a loss of control in this area is when actionable items are stored, unprocessed, in the same place as support material. In other words, if you are using only your folders and files to remind you that you have particular tasks related to a topic or project, you have blended items that have different meanings, which fosters psychic numbness. Support material needs to remain purely adjunct data—not a reminder of action. A notice that you *have* the project should be on your Projects list, and the specific actions you need to *take* about the project should be on your Action lists. Once those components are in their proper places, you'll experience a new sense of order and clarity, and your support material can be kept out of the way, accessible as needed when you work on the project.

There is a fine line of distinction between support material and reference material. In many cases, they are the same, and files can be kept together in the same filing system. But if your support materials on a project include your active plans, which themselves should be reviewed regularly, you need another trigger to remind you to look at them, such as a weekly assessment of the status of all of your projects, so you're not dependent on the plans themselves to alarm you. The specific plan review would be an active process that would update and identify current actions to be taken.

Often it makes sense to keep active project files in a more accessible and obvious place than you keep the files of pure reference material. I have two standing wire racks that hold files for the most current and active projects I'm working on. When the project is finished, or moves into the background, I will return the folder to my general reference filing cabinet. It's still easily retrievable, but no longer directly in my face.

REFERENCE MATERIAL

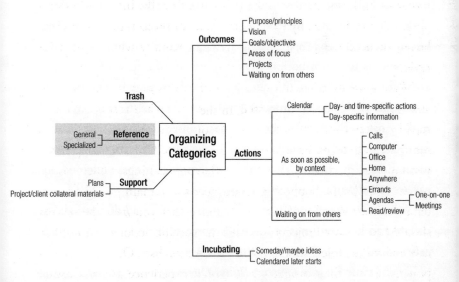

By far the category with the biggest volume of content will be "reference"—items that require no action but that you have decided might be useful to have access to in the future. These can range from simple historical or functional details about a person or company, to encyclopedic information about some project or aspect of your world.

From an organization point of view, in terms of meaning and location, this is a simple topic. Once you have determined that you don't have to make a commitment to do anything about information you receive or generate but think there could be value in having access to it, it should be placed into this category, and can simply be stored so that it is quickly retrievable.

The two most common issues that prove to be problems in this area are when (a) people store actionable items with their reference materials, or (b) the systems and logic for storage and retrieval are dysfunctional. The key strategies are (a) to ensure that actions required on any of your reference materials are captured, clarified, and organized where they belong (Action lists, Project list, etc.) and (b) to continually fine-tune both the content and structure of your reference systems.

It may be helpful to recognize an informal distinction here between "general" and "specialized" references. In the latter case, storage systems for information that is quite specific to work functions are seldom a problem. Contract files, client files, accounting files, and even recipes are specific enough to dictate their own structures that make sense to the people who need that information. If you're setting up those systems from scratch, it will take some thinking and experimentation to get them right; but for the most part these reference areas are self-defining and self-policing.

Where the situation gets sticky is deciding what to do with all the collated ad hoc information that has potential value but is not easily categorized or sorted into neat little buckets.

By the time I wrote *Getting Things Done,* I was already well aware of the potential bottleneck represented by general reference paper-based filing systems (or lack thereof), and I dedicated several pages in that book to describing the best practices we'd uncovered for setting up and maintaining an easy, accessible place for storing miscellaneous but potentially useful stuff. This would include documents like your cell phone manual, brochures about interesting topics, meeting notes and business cards, foreign maps you could use again, and so on. The key is to eliminate the unconscious resistance to immediately putting this kind of material away in an organized fashion.

When I first began coaching executives in this method, I would allow them to create a "to-file" pile. I haven't done that for years, though, because nobody ever wound up filing its contents. Even after they had decided that something needed filing, if it required anything more than a Post-it note to a secretary or a few seconds to label and store it, they might as well have thrown it away. Success clearly involved getting filing down to less than sixty seconds and making it at least a little fun. I'll repeat the GTD filing recommendations here, simply because making progress in this area has one of the most consistent rewards for GTD users. It's such a simple and mundane idea, and yet without it all kinds of information, physical materials, and mental concerns can back up into the rest of your system like bad plumbing. A great way to ensure the loss of control is to have no place to file useful information within a few moments of it showing up.

- Organize files by one A-Z index
- Typeset labels
- Require less than sixty seconds to make and store a new file
- Keep drawers less than three-quarters full
- Make your system fun and easy to use
- Purge files at least yearly

The volume and range of information that can gather is enormous. If it's not appropriately corralled, it will tend to bleed all over the rest of your physical and psychological space. It's precisely because its content is not that critical that it needs to be tightly managed—it can become an obstacle for the streamlined use of and access to more important material.

TRASH

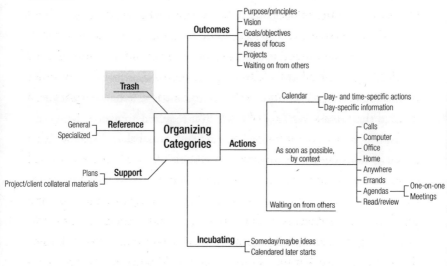

The final category of organization is one that in a sense needs no clarification. If something is irrelevant, not needed, insignificant, or meaningless, and it takes up any physical or psychic space, it's trash, so get rid of it.

While that may be self-evident, what's not is the avoidance of the executive decisions that actually determine what's to be classified as trash and what's not. Things have a way of accumulating around us like moss and mildew. It's all too easy to allow this to happen because we're either too busy or too uninterested in making decisions in the moment about relevance. This doesn't mean that you should be micromanaging to the extent of keeping everything totally current and clean and organized. By this point I hope you understand that GTD is not a moral judgment or a vote for seamless and totally clear organization being more important than the creative process and what it can produce. My intention here is to reinforce the awareness that trash, if left to pile up within our psychological or physical environment, will create drag on the system, which can only be relieved by moving it to where trash typically goes.

Most people, when confronted with the truth about what's going on in their life and work, will have some degree of guilt and remorse about the quantity of deadwood they've allowed to accumulate in and around their systems and spaces. More than once I or one of our staff coaches will recommend that an executive client order a Dumpster or similar large trash receptacle to be parked outside her office. In order to begin creating a functional self-management system for someone, a huge bulk of dross must first be removed.

For all your stored information it's also critical that you establish a procedure for consistent review and recalibration. As I've mentioned earlier, the meaning of things changes simply with the passage of time. You'll often want to keep notes about a company, a person, or a topic when the subject is fresh in your mind and at the moment seems as if it might become even more important later on. But by the middle of the next week it may simply become old news, so the best practice of keeping all kinds of potentially useful data has to be linked to the rigorous habit of regular reviewing, reassessing, and purging where necessary. If your system gets overloaded with out-of-date and unnecessary content, it will begin to repel you instead of inviting usage.

None of that may seem particularly mission-critical to you at the moment. So what if there are a few stacks here and there? The problem is that when you break that code of keeping things in their proper place, based upon what they are and what they mean to you, the negative syndrome feeds on itself. It becomes easier and easier to get lax about deciding what you collect, and to just toss stuff into your piles and "hunhhh" stacks.

Disorder can, without any conscious effort on your part, reduce everything to the lowest common denominator. One day you realize you're out of control—not because of any one traumatic event but because of the inherent entropy of "stuff." If you're not conscientiously transforming it, through the clarifying and organizing phases, it will overtake you. The best cure is prevention, and the best way to prevent that degradation of the effectiveness of your extended mind is to keep the edges clean and the categories discrete. You're not likely to throw a gum wrapper onto a clean lawn or floor, but if several are already scattered there, it's easy to accept the implicit invitation to drop another.

It seems that in our culture there is a serious propensity for creating but not for cleaning up. The universe abhors a vacuum, so whenever space becomes open and available, it will be almost impossible to resist filling it with new and more dynamic material.

As Simple as Possible, but No Simpler

How you may have related to these organizational categories depends a lot on what sorts of systems you are already familiar and comfortable with, and how important you feel it is to you to improve on this aspect of getting and keeping control around you. Many people believe that the framework I have laid out here is too complicated and ultimately unnecessary. Others believe it is too simple and not detailed enough. I stand by my contention that it represents the basic distinctions of meaning that are sufficient to stay on top of a complex life and work experience, but clear-cut enough to be intuitively functional, on the run, for anyone.

As with all the other aspects of GTD, I've tried to distill the successful processes into as few components as possible for the system to work. I don't think fundamental organizational structures can be made any simpler than what I have laid out. As soon as you attempt to simplify them, you almost inevitably blend one or more of these very specific categories and start to generate counterproductive confusion. You can delete a category, but that doesn't do away with its contents. They either go somewhere they don't belong, or they get reinserted into the amorphous blob of undifferentiated commitments with which you started. If you think having all of these lists, folders, and trays is confusing, try *not* having them.

Organizing on the Road Map

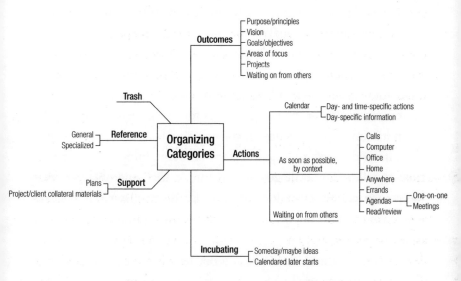

If you refer to this diagram at the next committee, staff, or project meeting, or in a conversation with your son, or if you simply consult it as a formula for what to do with all your e-mails, you'll begin to experience the power of organizing as a control function.

What should you consider when someone brings up a point, makes a suggestion, shares a piece of news or simply information that should be stored as reference? Where are you going to put it? Has she surfaced a project that needs to be identified, with action steps determined? Where does that go in your system? Should it be placed in a "parking lot" with no action now but with a review scheduled before the next meeting? Who's tracking that, and where? What about a new goal that should be clarified and put into the system? How is that to be organized so it's executed? And how do you deal with an identified behavior that needs to be affirmed and evaluated, trained, and installed in the group or culture? Where does that get parked, by whom, to ensure it's attended to? Clarifying what these various things mean is important, but having a way to sort and store the results of your thinking is equally so.

Obviously, tools are needed to implement this phase—both personally and organizationally—in the form of equipment that will store reminders and materials in intact areas that maintain the integrity of the type of contents you need to keep distinct. Lists, boxes, trays, folders—they can all work to this end. I'll address the range of options and some of the best practices for using them in chapter 19, when it's time to discuss tips on constructing your systems . . . which leads us to the next and natural stage of maintaining control: reflection. It will do you little good to capture, clarify, and organize what has your attention if you don't pay appropriate attention to it, once it's out of your head.

8 | Getting Control: Reflecting

	Purpose/Principles
	Vision
	Goals
	Areas of Focus
	Projects
Capturing Clarifying Organizing **Reflecting** Engaging/Actions	

P
E
R
S
P
E
C
T
I
V
E

CONTROL

Learn to pause . . . or nothing worthwhile will catch up to you.

—Doug King

Extreme busyness, whether at school or college, kirk or market, is a symptom of deficient vitality.

—Robert Louis Stevenson

If you worry about everything, then you don't have to worry about anything.

—anonymous

We must try to keep the mind in tranquility. For just as the eye which constantly shifts its gaze, now turning to the right or to the left, now incessantly peering up or down, cannot see distinctly what lies before it, but the sight must be fixed firmly on the object in view if one would make his vision of it clear; so too man's mind when distracted by his countless worldly cares cannot focus itself distinctly on the truth.

—St. Basil the Great

An Unused System Is Not a System

Getting something out of your head does not mean eliminating your responsibility to yourself to manage it appropriately. Too often people are inspired to create lists and reminder systems but then lose the motivation to stay involved with them as consistently as they've told themselves they should.

It's true that simply going through the capturing and clarifying processes with the important topics in your life and work will create value. Making decisions and maturing your thinking about strategic and sensitive situations by applying an outcome and action focus to them can make a significant difference in how you approach your personal and professional agendas.

But once you have externalized your inventory of commitments and interests into a structure for your extended mind, it will only provide its benefit of ongoing freedom and productive engagement with the multiple aspects of your life if it receives proper care and feeding. You have to engage with it—and not just in a cursory manner, but with sufficient focus to absorb the information in a way consistent with what the data mean to you. Hence I'm using "reflect" in place of the original GTD wording of "review."

This step is, or should be, obvious. There's no reason to have a calendar if you don't pay any attention to what's on it. Why draw up a list of calls to make if you don't look it over before you start dialing numbers? Why identify all your projects if you're not going to evaluate them individually and as a group with some regularity, to ensure forward motion on each of them and to foster a more solid sense of your day-to-day priorities?

The Dual Function of Reflection

Reviewing your system serves two distinct but equally critical purposes: (a) to update its contents and (b) to provide trusted perspective. Though these are conceptually different objectives, they almost invariably take place together. The process of reviewing the agendas you've been collecting to go over with your boss at your next meeting is likely to trigger more content to add to them or at least provide an update on their accuracy and completeness. Doing so also automatically increases your trust that your interactions regarding the material will be more coherent and inclusive of everything that's relevant. Because the content is current and complete and you've accessed your thinking and intuition for this particular horizon, you'll have a better meeting. That will be true to some extent for any list you've been keeping for any horizon or area of your work and life. To maintain control, you must review the data of your system and refresh it to match current realities.

GETTING THINGS CURRENT

Invariably, the world comes at us faster than we can keep up with its details. By the very nature of work, when you are doing one task you're not thinking about others—nor should you. You may be capturing along the way, but you won't be clarifying and organizing everything as it happens. And because there are multiple horizons within which we work and live, we may be caught up on one level but lag behind in our thinking and structures on another.

For instance, if you were to stop reading this book right now, and look over your calendar in detail for the last two weeks, for this week, and for the next two months, I'll bet you'll come across at least one if not several items that need to be updated. You'll likely notice events that have already taken place but still have some loop to close that you haven't captured yet. You'll see meetings and travel in days to come that you now realize need something done about them soon, something that you hadn't thought of before. Similarly, if you have a strategic or annual plan for your company or your job area and you pulled it out for a close look right now, would you find anything that might need some tweaking to make it current, given recent unexpected events? Would a review of your job responsibilities surface some changes in your focus over the last few months that might be useful to clarify for yourself and others you work for and with?

There are times when, during my own weekly review, I mark off quite a number of actions from my lists that I've finished in the last few days but not yet had the time to eliminate, much less figure out what I need to do next about them. I often ask in my workshops how many people have had at least a couple of situations turn up in the last few days that they knew they had to take care of, that required more than one step to do so, but they haven't had the time to sit down and clarify the precise nature of the projects or decide what to do about them next. Almost everyone raises his or her hand in acknowledgment. My question to them is, when are you planning to do that?

Because projects are likely to change their meaning over time, your system also needs to reflect that fact. What was an active project last week may now have turned into a "someday" one, given all the new demands that have arisen since then. Meetings on your calendar that you committed to last month may now need to be renegotiated because of recent changes in your travel schedule. An action on your Computer list to draft a proposal may, because of new demands from a client, need to be moved as a "have-to" to Monday's calendar. Overlooking such mundane but often critical catch-ups for yourself, due to failure to review your system contents, can throw you quickly into the Victim quadrant along with a load of stress.

REFLECTION FOR PERSPECTIVE

In addition to updating your inventory of commitments, the other equally important aspect of reflection is its obvious benefit for enhancing perspective. It is at this stage of the matrix of self-management that the two dynamics of control and perspective sit closely together. If you are feeling driven by the latest and loudest and have the feeling you're becoming overwhelmed by details, it is always healthy to stop, take a breath, and rise to survey the situation from a more elevated viewpoint. That, of course, is easier to do when you can capture, clarify, and organize what's around you, but at some point if you don't stand back and assess what you're doing and not doing from a broader perspective, you'll keep sliding out of control.

In the next section of the book, I'll describe the six Horizons of Focus and I'll share quite a bit more detail about the kinds of reviewing processes and techniques that are unique to each level. Usually the longer the horizon, the longer the time interval you can allow yourself between reviews to stay comfortable. In other words, your list of people to call needs to be checked a lot more often than your company principles or your yearly goals.

The basic principle to affirm here is that extending and parking your thinking in these more objective and reviewable formats primarily enables you to reflect on and maintain perspective about anything and everything you're doing, as efficiently as possible, whenever necessary. I can't state this too often: you can only feel good about what you're not doing when you know what you're not doing. And there's no way you can truly know what you're not doing without a consistent renegotiation with yourself. Your mind, on its own, does a pitiful job of that, given the complexities and subtleties of the multiple universes in which you have made your commitments. It does do a marvelous job of noting the reminders, making sense of them, and using them to foster an ongoing flow of creative intelligence.

This observation is tied to another reason that the reflection process is so critical: your mind's phenomenal ability to integrate and associate information must be used as the glue that holds your external system together.

An interesting dance takes place in the interplay between using your system to unjumble your thinking and then using your thinking to coordinate your system. There is no mind in the world that can objectively keep track of projects and reminders as accurately as a simple loose-leaf notebook of lists and no system in the world that can tie together what's on those lists in their infinitely varied associations like your brain. But you can't think about relationships between items when you're thinking about the items themselves, which is why during a brainstorming session you must write down the ideas. If you don't, your mind keeps trying to hang on to them. The value of reflection for perspective is perhaps best expressed by another basic GTD tenet: your mind should be used to think *about* your stuff, not *of* it.

Over the years the most common questions we receive about the structures we've recommended for setting up lists of actions and projects concern how people can link the various items on their assorted lists together. "If I have 'Call Susan re: budget' on my Calls list, but look at my projects and see 'Finalize budget,' how do I know that I have a call to Susan about it?" I understand that it would be ideal to be able to cross-reference everything in your system with every possible relevant association and meaning, and within the life of this book we may actually see software that will provide this capability in a manner that's not more trouble than it's worth. The truth is, however, that this kind of question almost never comes from people who are diligently reviewing their system contents. If you did a few seconds of focused thinking about the budget and what was happening with it, at least once a week (which is the best review cycle for projects) from the time you committed to it, and if you looked over your Calls list every time you had a phone and some discretionary time, you would have little or no need to be concerned about what was connected to what. Those kinds of associations are naturally made in a flash, and consistent review of a complete inventory of such details ensures cohesive perspective.

BLUEPRINTS FOR REFLECTION

It seems that no matter how hard we work, we always seem to be in a continual process of bringing up the rear guard. The faster you are moving and the more creative your output, the greater the demand to apply a disciplined habit of review and reflection to prevent outdated and irrelevant aspects of work and to keep life from becoming a heavy anchor pulling back on your momentum.

It's ironic that some people view a set of lists such as those I recommend as a burden, and basic GTD practices as unnecessary. "Write everything down? Decide the actions you need to take on everything? Keep all that on . . . how many lists? Keep an index of all my projects? And . . . what? Take two hours every week to review all of that and get all these lists complete? You've got to be kidding! I'm too busy."

This skepticism is frankly quite understandable. The majority of the systems that most people have tried to implement have not been complete, current, or clear enough to genuinely relieve sufficient pressure from the mind to be worth adopting. And even if at one point in time they did happen to approach some measure of truly having it all captured, clarified, and organized, they weren't able to maintain it with any consistency. The real rub in this scenario is that incomplete reviews of outdated lists create as much stress as they relieve.

The conundrum here seems to be that the success people experience in moving past the first hurdle of "getting organized" can easily create a false and temporary sense of freedom from what they got organized. It's almost as if they are telling themselves, "It feels so great to have it off my mind, I now don't ever want to put it back *on* my mind!" When they run up against the second hurdle of *reengaging* with the contents in appropriate ways to keep their central mental station clear, they come to a halt.

This is another paradox that I have come to accept in working with the GTD methods: to really get things off your mind, you must put them *on* your mind, appropriately. If you're not reviewing your goals as often as you think you should, in order to keep them vital and operational, they will begin taking up unnecessary mental space unproductively. If you are not doing a thorough weekly assessment of all your projects, some part of your brain will keep trying to review them continually and never finish the task. If you had a lot of appointments but never bothered to look at your calendar, you'd probably be taking up a lot of psychic energy trying to remember your commitments. In other words, if you're not consciously reviewing your commitments in a directed way, you'll compensate by attempting to review them in a foggy way, all the time.

To keep from having to be compelled by this incessant thinking about something while making no progress on it, you need to have already thought about it, sufficiently, and trust that you will again, when you assume you ought to. That means that a regular reflection about all your horizons at all the appropriate intervals must be maintained. Keeping to such a schedule may seem like quite a challenge, and it is, but remember that it is not the precept of some externalized morality or a rule imposed from some outside source. This practice is all relative to your own agreements with yourself. If you're truly fine and clear with a decision that you don't have to rethink your career goals every year, then you're fine and clear. It can't be said enough: these methods are about paying appropriate attention to what has your attention. I am simply attempting to elucidate what "appropriate attention" encompasses with respect to your commitments—big or little, obvious or more subtle. You need to remind yourself of them only as often as you need to remind yourself of them.

There's no question that it's very easy to fall off this wagon, if you were ever in it to begin with. The good news is that it's also relatively easy to climb back on. The key to doing so is to have a solid blueprint of a structure, plus some form of review process that will engage with that guide to fill in the blank spaces that may appear from time to time.

Most reasonably effective people utilize the structures of their environment to provide at least a modicum of reminders from this larger context. If you work at a desk in an office, simply sitting down with your phone, computer, stacking trays, briefcase, PDA, and calendar tools arrayed in front of you will provide a template for your thinking and focus. If you like to cook, merely walking into your kitchen and encountering the stove, refrigerator, cookbooks, dishes, and pans will frame your thinking about groceries and dinner. In either of those scenarios you are likely to notice gaps, things to catch up with, and new projects to consider, simply by being in a space that encourages a certain kind of reflection. Having a meeting with your staff or project team, in which whiteboards, computer projections, or printouts include agendas and relevant reminders, will automatically make it easier to bring the topic under consideration current and frame appropriate perspectives for constructive discussion and decision-making.

If you extend that principle logically into the more subtle area of the inventory of your interests and responsibilities for all of life and work, you'll come to appreciate the utility of the external, extended-mind format I've been describing, and how its real power is unlocked by engaging with its contents in an active, dynamic way. Thorough assessments of complete inventories of commitments promotes clarity, creativity, and self-trust—without fail.

9 | Getting Control: Engaging

				Purpose/Principles	P
				Vision	R
				Goals	S
				Areas of Focus	P
				Projects	E
					C
Capturing	Clarifying	Organizing	Reflecting	**Engaging/Actions**	T
					I
					V
					E
			CONTROL		

The world can only be grasped by action, not by contemplation. The hand is more important than the eye . . . The hand is the cutting edge of the mind.

—J. Bronowski

The fifth and final stage of getting positively engaged with your world is, of course, to engage, positively, with your world. I know that may sound absurdly self-evident, but bear with me. Many people tend to avoid making the decision about what real engagement involves, with respect to many aspects of their world. Even if their thinking is sufficiently advanced, they often remain in the dark about how to integrate the relevant physical actions that constitute real engagement with their commitments. The key concept to keep in mind here is that staying in control will ultimately be a function of how you manage to allocate your physical resources—quite simply, what action you are taking *now,* and how comfortably you are relating to that.

Are you in alignment with your choice? Is reading this book or listening to me or someone else narrating this sentence absolutely, positively, without a doubt *the* thing you should be doing at this moment? If you think it's not, or are afraid it's not, or if you don't know whether it is or not, then to some degree you're out of control. If you assert confidently, yes, indeed, this is the best thing for me to be doing and the best place to put my attention right now, you're probably in your zone. You will experience, at least in the existential moment, no sense of time, no feeling of overwhelm, no gnawing sense of amorphous pressure on your psyche. You won't be concerned about life/work balance, or even making a distinction about whether you are in "work" or "life" mode. You're just doing what you're doing, appropriately and without internal distraction.

Ultimately, every other best practice described in this book is designed to lead you to this point. Getting in control by capturing, clarifying, organizing, and reviewing clears your internal deck to ensure that you have an unobstructed view of all the concrete options available to choose from. Achieving a mature sense of perspective, and a willingness to evaluate your commitments at all six Horizons of Focus, will "hardwire" your intuitive judgments about relative priorities of all those choices. You can't actually *do* more than one thing at a time, with full conscious attention (although you can switch between activities rapidly). You can't actually *do* outcomes or standards—you only hold them as realities to achieve by doing specific behaviors. All your investments, commitments, and involvements in and about your material world only manifest themselves as action. It all comes down to hitting a key on the computer, punching a number on your telephone keypad, moving your body into your car, opening your mouth, and forming a word.

As unsurprisingly mundane as this conclusion sounds, I guarantee that profound magic and power are embedded in this level of involvement. You might ask yourself, of the people you know who most seem to maintain a sense of control and perspective about their world, how constructively active—how positively engaged with the physical involvements of their life—do they seem to be? And for those you know who you'd say lack that kind of control and perspective, how many of them flip-flop between lethargic inaction and manic hyperbusyness? The relevant barometer here measures not so much the amount of things people do, but the quality of that engagement.

The elements that are relevant to this level include defining what engagement really means at its most granular, and the specific factors to consider once that particular action focus is clarified.

What's a Next Action?

In this section I will continually risk restating the obvious, because no matter how long and how many times I have coached and taught about how critical specificity is in defining the physical action required to move things forward, it is a lesson that many people still avoid taking. Even for the thousands of people who have caught the vision of GTD and begun to implement its method, this one procedure of deciding and tracking the immediate next action remains elusive in practice. The most common cause of a list becoming listless and uninspiring is the lack of clarity about what to do about what's on it. If you have allowed yourself the laxity of placing a vague item, like "deal with Dad's situation," on an Action list, you will tend to avoid further thinking or doing with regard to it. If instead you decide that a call to your aunt is the next logical step to get some information to move you toward clarity, "Call Roberta re: Dad's situation" becomes a powerful catalyst for productive motion.

The fundamental engagement question is, "What's the next action?"

The answer creates the bridge from the invisible to the visible, from idea into reality, and (if you're not allergic to the term) from the spiritual to the physical.

In order to clarify some very significant factors, such as where you need to be to move forward on this or that commitment and how much time you need to do so, you must determine what subsequent physical, tangible activity is required. Without that determination, you will miss opportunities to make progress when you are in a context that could be utilized, and you will likely procrastinate about getting involved in a project because you think (but aren't sure) you don't have the time available to do so.

You could be in a hardware store, walking by the superglue you need to repair a lamp at home, and miss the opportunity to address a problem your partner at home has been nagging you about for weeks. If you hadn't determined that the next action on the project was to buy superglue, you wouldn't recognize the key ingredient when you walked by it. Likewise, while on hold on a call to the airlines, you might have easily taken ninety seconds to send an e-mail requesting a meeting with three of your staff to brainstorm and jump-start a major new project. But if you hadn't decided that this was the very next action to take, you'd be sitting in a bottleneck because your brain was focused on too big a picture to do anything about it.

Many people believe that what they have written on a To-do list represents next steps, but seldom is that true. Even if you have included on a list a task like "set meeting with Bob" (which is actually more specific than most people get about such things), there is still a gap between your commitment and what it means in reality. How, exactly, are you going to set that meeting with Bob? Delegate it to your assistant? Send an e-mail? Make a call? If you haven't moved it to that level of physical specificity, you have not finished your thinking about the situation, and a part of you will continue to wonder, Should I call? Send an e-mail? How should I arrange this? In order to silence that monkey in your mind, you must complete the thinking process: okay, I'll e-mail Bob to request the meeting. Now your brain is satisfied—as long as you either take that action then or park the reminder in a trusted place. Until then, it'll keep bugging you.

The best criteria to determine whether or not you've actually thought something through sufficiently to act upon it is how clearly you can answer these three questions:

- What has to happen first?
- What does doing look like?
- Where does it happen?

If you can't answer all three specifically, you still have work to do.

This exercise reiterates the part of the process that I laid out in chapter 6 about clarifying what you have your attention on. If something is actionable, there is a next action associated with it, and you need to get that clear and park the answer in some trusted place before you can really get the subject off your mind.

I am restating and reinforcing the principle again in this chapter and in this context because, of all the best practices I have uncovered across the years of my work in this field of personal and interactive productivity, this one is perhaps the most profound in its ramifications. By asking myself, "What's the next action on this?" I have generated more creative thinking, tough decision-making, critical conversations, innovative ideas, clarity, and motivation than by using any other specific technique I'm aware of.

Identifying the next action runs neck and neck with defining the desired outcome in terms of generating value in a given situation. But if I had to choose between those two questions that would be the most effective in increasing productivity, I'd unhesitatingly pick, "What's the next action?"

Why? Because I've seen too many people come up with a confident response to what they're trying to achieve, but have the whole effort falter because of a lack of clarity in what, specifically, to do about it. When, on the other hand, someone takes the responsibility to determine the next action on a project, he will almost without fail begin to bump his focus upward and integrate that thinking into the higher levels of his commitments. What's the next step? Yeah, but in order to do that, we need to decide if . . . Oh yeah, that brings up the key issue about whether we're really going to . . . and so on.

You actually can't have one without the other. Actions are determined and filtered by desired outcomes, and outcomes are achieved by actions. But because the primary instrument of involvement for people who need more control and perspective is their hour-by-hour inventory of action possibilities, establishing commitments at the physical level seems to provide a context that is energizing and solid. It's often easier to clarify the big picture when you start with physical action allocations than the other way around.

This is why in our many years and thousands of hours spent coaching, we'll use the "What's the next action?" question as the key driver for dealing with each item in our clients' e-mail, in-basket, and head. If that question is not addressed, all kinds of noble thinking will go to waste, allowing a pressure-laden fog to settle over the whole situation. Grappling with the answer to that question occasionally surfaces very fertile issues at higher horizons that often need to be dealt with, and often that's the only way we can actually start to identify and confront them.

AN INSTRUCTIVE STORY ABOUT THE UTILITY OF CLEAR NEXT ACTIONS

The one and only person I have ever encountered who had implemented, on his own, without any other coaching, a personal system of reminders based on specific next physical actions, was someone I happened to meet on a plane, serendipitously, flying into Santa Barbara.

The man who actually trained me in the concept of "next actions," Dean Acheson, didn't formulate that for himself, by himself—he discovered its value in working with many executives to unstick their thinking and work flow. For that reason it was especially surprising that another implementation of this practice had been developed by a seatmate. After initial icebreaking, our conversation moved to, "So, what do you do for a living?" We wound up sharing our personal systems and lists. Noticing the granularity of my entries—"call," "e-mail," "buy," "talk to," and so on—he remarked, "Wow, I've never met anyone besides me who ever tracked that level of actions." (His own list was equally specific.) I said that I hadn't either, except for the people I'd trained and coached, and asked him, "How did you come up with this?"

Jack Stuster, executive and principal scientist with Anacapa Sciences, in Santa Barbara, California, had advanced degrees in both psychology and anthropology and was one of the world's experts in understanding human behavior in high-stress, long-isolation environments. He had researched and written a major resource manual on the human factors that tend to be suboptimized under those conditions, and he consulted with groups like the builders of the space station and international teams exploring the Antarctic. These are situations in which people must dependably perform at high levels despite many of their psychic fuses having blown due to extended environmental and psychological stresses.

I probed about how he'd come up with the concept of specific next actions, and his answer has provided a clue to me over the years as to why GTD and its methodology continues to expand in its attraction and adoption. The instruction manuals he had prepared for the people in those isolated situations were designed so that when something out of the ordinary happened, they could look the procedures up and guide themselves through the assessment and correction of any problems. Guess at what level those instructions had to be formulated to be practical for individuals who were not firing on all cylinders? That's right—a typical sequence ran, Look at the panel. If there is a green light, do A. If there is a red light, do B, and so on. Jack found that there was remarkable value in prethinking specific actions required, so you could trust the resulting system to guide you when you had only enough energy to do, but not to think. He couldn't help but integrate that discovery into his own life.

Once You Know That the Next Action Is . . .

Having determined the next action to take, another set of decisions should then be brought into play to control the minute-to-minute flow (and often flood) of incoming stuff, reducing the volume of outstanding items you need to keep track of in your system. You should actually *do* the actions you can do on your own immediately, in less than two minutes, and *delegate* other feasible items to someone else, if possible. Once those two procedures are completed, what remains for you to track for yourself are the longer-than-two-minute actions. (Hence the popular "3Ds" in the GTD model—Do, Delegate, or Defer—which are described in more detail in *Getting Things Done*.)

The two-minute guideline is based on the fact that most things that can be handled in that time frame would actually take longer to organize and review again than to finish in the moment.

Anything that someone other than you can do, they should take over, assuming you have an agreement in the relationship that makes that appropriate. "Delegate" in this context doesn't necessarily mean down the chain of command (although it often will be)—it could involve passing something to a peer or even to a boss, if he is the most effective party to be handling whatever the action is.

These two practices—doing short actions as soon as they appear and delegating anything else that you can immediately—have proven themselves to be some of the most productivity-enhancing habits. Many of the thousands of hours I and my staff have spent one-on-one with clients at their desks are actually taken up with having them *do* the two-minute actions that result from processing their in-baskets, and having them *delegate* any tasks they can, on the spot. The increase in the experience of flow and productive use of time that these behaviors foster is dramatic. Some people have suggested that installing the two-minute rule gave them the feeling of getting an extra six months in their life!

Of course you won't be able to reap the benefits of these practices until and unless you understand the concept of "next actions" and actually implement that clarifying thought process when going through your in-basket contents. If you haven't yet figured out the next action for a particular item, you have no idea whether it will take two minutes or two hours. There are plenty of short actions lying untapped in the stacks of documents and e-mails, which, when discovered and unlocked, unstick all kinds of work and generate a very real sense of progress.

In a similar vein, the lack of next-action thinking works against effective delegation. In many cases you can't give someone else an entire project because you're the only one who can take responsibility at that level. The next action on it, however, can often be handed off, as long as you know what it is. Whenever we coach a senior manager or executive, we often find it useful to warn all of his direct reports that they are likely to begin getting a flood of things to do. It's not that their boss is suddenly inventing new projects, but rather his understanding that he has been the bottleneck because he hasn't thought through what the next action should be. When he does, more than likely a lot of them will be passed along to the staff—and appropriately so. Ideally anything that can be delegated within the two-minute guideline should be; and sending an e-mail is probably the most efficient way to do that. Some hand-offs, however, will require real-time conversations because of their sensitivity or complexity, and those should be tracked on your own lists as agenda topics, organized by the person with whom you're going to speak.

So, if you are maintaining maximum control of your work flow, quite a number of items will not wind up as actions for you to take yourself, logged in your system of reminders. Many will be completed when they first appear, so they never need to reach the list stage, and many others will be handed off to someone else as they show up, leaving you only to track what you're waiting for (if you need to place attention on getting something back).

A lot of thinking and decision-making takes place as you're defining the work as you process your in-basket; a lot of that work actually moves forward when you've driven those in-baskets to zero backlog.

But you will still have a significant number of actions on your plate—more than you can possibly do today. How do you stay in control of this work load?

Incorporating All of the Engagement Factors

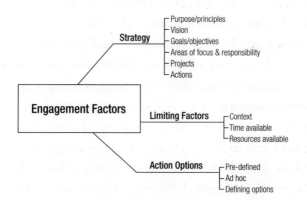

Now that you've held yourself to the task of deciding what, exactly, needs to be done next—about your mom, your next vacation, the summer stuff with your kids, and the possible merger with a competing organization—how on earth do you assign an appropriate priority to that action, amid and against all the other things that you have your attention on and about which you know you need to do something?

Let's examine the variables that have an impact on that decision, which are too numerous and complex to allow you to use a simple priority grading method such as A, B, C, or 1, 2, 3, or High, Medium, and Low. You must continually take into account the six horizons of your commitments, the three limiting factors for action, and the three options about what kinds of actions you choose to do.

The unique combinations and configurations of all of these variables can change many hundreds if not thousands of times in a day. As a matter of fact, every time you decide to turn your attention to a new task, you are at least implicitly attempting to match up your reality with the shifts in your unique priority pattern at the moment.

When you decide to stop working on the monthly report, stand up and stretch, and go get a cup of coffee, you make a decision about reallocating your resources. Theoretically you are making more than fifty thousand such priority judgments a day—someone has estimated that that's the number of different thoughts you're likely to have during that period—and what you think about is always an option (in principle, anyway). If you put too much weight on the conviction that there are only a certain small number of items that can genuinely be considered a "priority," you're likely to feel some degree of angst whenever you're not doing them and that you're consequently being somehow less than productive. That's doing yourself a disservice, as well as being inaccurate.

STRATEGY

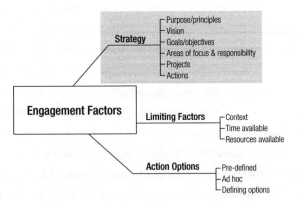

Conceptually and logically, your choice about which action to take should be aligned with the commitments you have identified at the highest levels and cascade from there down the hierarchy. This is the strategic and tactical thinking framework that a consultant might use to facilitate organizational alignment, goals, and plans. Which e-mail you should respond to first should be the one that most fulfills your personal and organizational purpose and aligns with your core values.

In order to make more operational sense of what that means, though, some amount of fleshing out and detailing at lower levels of focus has to take place. What is the vision of the higher purpose and values being fulfilled and expressed in the long term? What are the shorter-term goals and objectives that should be quarterly targets, in order to ensure that the larger desired outcome is achieved? What needs to happen to maintain all the key areas to ensure you have a functioning system to get you there? What are all of the resulting projects that need to be finished? And what are all of the next actions you could possibly take right now that would move all of those elements forward, with consistent progress?

Another way to understand these strategic criteria is from the bottom up. When you or your enterprise takes an action (runway), it will be in the service of projects (ten thousand feet) or maintenance standards (twenty-thousand feet). Your projects fulfill areas of responsibility (grow sales, maintain health, serve customers, control quality, manage assets, etc.) and move you toward bigger goals and objectives (thirty thousand feet). Their outcomes are there to help move you toward the long-term vision of where you want to be (forty thousand feet), which itself is the ideal manifestation of your purpose (fifty thousand feet). All of which is to be done within the framework of your core values (fifty thousand feet).

This stacking model of thinking about priorities is logical common sense. Although the concept is relatively simple, using horizons as markers to maintain a focus can be an extremely practical way to keep discussions under control and pointed at the right targets. Because this hierarchy of prioritizing is such a key source for establishing appropriate perspective and each of the levels has its own type of content and processes, they will all be explored in greater detail in the final chapters in this book.

It would be nice if you could maintain maximum control in your environment simply by maturing your thinking and decisions at all six of these levels. But it's not quite that easy. The interplay between the levels of commitment you have with yourself is complex enough, but there are still two further frameworks that you'll have to consider in order to make a choice about what to do, and that have to be integrated into your day-to-day functioning in order to stay on top of your game.

LIMITING FACTORS

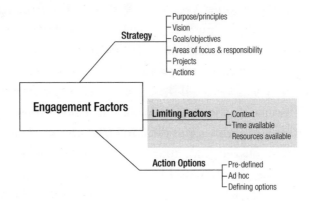

Assuming you have captured, clarified, and organized all the possible actions you need to take about particular items in your life, and assuming you have matured your thinking at all the relevant horizons of your engagements, there are further realities to factor into your decision about how to move forward. These involve considerations of the potential limitations imposed by context, time, and energy.

Context

What can you possibly do right now, of all the options that face you? There is never a moment at which you could do everything you've decided you need to do, simply because most of those actions require a specific tool or location. You have some tasks at your office and others at home, and unless they happen to be in the same place, you are limited in your choice by where you are. You will usually have several things to do on a computer, but if your server is down, or your laptop is in for repair, that option is moot. If you're being driven in a car to an appointment but you notice that you don't have a strong enough signal for your cell phone, the possibility for calls is precluded. At any single point in time, you can only do what you can do.

This is why I recommend that reminders of all your actions be organized by context. That's not an arbitrary consideration—it's the first criterion that limits your options and keeps you from being reminded of things you simply can't do. If you're out doing errands, the only lists you really need to pay attention to are tasks along your route and perhaps the calls you could make. If you're sitting on an airplane and have your laptop, you could do anything that requires a computer (as long as it doesn't require a Web connection). Of course, if you're taking off or landing, the only thing you could do would be to work through your Read/Review folder. That doesn't mean that you *have* to do those things—it's just easier to consider your possible range of choices moment to moment when your reminders are structured to reflect a particular context.

If you're like me, and find utility in keeping objective track of all the actions you have to do, you'll discover you probably have more than 150 of them at any given time. If you put them all on a single list, how would you feel when you tried to look for the calls you had to make, while you had a few minutes before picking up your daughter from school? It would be overwhelming to try to hunt down all of your calls strewn among your errands, things to talk to your husband about, stuff to pick up at the hardware store, and e-mails you need to compose. It's a lot easier to simply turn to a list that already has things to do sorted by their context, where you can see your eight calls in one quick glance.

Time Available

The next limitation that affects what you can do is the amount of time you have. If there are fifteen minutes free before the staff meeting starts, you wouldn't want to try to take on a task that required a half hour of uninterrupted time to do well, no matter how important it was. Typically, some of the most strategic next actions you're likely to have may require a solid chunk of quiet time. As I was putting together my first book, I learned a painful lesson about how much of a time window I needed in order to get into the rhythm and flow of my writing. When I tried to do any new, constructive, and creative thinking in anything less than a two-hour space, I felt as if I was stepping on my own feet, mentally, and it was almost impossible to get into a productive groove. I was better off writing nothing at all than trying to cram the process into an inappropriate time frame.

If you only have ten minutes available, and you want to be productive, you're best off choosing a task you can feel comfortable working on within that limit.

Obviously, based upon all the other prioritizing factors, you may need to create specific structures and block out sufficient time slots for the important actions that require them. That is the kind of thoughtful planning that will tend to occur in a weekly review mode, where you lift up to ten thousand feet and survey the next couple of weeks, integrated with some deadlines that have changed and numerous other factors that have come into play.

But the key point here is that your choices have to take into account, in addition to the context you're in, how much time is available and how much time your actions require.

This is obviously another great reason to have a total-life action inventory at hand. No matter what your time parameters and constraints, there are likely to be things you can get done within them.

Energy

The third factor to consider in planning your actions is how much energy you have. Given your mental, emotional, and physical resources at the moment, could you effectively carry out what you've elected to do? Even if you have a computer and an hour of time before you leave work, do you have the horsepower you need to craft that new proposal for a major project? If you're feeling refreshed from a nice break, caught up, and clearheaded, sure . . . start that draft. If you've just come out of an intense meeting with one of your staff and are still recovering from a bad head cold, you might have some things to do that would be more suitable to your condition. Cleaning up a bunch of e-mails or replacing a printer cartridge may be a better way to stay positively engaged with your world.

This is another justification for maintaining a complete set of reminders of all of your possible actions—you'll be operating more as Captain and Commander when you match the task at hand to your state of mind and body. If you have taken part in three back-to-back teleconferences, each of which demanded a lot of concentrated thinking and careful politics, you wouldn't want to instantly get on the phone again to call some senior person to discuss a challenging issue. If you wanted to do anything at all besides get a cup of coffee, you might make a call to change a hotel reservation or book a car. It's great to always have a batch of simple little tasks to do, that still need to be done, so that when your energy is depleted, you can still be good for something.

Of course the line between doing simple things because that's the best you can manage and doing simple things as a way to avoid the more challenging ones is very thin! But if you're going to procrastinate anyway, you might as well enjoy the downtime but get *some* constructive things done. Doing something and feeling slightly anxious is probably better than doing nothing and feeling seriously guilty. As long as you're at least willing to engage with your world in any kind of constructive manner, taking any action at all will often start moving your energy in the right direction, and you might actually reach a level of sufficient strength that you need to tackle a project a little riskier with a higher payoff.

ACTION OPTIONS

The last set of variables that come into play regarding your action decisions is the choice about whether to follow up on the actions you've already defined on your action lists; to do work that shows up ad hoc, when it shows up; or to spend the time actually processing your incoming stuff, so you can have an updated inventory of all your possible tasks.

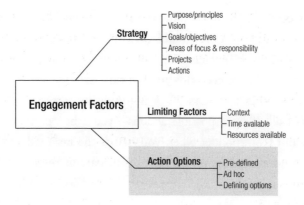

Predefined Work

"Predefined work" is a fancy but accurate description of the contents of your lists of actions, projects, goals, and so on. Of course you can only do things at the action level, but assuming you have thought through the higher-elevation descriptions of your commitments to bring them down to the level of next actions, you'll have plenty of choices from those lists (given the limitations I previously covered).

A big part of the control stages of capturing and clarifying is to define your work at the various levels on which it exists, a majority of the reminders of which wind up on your next-action lists. A typical professional, sitting in his office, could have fifteen calls to make, thirty things to do at the computer, twelve things to talk to the boss about, seven things to see to around the office space, and three things that can pretty much be done anywhere. So, assuming he has the time and energy, there's plenty of work to choose from.

Ad Hoc Work

Life would be challenging enough if your predefined actions were the only options. As you probably have realized, no matter how complete and current you keep the lists containing them, all kinds of unplanned-for things can show up that fall outside their range.

First there are a vast number of maintenance activities that simply need to get done in the course of a day or week that aren't necessarily planned for or listed ahead of time: picking up the cleaning, walking the dog, chatting with your assistant about his family, checking a stock price, taking a colleague to lunch, napping. The number of those kinds of unplanned events, if you took the time to track them, might surprise you.

What will probably come as no surprise, though, is the second category of ad hoc stuff you have to deal with—surprises. Your boss walks in unexpectedly with a new need-it-now project. You get a call from school because your son just broke his arm on the playground. A client just called and wants to give you a big piece of some extra budget money she found.

Ever had a whole day that was a string of surprises, when you couldn't get to anything on your lists? We all have. Is that a bad or good thing? It depends. If everything you did that you didn't previously expect was actually more important than anything else you had to do or could do in the moment, your decisions were a product of mature, sophisticated self-management. If, however, you weren't quite sure what else you had or needed to do, and faced a huge backlog of still-undefined work and "stuff" piled up and pulling on your psyche, being surprised and interrupted with new and additional demands is only laying ground for an ulcer. You'll not feel comfortable about making quick, clean judgment calls about priorities within your entire inventory of commitments, and you'll probably feel compelled to drop everything and deal with the new task right then, simply because you won't trust your ability to easily capture it and establish a placeholder for getting to it at a perhaps more effective time.

How well you deal with surprises and how you feel about them in general are dependent on the accessibility of the complete view of your work at hand and your ability to evaluate the new input against the trusted inventory. If you have to walk down a dangerously dark alley, you don't want your mind to be distracted by unclear projects and unprocessed e-mails. If you are surprised, you want full access to all your faculties and the freedom and facility to shift your focus from the big picture to the small and back again, to enable you to navigate effectively in the current situation.

That's why when you're not doing anything else, it's a good idea to clean up your backlog. A surprise is coming toward you that you can't anticipate, and when it hits you should have as little residue as possible in your psyche, with minimal unprocessed and undecided stuff. Life seems to be increasingly taken up with unexpected events and opportunities. Probably 90 percent of my usage of my own personal action management system is to have a quick and easy way, when an unexpected item appears, to renegotiate with myself about whether I can afford to stop doing everything else and take it on. But I can't trust my judgment on that score if my lists are incomplete and my previous commitments are unclear.

Defining Options

The third possible work focus is the activity you need to do that actually clarifies your work: processing the contents of your in-tray, cleaning up your e-mail, emptying your voice mail and answering machine—all those things that you need to do that ensure you're not overlooking anything that should be considered in your mix of work at hand. This usually takes from thirty to ninety minutes a day. Thinking demands time, and thinking is required for defining and managing your work.

So, how do you decide which of these three options we've discussed is the best choice? That's part of the dance creative and productive people must continually take part in, minute to minute. This third aspect—processing IN—often gets the short end of the stick, given the incessant amount of work at hand. But practically speaking, how long can you go without checking your voice mail and still feel comfortable that you're not missing something that should be included in your mix? How large an inventory of unprocessed e-mail can you tolerate and truly trust your judgment about what to be doing and not doing right now?

The methods of GTD are designed to make defining work as easy and complete as possible, and to provide a way to keep the resulting inventory as clear and accessible and conscious as possible.

If I suddenly decide that I want to take a nap—one of those ad hoc situations that in my later years I'm learning to value a little more—the more I'm aware of what I won't be doing if I decide to lie down, and the more comfortable I am with it, the better I will rest. I don't want to sleep as a way to avoid my amorphous cloud of commitments, but rather because it's the best choice to be making right now vis-à-vis everything else. It's the "everything else" part that I need to be conscious about.

What will never work over the long term is to live and work only in "emergency scanning" mode, if your inventory is eternally unclear and unable to be fully, cleanly, and quickly renegotiated. If you never quite know all the things you have to do, you'll expend much of your energy plugging up leaks and fighting the fires only as they pop up. You'll be living in the realm of hope instead of trust, which is not a way to win at this game.

The Priority Challenge

So, taking into account all the factors that affect your choices, here's the big challenge: if you understand the driving purpose and core values of your life as well as the purposes and values of the enterprises in which you are significantly engaged; if your vision is clear regarding your own ideal success scenario in the long term, as well as that of your organization; if you have identified any key goals and objectives to accomplish in the next year or two; if you have reviewed and evaluated your progress in all the key areas of interest and responsibility in your job and in your life; you will recognize many dozens of projects you are committed to finish within the next few months, projects that will involve one hundred to two hundred next actions to move them forward. You will need to follow through on those actions in conjunction with hundreds of other daily activities that are required for maintenance, all of which you have to negotiate within an increasing volume of unforeseen inputs. Then, at any moment, given your context, time, and energy, you might have a chance of really trusting that what you're doing is what you need to be doing.

How *are* you doing?

Wherever I have laid out that description of prioritizing factors that almost all of us must navigate, the majority of people express at least a mild form of shock and awe. I've never run across anyone (myself included) who can honestly state that he is typically clear, stable, and totally on course with all of that. Have I overstated the ingredients and the complexity involved in deploying them? I don't think so. Again, applying my own standards in researching the best practices of productivity, if the model is too simplistic or incomplete, it's not really an effective one, and it will always leave some aspect unincorporated that then undermines trust in its functionality. I've tried, but I can't get the prioritizing game any more condensed. Every factor I have included affects every action choice. If you try to do without any one of them—time required for actions, your location, your areas of focus (such as health or personal finances), core values, well-defined projects, concrete action decisions—you will be ignoring an essential element that will at some point cause your prioritizing model to unhinge.

If you are not moving on your priorities because you are avoiding them, you refuse to acknowledge their complexities, or you simply don't know what they are, you will inevitably experience some degree of lack of control in your life. If you don't have any priorities, or they are all equal, there's no problem. But assuming you have any desire to improve, to express yourself, or to expand your experience in any way differently from what you are currently doing, the way you are doing, you will have priorities. You have a sense of direction and a need for movement. If forward motion is not happening, or not happening on target, then you will sense being "off" instead of "on." In what direction and at what speed you proceed will be up to you. At any and every arbitrary point in time some things will be better to do than others.

Ultimately you must trust a combination of your intelligence and your intuition. You'll never be able to integrate enough information consciously and then apply to it some logical or mathematical formula whose results you will always trust implicitly. There are just too many factors and subtleties that only the brilliantly integrative part of your mind, which recognizes patterns with both associative and sequential thinking modalities, can possibly process.

But your mind's ability to do that is greatly enhanced when the prioritizing factors that *can* be identified and supported in a systematic way, have been. I now can say with relative certainty, given the years I have worked with these models, that every one of the practices that I have been describing in this book, when implemented to any degree at all, gives you more control and perspective and produces a heightened confidence about and clarity with respect to what you're doing.

A common criticism of my earlier writings was that I tended to ignore the question of priorities, because so much of my focus was on the tactical aspects of controlling the immediacies of hour-by-hour flow of work. Actually, the basic principles that I've shared here can be found in chapter 3 of *Getting Things Done*. I didn't delve into as much detail there, nor give the subject the kind of emphasis that people may have expected, because (a) the primary need for most people, before they could even focus on priorities with any degree of clarity, has been the tactical best practices for gaining control; (b) without a trustworthy and systematic process for translating your priorities into real actions, merely setting them creates more stress and frustration; and (c) the subject of prioritizing deserves a treatment that incorporates much more depth and detail than oversimplistic daily To-do lists or ABC coding techniques can address. I needed more years and experience to really understand this area better, and the room in a book like this to lay out the full extent of my ideas sufficiently.

THE SUCCESS FACTOR OF MOVEMENT PER SE
Sometimes I think we all need to lighten up a bit about goals, plans, and priorities. Do your best to capture, clarify, and organize what

you can, have the basic conversations you need to have with yourself and other key people at the horizons that are calling you, and then *just get moving.* If and when you find yourself off base, course-correct and then get going again—ad infinitum. Frankly, that's what you've been doing all along and will continue to do, so let's not set ourselves up with overly romantic or idealistic standards for attaining some perfected state of total clarity about everything we're doing, all the time.

That's the primary reason to have a road map for your life, like the one I'm laying out in this book. Its five stages of control and six Horizons of Focus are designed to provide guy wires that you can count on to bring you back in line when things get too unsteady. The more you trust that you have a reliable safety net, the more risks you'll be willing to take and the more permission you'll give yourself to explore freely. The structures I'm putting forward here should not be regarded as constraints. They're intended merely to offer some dependable frameworks as you move forward in the game of work and business of life.

Ultimately, motion is key. Truly, taking *any* action will give you more of a sense of control than hanging back in hesitation, even if the action might not be the "right" one or best one to take. One of the critical things that I learned while training in the martial arts was that being in motion is the optimal state in which to be effective. It takes less energy to change direction 180 degrees while moving than it does to start in that direction from a standstill. That doesn't mean, however, that you should allow yourself to get wrapped up in frenetic busyness. There are times when slowing down and retreating into a more reflective mode are called for. That's not actually slowing down, however; it's slowing the body down, so that the mind can continue to be active at a more dynamic level.

10 | Getting Control: Applying This to Life and Work

Meet Ron Taylor. One afternoon Ron finds a letter in his mailbox from an estate attorney in another city. The letter informs him that a long-lost great-aunt, Gracie Kotter, has died and left Ron, her only living relative, her small estate. The main asset in that estate is a business—Gracie's Gardens—which apparently still exists in a small town in another state. The letter requests that Ron contact the attorney and make some decisions about the disposition of the business.

Ron travels to the small town to assess the situation and details of this surprise inheritance. With rental car and map in hand, and help from a few locals, he manages to find Gracie's Gardens on the outskirts of town.

What a sight! It appears to have been a garden supply store and small nursery, which also provided landscaping and gardening services; but no one's around, and it looks as if no activity has been going on there for many weeks. Hundreds of overgrown or dying plants in pots are strewn all over the lot. Entering the padlocked office with a key he'd been given, Ron's confronted with stacks of mail that were shoved through a postal slot in the door. Loose papers lie scattered over the small office, and the store has a disheveled inventory of fertilizers, seed, garden tools, and equipment. It's a mess—obviously an enterprise out of control.

So, how should someone handle a situation like this? Though what follows will seem like a commonsense course of action, I'll frame it in light of the five stages of gaining control—capture, clarify, organize, reflect, and engage.

Getting Gracie's Gardens Under Control

You might think it logical for Ron to start by addressing the questions of what he might want to ultimately do with this business. There wouldn't be any harm in having that conversation, of course, and he'd hardly be able to stop having lots of thoughts run through his head about his possible options.

But the most immediately present task is to get the situation under more control. Any informed decisions about what to do with a business will be seriously hampered if you don't even know what the business is and what shape it's in.

So Ron blocks out a long weekend, rolls up his sleeves, and dives in.

CAPTURE

The very first thing Ron does is to take a quick site walk-through, just to identify the property lines and to notice what the obvious things are within them. Next, he clears off the top of the old oak desk in the small office, sets up an in-basket, gets a legal pad and a pen, and does another site walk-through, this time making notes about anything that grabs his attention and gathering any paper-based or physical items that look as if they might have some meaning, using an in-tray and a couple of empty boxes in the office as a big, temporary in-collection spot. What's obviously broken? What might be functional? What's unknown but could be relevant?

At the same time he starts a junk/trash pile and begins to eliminate whatever is obviously useless, or dead and gone.

Once the area is relatively cleaned up, he then starts a more detailed inventory of the assets. What are the resources, equipment, viable inventory? What's in the files? What's the nature of the business? Where are the ledgers? Who were/are the customers? Who were/are the vendors, suppliers, bankers, accountants, attorneys, employees?

As the last and most subtle part of the capture process, Ron does a thorough "What's true?" session of discovery about Gracie's Gardens. Given its small scale, he begins assessing the market it's in, the competition, its reputation, the local economy, the environment.

CLARIFYING

Now Ron has to start making some "businesslike" decisions. What assets are worth keeping? What of the viable inventory is worth keeping? What files need to be saved? What supplies are still useful?

He begins formulating some outcomes on which to focus. What are his objectives? What needs to happen to produce more clarity and more information that will enable him to make intelligent decisions about what to do with the business? Whether he chooses to keep it or sell it, there will obviously be some immediate and short-term projects that need to be defined.

And for each of those outcomes and projects, what are the next steps that need to be taken (calls to make to resource professionals, things to buy at the hardware store, tasks to do around the property, etc.)?

ORGANIZING

So Ron starts getting organized. He creates a list of his projects and lists of actions to take, organizes reference files, and sets up folders for the various projects. Assuming that he'll be able to connect with the employees who were and perhaps still are involved in the business, he'll draw up a simple organization chart, structure some meetings, and so on.

REFLECTING

At the beginning stages of this new adventure, Ron will probably need to stop and reflect on what he's discovered, what's been done, and what still needs doing, many times a week. There's a good chance he'll also be setting up meetings with friends, consultants, attorneys, accountants, local officials, and anyone else who can contribute perspectives on the situation and his plans.

ENGAGING

Ron's day is filled with making calls, taking notes, filling out forms, researching, buying things, having meetings, and running errands that have emerged, and continue to, from the previous steps.

Ron Taylor Getting Himself Under Control

The unexpected inheritance of a small business you know nothing about is a good example of the kinds of input most of us receive from time to time—a novel event that could be either good or bad, or both. But no matter what the ultimate evaluation of how positive or negative this experience might be, it's certainly new, different, and demanding of our attention in the moment. And, since Ron already has far more to do than he can keep up with in the rest of his life, one more demanding project can certainly jangle his system to the point of knocking him off balance.

So now that Ron has been able to stabilize Gracie's Gardens to some degree, he knows he needs to do the same thing for himself, given the unexpected complication this has brought to his world.

Soon he dedicates another long weekend, back at his home and office, to get control in and around his own total universe.

CAPTURING

Ron takes a couple of hours to gather up all the loose stuff that's piled and accumulated during the rush to get away to deal with his great-aunt's estate. He makes sure that his voice mails and answering machine are all cleaned out, notes put into his in-basket, and briefcase emptied into the in-basket with all the miscellany he collected back at the Gardens. He takes another stack of paper and does a complete "mind sweep" to grab any of the loose ends from his somewhat crazy last couple of weeks.

CLARIFYING

Ron then cleans up his in-basket and all his notes by making decisions about new projects that need to be identified and actions to be taken. He decides what's irrelevant, what might be useful later on, and what is good information to keep.

ORGANIZING

Ron then sets up (or cleans up and refreshes) his systems for sorting the things that he needs to keep track of. He incorporates all the actions from Gracie's Gardens into the inventory of everything else to be done in his life and work, identifies and parks commitments appropriately, and verifies that his structures and lists are all appropriately configured to incorporate the data and reminders from another whole enterprise that he now has to integrate.

REFLECTING

Every few hours Ron finds it necessary to back off from all the hectic minute-to-minute activity, to make sure he's not missing any critical, outstanding stuff. At the end of the week he allows himself the luxury of a two-hour overview of all the projects, actions, and scheduling details, given that he has absorbed so much new input. He brings all his content up-to-date, demoting some projects that have fallen back in priority, and generating more new thinking and commitments to reflect his progress.

ENGAGING

. . . All of which lead back to the physical actions Ron continues to take, day to day.

So what?

As straightforward as this hypothetical scenario may appear, it reflects the set of behaviors that normally and naturally promote a sense of control and balance, whether applied to an enterprise or to an individual. Although it is a fictional and obviously highly compressed account of all that would actually be part of a situation like this, all the procedures described here represent the methods I have spent many thousands of hours implementing systematically with actual people in their work and life.

It may be instructive to realize that, had I removed the headings marking each of the five phases, the narrative would read as a very logical and perhaps obvious sequence of events for Ron Taylor to walk himself through, getting a grip on Gracie's Gardens and then on himself.

Indeed, this simple case study illustrates another example of the paradoxical nature of the GTD models: they are distillations of what most of us typically do to keep ourselves productive. They are intuitive, effective, and familiar. That flow through the five dynamics is how we maintain a sense of equilibrium and order, all the time.

What's less familiar is how to learn from and work those models when the situation is not quite so obvious and naturally self-correcting. You already know how to win at this part of the game of work and business of life, that is, you demonstrate the successful application of the model constantly. The challenge and opportunity are to apply that success formula to take you to the next level.

What have you not yet fully accepted and acknowledged that is pulling on your psyche, or on your company, or on your family, right at this moment? What projects, committees, situations, and relationships need a good current-reality and distractions inventory brought to light?

What have you not yet clarified or decided about any of these issues, in terms of what you're actually going to do about them?

What is out of place in your mind and in your world, potentially creating a drag on your energy?

What projects have you not reviewed sufficiently, to ensure that you have captured, clarified, and organized everything you should? What creative, forward-looking thinking have you neglected to spend enough time on?

What actions are not taking place, because they haven't been defined, because you haven't reminded yourself about them, or because you're simply avoiding them because you're not trusting enough that they are the right ones?

If you're feeling at all out of control, there is a good chance that one or more of these questions will ring as relevant.

Though we're familiar with how to work the patterns I've discussed in our common, ordinary activities, the complexities of our involvements in the world can quickly undermine them. Inheriting a huge amount of new responsibility at work and letting e-mail overrun you as a consequence can shake your sense of stability and require a very conscious effort to get on an even keel.

Getting control by capturing, clarifying, organizing, reflecting, and engaging—whether it's applied to your vacation or to your management team—is not difficult per se. Recognizing when and how to take charge of the process, though, instead of simply reacting insecurely, is both a continual challenge and an opportunity.

11 | Getting perspective

Never look down to test the ground before taking your next step; only he who keeps his eye fixed on the far horizon will find his right road.

—Dag Hammarskjold

Everything is created twice—first mentally, then physically.

—Greg Anderson

Either you focus, or you hit something really hard.

—Jeff Gordon, race car driver

Once You're in Control, Keep Going!

Let's assume that, having read or listened to the first part of this book, you've gotten things under control. Now the question is: Where do you put your focus? The purpose of getting control in the first place is to be able to be clear of distraction. But why? And distraction from *what*? Admittedly, feeling and being clear is a wonderful end in itself. Having a totally unencumbered psyche could be one of the most exhilarating goals you could attain. Because the implementation of GTD methods began to give people a taste of such freedom, the most popular notion of the model was related to its success as a source of the experience. For that kind of equilibrium to be maintained, however, the qualitative aspect of the contents of your focus and commitments needs to be addressed.

A good example of the relationship of control and perspective that many people can relate to concerns reading material that may have gotten out of control. Have you ever felt that everything you've told yourself you want to or should read has just wound up spreading itself all over your world? Piles of books, printouts, brochures, manuals, magazines, catalogs . . . they've managed to crawl onto shelves, desks, and coffee tables; into drawers, briefcases, and other nooks and crannies.

A quick way to get control of this situation is simply to dedicate a stacking tray, a box, a shelf, or some combination of those to "Read/ Review." Label the location as such, and collect every single item in your universe that fits that description. Don't neglect anything—gather it all. Once you think you have thoroughly collected everything in that category, seeing it all in one location with a very clear boundary will make you feel terrific. If it were me coaching you through this exercise (and I have done something similar with clients many times), you'd probably want to buy me dinner. Though you may now be facing a mountain of reading material, you would have a gratifying sense of control—not only because you've got your psychological and physical arms around the problem, but because there is *nothing of that nature lurking anywhere else.*

But to really complete the equation, another process needs to be applied. What, of all the things you've captured that you think you ought to read, should you *really* be reading? Here comes the perspective part. Is there material in the stack that was interesting a while ago but has since lost its luster for you? Which of the reading is truly important to you? Ever find yourself still collecting magazines about some pastime that you haven't been that interested in for quite a while? What magazine subscriptions should you cancel? What *new* magazines should you subscribe to, given your current aspirations and curiosities?

These are, of course, good questions to be asking. But to reinforce the point that the most effective approach to winning this game is to gain control before tackling perspective, how would you feel if, before capturing and organizing all your reading material, I asked, "So, what should you be reading now, given where you're going in your life and what's really important to you?"

Most people would attempt to do their best to come up with a good answer, but for the most part they simply wouldn't have all their appropriate thinking and focusing faculties in working order, given that their reading material was still in disarray. Until that material is given at least a modicum of order, it would be something of a waste of time to pursue any higher-level prioritizing approach.

You Need Perspective to Stay in Control

The problem, however, with stopping too soon in dealing with your reading matter—just getting a sense of order by corralling the chaos but not yet bringing any additional focus to the pile—is that you will be prone to letting it get out of control again. If you neglect the perspective component, it will be very easy for the piles to once more spread themselves around your life. If their meaning is not frequently refreshed, recalibrated, and enlivened, they can easily revert to so much "stuff." In truth, without an appropriate focus and perspective from which to evaluate your relationship to the books and magazines, you can never really bring them under control. It will be *relative* control, but not yet a truly clear space.

Because there is such a close relationship between control and perspective, it can be easy to neglect the second part of that equation, especially since achieving relative control feels so good. In our work with individuals, simply establishing a greater sense of order automatically and significantly enhances perspective for virtually everyone. Cleaning up backlog really does facilitate clearer thinking. Applying the five-stage model of mastering work flow brings everything into greater focus. And building in a trusted, solid, systematic approach to enable you to get back to that state when required really allows for much greater freedom and confidence. What more could be required?

When once-disorganized people achieve relative control, it's wonderful. Compared to chaos, numbness, and confusion, it's an ecstatic feeling. Whenever they actually find the GTD "holy grail" of an empty in-basket and e-mail, they feel as if they now have a significant key to life! They actually have, but there are other keys that need to be applied in order to achieve the fullness of the Captain and Commander experience.

Getting a Grip on the Horizons

In actuality, if you were to *fully* implement the five stages for gaining control, there wouldn't be a need for any additional process to get you "on." Perspective develops with sufficient control, if you consider the idea of "control" to mean the achievement of ultimate balance and harmony. If you were to adequately capture everything that had your attention at all of the more subtle horizons, and if you were to appropriately clarify and review all of the contents of each of those horizons at the appropriate intervals, your choices about what to do in work and life would be as good as you could expect them to be.

In practice, however, there is often a need to address the Horizons of Focus in separate, dedicated processes. There is so much complexity in the human experience that it would be almost impossible for anyone to fully identify in a single sitting every detail and aspect of what has his attention. Even if he did, that very act of rigorous self-examination would change the content itself. This makes perspective a moving target. The exploration of any one level will trigger thinking and discovery on another. As you start to fully lay out a list of your projects (ten thousand feet), for instance, you will likely be reminded of a goal you might want to tweak (thirty thousand feet), another responsibility you may have with your family you hadn't thought about (twenty thousand feet), and certainly new actions you need to take (runway).

Our experience in implementing these models with thousands of people has taught us the efficacy of focusing on one horizon at a time. The associative part of your mind will certainly bounce all over the place in the process, and you wouldn't want to attempt to limit your thinking. On the contrary, it is highly creative and productive to give yourself permission to make those kinds of free-form connections and have a systematic way to capture and integrate them. But it's the holding of a steady focus in one area at a time that actually allows the process to work to its fullest.

The rabbit trails your mind is tempted to traverse can by themselves be a distraction, and the rabbit itself will often want to run— sometimes out of inspiration, and often out of desperation. As you ascend up the scale of your horizons in your contemplation, the issues, sensitivities, and insecurities that may be revealed can be quite disturbing. It's all too easy to feel yourself slipping out of your comfort zone when you need to think about where and how and what you want to be, in the long term, and what your most important values are. You will tend to procrastinate the most about the issues that touch you the most deeply, in terms of expressing and awakening to your potential.

So there's really no apparent safe haven emotionally in any of these exercises of focus, until you have actually done them. Then, because of the relief and boost in your esteem and clarity, you will wonder why on earth you could have been so resistant. It's not necessarily that easy to initiate this process, however, and step into territory that may be unfamiliar. Nor is it the most immediately attractive prospect to cause to surface and address areas you may have been avoiding for whatever reasons. When a client once expressed exasperation about why he should acknowledge and capture *all* the stuff he found himself committed to, our coach challenged him succinctly: "Well, how conscious do you want to be?"

Going Up or Down the Hierarchy?

The potentially daunting nature of attempting to address all of these areas of your involvements with life and work is part of the rationale for starting at the mundane end of the spectrum and moving up from there. But there are two additional reasons: it's usually easier to gain control on the lower rungs, and the more subtle commitments are more attractive to engage with when you have a trust in your ability to control their implementation.

I have been reminding people for years that it helps immensely to achieve a sense of control before they can stretch into the horizons that require a lot of clarity and reflective space. Indeed, the success people feel when they begin to work the GTD processes at the most basic levels very often triggers a flood of inspiration that occurs naturally, without their having to work at it. Much of the most durable value that is experienced by GTD users is not in the nitty-gritty of paper and e-mails and lists of things on their mind but rather in the creative, dynamic thinking that spontaneously develops when they get on top of them.

I've rarely seen the process work the other way around. Getting clear about your goals for the following year can certainly be inspirational, at least in the off-site meeting, but it seldom gives rise to the motivation to go clean up your in-basket, your e-mail, and your head, let alone install a process to keep them that way. Trying to get a senior team enthusiastic about long-term goals and strategies when there is a major cash flow crisis not being addressed does not have much chance of being successful.

The great psychologist Abraham Maslow had it right—the survival aspect of life and work must be addressed before humans have any capacity for dealing with matters of a loftier nature. But survival mode in the psyche is often not nearly as evident as its physical counterpart. I have witnessed many clients in whom the outer appearances of stability and order have masked a serious undercurrent of insecurity and vulnerability, and with whom attempts to do bigger-picture thinking and alignment could simply gain no footing. Drowning in the ocean is an obvious and immediate catastrophe. Drowning in unclear over-commitments is easier to tolerate, thanks to its numbing effect, and often much harder to recognize.

I've often noticed that people are much more open to taking on new goals and challenges once they really have a basic trust in their abilities to capture, process, organize, and integrate anything and everything that crosses through GTD's systematic approach. Knowing in your gut that everything you toss into your own in-basket will soon turn into a single, simple, easily accomplished physical action will encourage an openness to tackle bigger and better things. (It's also one of the biggest dangers you will face in fully practicing GTD—it can easily create the confidence to take on exponentially greater tasks and re-sponsibilities, and *really* throw you for a loop!)

Again, I don't see that happening in the opposite direction. Know-ing that you can set goals and have visions does not translate into greater facility and confidence at the operational nitty-gritty level where the work really takes place.

That said, there is no "right" way to approach all these levels and all the thinking that underlies them. The model is holistic, meaning that you can't really ignore any part of it and still assume that you'll be functioning fully in Captain and Commander mode. If you want to start by clarifying your job description, before you clean up your e-mail, have at it. If you want to make a list of your core values and principles before you begin identifying all the projects on your plate—fine. Sometimes we'll discover that a senior executive's biggest distraction will be at thirty to forty thousand feet, when, for example, he is feeling huge pressure to clarify the strategic vision for his organi-zation. That's obviously the best place for him to put his attention first.

If you try to ignore what most has your attention, attempting to focus on some other horizon can easily become a waste of time, or at least a less effective use of it. Trying to "set goals" because you think you should, without first dealing with major issues and projects that are running amok, would lead to a lackluster effort at best and undermine your resources at worst. You'll set much more aligned and engaging goals if that exercise is conducted without the pull and distractions of another level that's out of control.

Once again, because of the differing nature of the depth and breadth of the content of each of these horizons, there are circumstances in which it can absolutely make sense to go top down. A division of a major corporation has used our Horizons of Focus model as a way to facilitate the merger of two cultures following an acquisition. Once the core values of the two entities had been objectively identified and compared, a mutually inclusive vision for the new entity could then be formulated. The participants could then agree on the goals and objectives. If they had started any lower, they might never have achieved alignment so quickly.

As you can see, there is no hard-and-fast rule that can encompass all the possibilities. I have already offered the one guideline that will be your best indicator for achieving control and perspective: pay close attention to what most has your attention. With that in mind, you can start putting the grand puzzle pieces together in any order. I simply suggest, however, that you'll finish the puzzle more quickly, more easily, and with fewer missing pieces when you start with where your attention is most invested. Don't be surprised, though, if that means, in your case, or for whatever enterprise you're involved with, that moving from the bottom up may make the most sense.

Working with the Horizons of Focus

In the following chapters I'll describe the specific horizons, their scope, the typical formats associated with tracking and managing them, how and how often you will probably want and need to engage with them, and their relationship to gaining and maintaining perspective. I will also lay them out in the sequence that is typically the most effective—from the bottom up.

The altitude analogy that I have been using for the different levels of perspective does not correlate with any inherent value of the content on that level. It merely represents the breadth of view involved. The phone call that you need to make (on the runway), which is directly on task to your life purpose and core values (fifty thousand feet), is essentially as "important" in the grand scheme of things as your loftiest thinking.

By their nature, the higher altitudes provide reference points for correspondingly higher priorities. An organization's annual plan (thirty thousand feet) should be supportive of, and subservient to, its long-term vision (forty thousand feet). Your projects (ten thousand feet) serve your areas of focus and responsibility (twenty thousand feet). But none of these horizons is viable by itself. Each is part of an integrated set of viewpoints that serves as a road map for appropriately directed focus.

12 | Getting Perspective on the Runway: Next Actions

				Purpose/Principles	P
				Vision	E
				Goals	R
				Areas of Focus	S
				Projects	P
Capturing	Clarifying	Organizing	Reflecting	**Engaging/Actions**	E

CONTROL

Thought is useful when it motivates action and a hindrance when it substitutes for action.

—Bill Raeder

Nothing is more revealing than movement.

—Martha Graham

Scope

The pertinent question for the runway level is: What do you need to *do*?

Wash the car, call your mom, draft a proposal, talk to your boss about a new idea, surf the Web for a gift for your brother, buy nails at the hardware store, check your voice mail.

This category refers to all the physical, visible actions that you can take. They could be the next things to do on your projects or larger outcomes, or simply single-step events that you pursue because of some area of interest or responsibility. Once they have determined them, most people have more than a hundred such actions to take, as a running inventory of still-undone items, at any point in time.

Typical Formats

Once you have determined your next physical action, you can either complete it in the moment, hand it off to someone else to do, or keep track of it in a way that you will be reminded of it appropriately. In chapter 7 on organizing, I described the various categories of things that needed to be managed in your system, with "next actions" constituting such a large one that I also recommended various subcategories as the simplest way to keep them sorted. Those included your calendar, for actions tied to specific days and times, and another set of lists organized by action contexts, such as calls to make, things to do at the computer, actions for the office and for home, errands to run, things to do anywhere, and topics to talk with people about, either individually or in a meeting.

How and When to Engage

You will need to be involved with deciding what actions you have to take as well as making particular choices about how to carry them out, all day long, every day. Most of your actions will never need to be tracked, as you'll do them almost automatically when you think of them or simply when the circumstances demand—eat lunch, take the dog for a walk, put paper in the printer, say hello to your secretary, check your e-mail, replace the lightbulb that just blew out, pick up the phone when it rings, contribute a thought in a staff meeting, and so on.

The other actions, those that are not as self-reminding or immediately and obviously present, would be the ones on your calendar and on your additional action lists. You probably look at your calendar whenever you have a question about where you need to be and when, which can take place many times in a day or merely once or twice, depending on the complexity and detail of the content. The additional action lists would be reviewed whenever you had discretionary time and wanted to be clear that you were considering all your options.

The Runway and Your Priorities

You will automatically feel better about what you're doing if the inventory of defined actions available to you is as complete as possible. At the risk of stating the overly obvious, the more aware you are of what you've told yourself you need to get done, and the more accessible the options are for you to consider, the more you will trust both your plan of attack and your choices about the actions you're *not* taking.

But if this is so obvious, why do so many people avoid creating and maintaining that inventory? In most of my seminars I give the participants the chance to spend a few minutes to begin to capture, clarify, and organize their next actions. When I ask, "How many of you feel at least a little more confident about your priority choices now?" virtually everyone raises a hand—and that's after only ten minutes. Imagine how much improvement is possible when they invest the several hours most people require initially to catch themselves up to present time with that drill.

As is true with each of the Horizons of Focus, there is an exponential difference between partial and complete management. The bad news is that doing even a little feels so great that most people don't give themselves permission to keep going to discover what *really* great is by taking the process fully to its conclusion. When the subliminal part of you recognizes that you don't have it all—that something is still missing or incomplete in your system—you experience some limitation of trust, clarity, or freedom to lift to another horizon, with the result that it will be almost impossible to commit 100 percent to whatever you're doing as the best choice you could have made. You will experience *relative* value—a degree of *more* trust and clarity—but that's not the same as being fully invested. It doesn't mean your choice is the best one as measured by some external standard, but simply that you know you've done your utmost to make the wisest call, given all your options.

That hypothesis may be difficult for you to accept, especially if you see yourself as a reasonably effective and successful person. Part of having healthy self-esteem is a general trust in your decisions. If things are fine in that regard, why exert the disciplined effort to ensure that your lists are truly complete? All I can say is, try it and decide for yourself. You may discover a new reference point for "clear." I've never known anyone to implement this model fully who has disputed that conclusion.

The Action Level as the New Frontier

The runway may be the most challenging horizon to really master objectively and completely, simply because though it is the most mundane, it is also the most complex in terms of volume, variety, and changeability. As I mentioned in chapter 7, the lower the horizon, the more sophisticated the system must be to manage it, for those reasons.

Systematizing your approach to the action level may require the greatest amount of initial thinking and exploration, the longest time to install, and the most training to establish the necessary habits to maintain it consistently. In our two-day intensive coaching with individuals, usually 90 percent of the program is focused at this horizon, simply because its approach is so unfamiliar and the volume of material to deal with is so sizable.

The best practices for managing the runway have been responsible for the most resounding positive uptake of the GTD model. The powerful practice of next-action thinking and the novel but highly effective way to organize action reminders by context have become two of the most well-known and popular aspects of this material around the world. When people get a chance to meet me, after having previously discovered GTD through my first book or some other channel, their first inclination is to show me with pride how they have set up and are using their own "next-action" lists.

The professional world has come around to an acknowledgment of the importance of this horizon. "Execution" has reached the top of the business buzzword and no doubt will remain a hot issue and criterion for management and leadership skill. Lack of execution is often cited as one of the top reasons for the failure of start-ups. Most of the writing and training about execution, however, focuses primarily on the organizational and management-practices level. Those are valuable concepts and principles, but they don't usually reach down to the arena where the real work actually takes place—the physical action steps that individuals have to decide and take.

The defining index that I use to determine whether a management group, a couple, or a project team is aligned and clear is whether there is consensus about the very next actions that need to be taken, by whom, and by when. If that consensus is present, there's probably no need for further discovery, organization, analysis, visioning, or any other work in order to gain control and get appropriately focused. But if there is any discrepancy, disagreement, or lack of clarity about what, exactly, the next action steps should be, at least one if not several of the stages of control or the Horizons of Focus need to be revisited.

Simply bringing the focus to the action level, in any situation, will ground the energy in reality (in keeping with the same principle as grounding an electrical connection). Physical resource allocation is the end result of all the loftier thinking and decision-making in organizations, and where you direct your body is the culmination of all of your personal commitments, intentions, and values. Sometimes it's easier to get to the real crux of any issue when you are challenged to get to the point of asking, "So what's the next action?"

If posing that core question a little more frequently in a few more key situations is all that someone gets out of reading my books and working with this material, I guarantee it will be worth far more than the effort expended in learning it.

The Ultimate Mystery of the Mundane

It is at the action level that control and perspective meet head-on. No matter how elegant, sophisticated, and intelligent your thinking, your vision, and your focus, they must translate into physical action or they're ultimately vacuous. And no matter to what degree you have achieved a level of control—having collected, processed, organized, and reviewed all your commitments—you must take action to maintain it.

At that place where the rubber hits the road—what you decide to do at 11:36 tomorrow morning—there will always be the risk of the unknown. Perhaps that is why there has been so much spin and hoopla in so many forms since the 1980s about time management and personal productivity—there is no universally accepted and verifiable formula for making the judgment call about action. Like religion, the vehemence of the discussion is often inversely relational to the provability of the model.

No matter how assiduously you implement and practice the models I'm laying out in this book, no matter how much control and perspective you have and "on your game" you are, you will have to make at least a small leap of faith to actually *do* something. But the more control and perspective you *do* have, the more you will minimize that risk and be willing to stretch and expand into new territories.

13 | Getting Perspective at Ten Thousand Feet: Projects

Purpose/Principles	**P**
Vision	**E**
Goals	**R**
Areas of Focus	**S**
Projects	**P**
Capturing Clarifying Organizing Reflecting Engaging/Actions	**E**
CONTROL	**C**

Fulfill the agreements that you make with yourself and with other people around you. Fulfill your agreement to your family, your employers and employees, your friends, your landlord, your doctor, your dentist, your creditors, etc. When you fulfill the obligations that you have agreed to, you'll be surprised at the freedom you manifest in your life.

—John-Roger

Scope

The fundamental relevant question at the project level is simply this: What do I need to *complete*?

As the next level up from actions, this horizon is the source of many of the physical things we need to do. I define "projects" very broadly as outcomes that can be finished within a year that involve more than one action. That can obviously include quite a range of possibilities, from "fix washing machine" to "finalize acquisition of Acme Brick Company." In our experience, given that definition, most people have an inventory of between thirty and a hundred outstanding at any time, if you include every aspect of your life and work.

A project is essentially a miniature goal, something that can be finished and marked off as "done." The reason for the "within a year" parameter is that any commitment you have that can be completed in that time period—even very big ones—should probably be reviewed at least once a week. Though every project will have its own unique degree of complexity, the status of all of these current "open loops" at the next level up from actions ought to be evaluated regularly.

A project, like a goal, is not actually something you *do*. You can only do action steps. Once you've completed enough of the appropriate actions, though, you will cross some predetermined finish line, having achieved some final result, and you can then say the project has been accomplished. You never actually see anyone "take a vacation" or "finalize yearly taxes"—you would only see them packing clothes, moving their body to a different location, and buying sunscreen, or turning on their computer and filling out forms. But having undertaken a sufficient number of certain specific actions, they can be said to have "taken a vacation" or "filed their taxes."

The following verbs point to typical outcomes that I refer to as projects:

Finalize
Implement
Research
Publish
Distribute
Maximize
Learn
Set up
Organize
Create
Design
Install
Repair
Submit
Handle
Resolve

If you're curious about what and how many projects you actually have, just use the above as a checklist, and include everything that can be linked with one of those verbs. What, right now, do you have a commitment to finalize, research, repair . . . and so forth?

Typical Formats

Managing this horizon usually involves compiling some sort of overview index of outstanding projects, assembling all the various tools for holding and building project plans and support materials, and setting aside a dedicated time to facilitate your review of your world from this level.

One of the best tools you use for managing this level is a Projects list—one simple list of all of your projects, one per line, or one per page (if you want to keep them in a folder). This would function much like a file drawer that has a file for each one of your projects, which you could survey by scanning the labels of the files. Like the wide range of types of calls that can appear on your single Calls list, the Projects list can contain quite a diverse mix. Many people maintain a version of this kind of index by having a file drawer or cabinet dedicated solely to projects, with a folder for each one. The disadvantage of this method, though, is that you won't think that many of your real projects (by my definition) deserve a whole folder. Few people feel comfortable making a folder for "Install new set of tires" or "Get away for a long weekend in New York with Kathryn." Also many haven't even considered a topic like "Handle summer schedules and events for the kids" as belonging in the same category as "Launch the ad campaign" because of a resistance to thinking of "personal" projects as being as worthy of a place in their systems as "professional" projects. But for the purpose of maintaining control and perspective on this level, *all* of these projects need to be identified as such, with each being reassessed as often as any other.

How and When to Engage

There are three distinct times that this horizon review should come into play:

- once a week in a regular one- to two-hour executive session with yourself to tune up your awareness of the status of all your projects
- whenever you have a sense that some of your key projects are lagging behind in keeping next actions current and in motion
- whenever you're feeling as if you've lost your grip on priorities in the short term.

The "weekly review" that I have championed for these many years has become one of the hallmark success factors for maintaining and utilizing the systematic approach that makes GTD work. It defines a set of specific procedures for "pulling up the rear guard"—ideally at the end of a workweek (although anytime will be fine). Its function is to get you clear, current, and creative.

The "get clear" review is intended simply to shore up and capture systems and their contents, that is, to gather all the loose ends that may have accumulated in and around your world and your head that you haven't yet gotten into the system for processing and organizing. These include cleaning up e-mail, cleaning out your briefcase, and gathering all the scraps and strands of receipts, telephone notes, sticky notes, and the like that have managed to creep into your pockets and onto your nightstands and computer screens.

The "get current" review is to update the inventories of actions and projects that you haven't been able to keep totally caught up with during the week. Life moves too quickly most of the time for you to be able to keep track of everything in progress, in terms of maintaining accurate bookmarks about the status of projects and what the next steps on them are. Many times as I sit down for my own weekly review, I'll find actions on my lists that I've finished but haven't had the chance to mark off as "done" yet. And very likely there will be circumstances that have emerged over the last few days that have actually morphed into projects, but I haven't had the opportunity until my review time to recognize and identify them as such. Once I'm clear that my Project list is current, I ensure that I have all the operative next actions for each one in their proper place in the system—usually on the calendar or action lists.

Probably the most graphic example of getting current is our recommended review of your calendar—scanning the details over the last two weeks and looking as far ahead as you might have commitments that you should be noticing in advance, making critical catches. This will be especially true if other people have permission to add items to your calendar.

Reviewing your calendar, which is your time-based tool, in conjunction with your project inventory also brings you current with the eternal issue of juggling deadlines and the constant recalibration of how your time is allocated. Many commitments are time-sensitive to some degree, but seldom is everything so perfectly planned and coordinated that you can easily renegotiate your schedule when one appointment changes or you have new input that impacts the allocation of your focus. Realizing, as you look through your calendar while considering what's changed in the last few days, that you had now better block out two hours for yourself in the coming week so that you can finish drafting a document on time, is the kind of "aha!" moment that can help prevent the loss of control.

"Get creative" is the one part of this weekly review process for which you won't need any discipline at all—it'll just happen, at least if you allow enough time for it. If you follow my prescriptions for populating your systems with the appropriate contents and reviewing them all from this horizon, you will invariably trigger a wealth of useful thinking and good ideas that you would likely not have had otherwise, or not have had until you *had* to have them because you've waited until the immediate demands of your world forced the situation. Deciding to research possible entertainment events taking place in San Francisco while you're there with your partner to celebrate a birthday is usually best done a month ahead of time rather than waiting until you're in the city and trying to obtain good tickets.

Looking through the lens of this level seems most appropriate at least about every seven days. Some projects will need constant surveillance and review, especially if you inherit a big one on Monday and it's due on Friday. And some of your projects, like researching how you might want to spend your next long holiday nine months from now, might cruise along without notice for a couple of weeks.

One of the great values of having the "extended mind" that this model supports is not only its relief of the pressure on your central processor to keep running the programs, but also the automatic productive thinking that happens when you pay a visit to the programs. In other words, by using effective placeholders for the projects you're committed to develop and complete, when you "make the rounds," focusing on each in turn, your creative intelligence is then being maximized for what it does best.

The perspective at ten thousand feet is not simply taking stock of the inventory of discrete projects you have defined. That's a core part of the process, certainly, but it really encompasses a slightly higher-level assessment across the entire playing field. It's the time-out that will allow you to catch your breath and rethink your game plan. It's the quality time you need to spend, detached from the daily grind, that will enable you to regain control of the daily grind. Most people get ground up in the work that they leave on Friday and hate coming back to it on Monday.

Higher-level reviews increase comfort and direction overall, but this horizon—closer to the flux of day-to-day work—is a key component for sanity. It allows you to unhook from the busyness of what you're doing, but not too far. This is the tactically important scan from the crow's nest, not the ivory tower.

The Power of Project-level Thinking

Doing a weekly look at all your projects, actions, and schedule provides an "inner coordination" that is fundamentally intuitive because of all the shifting factors involved in the complexities of your life. As with all the upper Horizons of Focus, your engagement with this level will assist greatly in what I call "hard-wiring your intuitive judgments," as you can sharpen the functioning of this subjective algorithm with better preparation.

I often somewhat jokingly say that I only think about once a week. The little bit of truth in that statement is that the weekly horizon review demands the kind of dedicated thinking that really only needs to be done, at the appropriate level of concentration, every few days. As Whitehead put it, "Operations of thought are like cavalry charges in a battle—they are strictly limited in number, they require fresh horses, and must only be made at decisive moments." The time in which you're taking physical action is not a suitable time in which to be thinking about what all your actions should be. That ought to have already happened. You need to lay the groundwork internally for mature responsiveness to your environment by consciously focusing from this elevated level at some consistent interval.

If you're not really doing a thorough weekly review (with fresh horses!) so that you can achieve that level of renegotiation with yourself, some part of you will always be trying to do it, but never really get there. You need to have thought enough so you don't have to think—just act.

A compelling reminder of this principle came from a business coach I used for myself for several months. Having been on a Super Bowl team in a previous career, he observed that GTD was very much like pro football. Once you're on the playing field and the whistle blows, you don't have time to think. You need to have spent the previous six days thinking, strategizing, planning, and preparing, and hope you did them all sufficiently so that your instant, gut-level responses in the heat of battle were the right ones. It made me think how strange it was that in high-level sports, the vast majority of players' time is spent getting ready for doing. In the typical office and family, however, my educated guess is that it would be rare to find anyone dedicating even an hour or two out of a full week to do that kind of operational assessment and reflection.

A general in the U.S. Air Force, who's a big champion of the GTD processes, told me that the reason he gives *Getting Things Done* to all his officers is that it galvanizes "situational awareness"—the critical ability of fighter pilots to intuitively integrate an enormous variety and amount of input coming at them at mach speeds and to make informed life-and-death judgment calls in a split second. A comparison between the world of jet combat and office-working professionals or parents may be a little extreme, but maybe not! In fact this officer, once he discovered the real power of the GTD weekly review (and he admitted it took him a while to fully appreciate it), began to request a status report on Monday from each of his staff, which by its nature required all of them to do their own weekly review to supply the data.

A wide range of examples of this kind of productive use of this project-level horizon focus have been shared with us. We know of managers who have built in an hour of quiet time at the beginning of their weekly staff meetings, effectively creating an oasis for everyone to catch up with (and share) the current realities affecting the group. Many bosses have discovered the great value of decompressing the stress of their staffs by coaching them in how to keep track of the inventory of their projects, which they can then review together regularly to keep one another's expectations appropriately renegotiated.

At the end of our GTD in-house seminars, a huge corporation in the retail industry gives all the participants a small roll of yellow police tape. We have often said in jest that, in order to get some quiet time for their weekly review, people who work in open office spaces should post warning tape across their cubicles. The company picked up on that idea and uses the tape as an icon to represent permission in its culture for employees to hold the world back every so often, in order to regroup.

Another wonderful example of the value of having this level in optimal condition is how seamless it makes the handoff of jobs. I know of one case in which a senior executive in a Fortune 50 corporation was changing her position in the company, passing her previous job along to someone she had never met. In the first meeting with her replacement, they both discovered that they had been through GTD training. They each had up-to-date Projects lists and agendas of details to go over already prepared, facilitating the smoothest transition and one of the most productive interactions either had ever experienced.

One of the most inspiring examples of how this elevated look at your commitments can add huge value to your life is the family weekly review. Establishing a context in which life partners (and children) can mutually debrief their past week, share a thorough and concrete overview of their commitments and projects, compare calendars, look ahead to the immediate future, and make decisions and plans together can be a phenomenal way to experience winning at the business of life.

The whole concept of work *versus* life and personal *versus* professional is nonsense. Life is work and work is part of life, and the professional is the personal. Understandably the split occurred when the breadwinner(s) began to go *off* to work, in places separate from where they lived. At the end of a long, grueling day at the factory and a long, tedious day with the household, there was little energy left in either partner for updates. To a large extent that's still likely to be the case—couples go into different worlds for a majority of their day for a majority of the week. But GTD now provides a common *format* of work that *can* be shared.

We were recently invited to conduct a seminar in Latin America exclusively for businessmen, but the host had the prescience (or audacity) to invite their wives. By the end of the seminar the spouses were all sharing Project lists and setting up schedules to do so regularly with each other. They were all enthusiastic about the new level of awareness and interaction they could now incorporate into their relationships with the people most important to them. Parents who become frustrated when they get little response from their kids when they are asked, "So, what did you do today?" should ask themselves to what extent they are actually modeling such behavior. There's no question that it's difficult to keep people abreast of all that's really going on in your world, even when they are very close to you.

This exercise of focusing at ten thousand feet—an operational level above actions but more tactical than goals—is, in my experience, the horizon least visited in a consistent and systematic way by most people (though the twenty-thousand-foot level—areas of responsibility and interest—comes close). Actions have to be dealt with, to some degree, because they're the most obvious and the most pressing elements of life: bills have to be paid, calls returned, e-mails dealt with. Goals and objectives, though often avoided, are still relatively familiar, as are visioning and long-term thinking. Setting a purpose and clarifying values are likewise at least easily recognizable concepts. But regular thinking about what's going on at the one-week to several-month level seems to go untapped as a perspective-building resource. Accustoming yourself to this horizon review as a consistent practice will likely provide you more durable relief and productive thinking in the game of work and the business of life than any other practice I know of.

14 | Getting Perspective at Twenty Thousand Feet: Areas of Focus and Responsibility

Purpose/Principles	**P**
Vision	**E**
	R
Goals	**S**
	P
Areas of Focus	**E**
	C
Projects	**T**
	I
Capturing Clarifying Organizing Reflecting Engaging/Actions	**V**
	E
CONTROL	

It is easy to dodge our responsibilities, but we cannot dodge the consequences of dodging our responsibilities.

—E. C. McKenzie

Scope

Once you reach twenty thousand feet, the relevant question to ask yourself is: What do I need to maintain?

This level functions as an abstraction of your reality, a tightly focused series of ten to fifteen categories in areas that you are particularly responsible for, interested in, or pay special attention to, just to keep your ship afloat and sailing steadily. Your commitment to them motivates you to take on projects and do actions.

For instance, to work and live comfortably, you need to keep your health and physical energy at a reasonable level, so you must pay some degree of attention and interest to your body (and perhaps even more to subtle factors that affect it). Exercise, getting your teeth cleaned, eating, sleeping, and physical checkups are the typical items that fall within that arena.

If you work, your job could probably be defined by identifying the four to seven areas you are responsible for maintaining or doing well. One way to think about that is to imagine your year-end review by your boss or your board for what they are going to hold you accountable to have done well. Typical duties here might include asset management, staff development, administrative support, customer service, product design, quality control, client development, shop-floor efficiency, employee morale, increasing shareholder value, and so on.

With a few exceptions, such as being hired simply to write code or to ensure security, most people are expected to wear several hats in their job. If you run your own enterprise, or simply work alone, you have to handle all seven categories of organizational focus—executive, administration, public relations, sales, finance, operations, and quality. If you are part of a larger organization, you will be more specialized in one or more of those areas, but you could probably come up with an equal number of separate responsibilities in your bailiwick.

Organizationally, this horizon would be represented by areas of an enterprise, project, or endeavor that need to be managed well in order to have them run smoothly. If you were organizing a conference, for example, you would need to ensure that items like food, media support, content, PR, registration, and budget were all present and accounted for.

In your life, overall, you probably have seven to ten areas into which you could logically group your interests and activities. Typical categories here include your relationships, your household, parenting, finances, self-expression, career, service, and health. The roles you have taken on and the key components of your lifestyle maintenance and involvement would serve as a horizon checklist at twenty thousand feet.

Each one of your projects and actions reflects your commitment to maintain work and life responsibilities and interests at some self-assessed standard. One easy way to identify your own relevant categories at the Areas of Focus level for yourself is to examine your projects and your actions and ask yourself, "Why am I doing that? What area of interest or responsibility does it reflect?"

For instance, if you have a project described as "Develop proposal for Acme Brick Co. for new computer system," then you probably have some agreement with your organization regarding growing sales, client development, and/or custom system design. If you have a project involving throwing your aunt a special birthday party, you have an interest in extended family.

EXAMPLES OF TWENTY-THOUSAND-FEET CONTENTS

WORK	LIFE
Asset management	Finances
Quality control	Health/vitality
Staff development	Family
Planning	Career
System design	Household
Administrative support	Parenting
Product development	Partnering
Public relations	Recreation
Customer service	Creativity
Client development	Self-development
Research	Service/spirituality

Typical Formats

Areas of focus can most usefully serve as checklists for ensuring balance and inclusion of the most significant components—of your life, a project, or a department. Typical forms these might take include:

- High-level job description
- Personal lifestyle checklist
- Organization chart
- Departmental structure chart
- Project component checklists

As of this writing, this is the checklist I use.

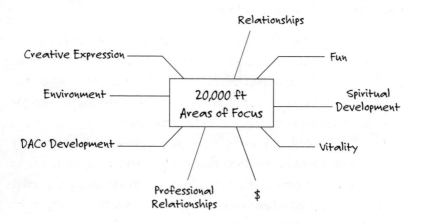

Each of these headings has a subset of associated details. For instance, the one that tracks my professional focus with my company (job) includes the following topics:

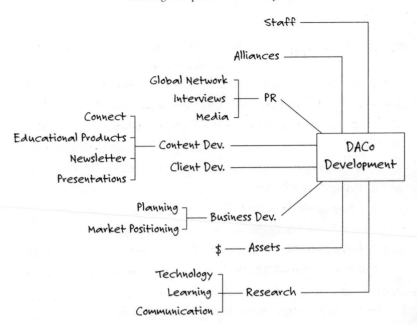

How and When to Engage

The Areas of Focus horizon is not one that requires as frequent a re-view as projects and actions. Its contents are not meant to be finished. They are markers for ongoing areas of your life and work that gener-ate projects and actions as well as many ad hoc activities that simply maintain these areas at some satisfactory standard.

You'll probably find it useful to revisit a high-level checklist every month or so. Frankly, anything that can give you an opportunity to view your involvements in the world from a more elevated perspective than you can afford when you're "down in the weeds" is going to be valuable, to some degree.

One of the situations that might give rise to a need to think at this level specifically would be when things have changed dramatically in your world in a given time period, and you have the sense that you should be rethinking the mix of all of your projects. The most common example would be in the case of a significant shift in your job or role at work. In most companies very few people are doing what they were hired to do, and job descriptions can become moving targets, especially with so many organizations in the midst of rapid change. It helps to keep an occasional bird's-eye view on the various aspects of your work that demand some level of attention, to ensure that nothing of consequence is slipping through a crack as a result of new conditions.

In a company this level would be represented by an organization chart, which is usually set up to reflect the different components of a company's functions and who's responsible for them—finance, sales, operations, human resources, administration, marketing, and so on. If you run an organization, one version of a twenty-thousand-feet review would be to assess the organizational chart, asking yourself, "How is it going in that division? Is everything being handled that needs to be?"

Aside from a regular review, the other time at which it's useful to take an account of various areas of your life from this altitude would be when you have a sense that you could use more balance among them. For instance, if you've been going through an extended period of very intense work in your job, with little opportunity to engage in relaxing activities, you might need a reminder to pay some attention to the fun and recreational aspects of your world. Or if you think you may be getting a little stale mentally, you might want to jog plans to take a workshop or training program to boost your professional skills.

I have personally found that the simple act of making a diagram or list of this horizon from time to time is a productive experience, even though I may not consciously refer back to it very frequently. As with much thinking that you may do at the upper altitudes, the very process of focusing there sufficiently to be able to generate a list will update and mature your awareness naturally and automatically.

Hopping into the Realm of the More Subtle and More Strategic

Often the benefits of visiting the more elevated horizons will be the opportunity to identify a number of important topics that have had your attention but that have tended, at least initially, to lurk further back in the recesses of your mind. Some of the most significant changes and improvements you consider making in your life and work won't be obvious, polished, and ready to move on. More often they will develop slowly and creep up on you.

For instance, when I have coached executives and introduced them to this horizon via a review of their own roles and responsibilities in their organizations, many have realized that some version of "staff development" has been on their mind for a while. They may have been reading management self-help books or listening to motivational business gurus talk about "growing your people" and "creating a culture of trust" and such, with an increasing sense that they probably should be doing something to engage with their own staffs in a more proactive way. While that's certainly a valid long-term strategic goal, it doesn't present itself as a neatly packaged project, but has to be captured and clarified before it can be acted on.

"You know, David, I've been thinking . . . our whole performance review process should be reevaluated." I often hear statements like this from executives when they step back far enough from their day-to-day activities to look through the more refined filter of Areas of Focus. As they're sitting with me, they accordingly gird their loins, turn to whatever list-management tool they've picked to hold their reminders, go to their Projects list, and add "R&D performance evaluation process."

It's this kind of self-notification of issues that are roaming around in the background of your thinking and turning them into real projects with specific next actions that produces real magic and enlightened engagement with your world. Few experiences can contribute as gratifyingly to heightening your sense of self-esteem and flow.

I would be willing to bet that if you did a thorough analysis right now of all the areas of interest and responsibility in your life, you'd come up with at least a few projects crouching in the background that you would still consider relatively important, in terms of your values and personal and professional directions. Here is where we often see extremely valuable projects get surfaced, clarified, and put into motion, such as:

- "Implement a structure of spending regular, quality time with my kids"
- "Research options for getting an MBA"
- "Set up a regular exercise routine"
- "Start working within a personal budget"
- "Start drawing again, regularly"

Twenty-thousand-feet themes do not lend themselves as such to specific projects, but rather they serve as reminders and affirmations of activities that we simply want to be doing and thinking about more consistently—reading more, exercising more, paying a little more attention to the extended family, being open to more ways to assist in the community, being more conscientious about health, diet, and exercise habits, and so on. It's fine if you don't have or want to set up a specific project related to any of those, but do ask yourself if there's something that could be done or completed (i.e., a project) that would greatly assist in getting you more dependably engaged. In other words, what project, if implemented or completed, would automatically get you doing more of what you want to be doing? If you want to start doing more painting, perhaps a commitment to research water-color classes in your area would give that motivation a good kick-start.

To some degree the twenty-thousand-feet horizon is similar to the fifty-thousand-feet one—it identifies areas that you consider especially important, not so much as a goal or direction, but rather as a definable sphere of experience. For instance, "family" could be viewed either as an area of responsibility and interest or as a fundamental core value. When you are ruminating about your life at twenty thousand feet, the idea of "family" is more likely to trigger thoughts about summer activities to set up for your kids and the birthday party you want to give for your brother. At fifty thousand feet (core values), your concerns will be more along the lines of "Research trust fund options" and "Structure regular quality time with Sarah." No matter what the assigned altitude, these important components of life and work should be appropriately considered to ensure that they are incorporated into your endeavors.

15 | Getting Perspective at Thirty Thousand Feet: Goals and Objectives

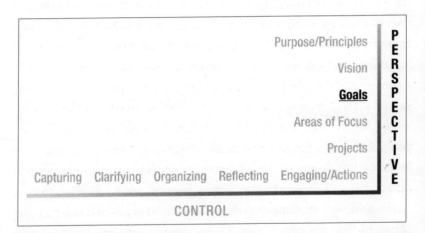

Our acts of voluntary attending, as brief and fitful as they are, are nevertheless momentous and critical, determining us, as they do, to high or lower destinies

—William James

Scope

What do I want to achieve?

This is the fundamental question at the Goals level, the next horizon upward, which incorporates the commitments you may have to complete or goals you're eager to accomplish over the next year or two. Any project that is likely to take longer than a year to finish should be parked in this category. The reason for that one-year time frame is based purely on how often you think you ought to reexamine your progress. If you really need to check the status on an item weekly to feel comfortable, I would call it a project and include it in that grouping. If you can honestly conclude that you only need to reassess your position on a monthly or quarterly basis, then you would most likely want to categorize it as a thirty-thousand-feet item, commonly referred to as a goal or objective.

Goals, like projects, are outcomes that can be completed and checked off as "done." Restructuring an organization, publishing a book, getting out of debt, sending your son off to college, launching a new product line, running a marathon—these would be the kinds of aspirations you might expect to have on this list.

Typical Formats

As you move upward through the levels of perspective, structures become less complex, though formulating the actual content can be challenging. The formats are simpler because what you want to have come true over the longer term can usually be organized in a straightforward list, outline, or plan. If you were to stop and consider your goals for the end of this year or next, you might only come up with fewer than a dozen. Of course, if you were responsible for strategic and operational planning for a medium- to large-size business, you might have quite a complex planning document, with numerous outcomes and suboutcomes delineated for each division. In most cases, though, a simple list or document will suffice.

This is the realm of typical annual goal-setting and planning meetings for organizations—corporate boards, senior management teams, partners, and so on—that are often held off-site, away from the distractions of the work environment.

When and How to Engage

It makes sense to rethink the substance of annual and longer goals at least once a year. In most organizations this process is fairly automatic because of planning and budgeting meetings, which can be tied to the start of a fiscal year if that's different than the calendar year. It's also common to revisit the annual goals on a monthly or quarterly basis, for course correction and recalibration, if required.

Unless you have internalized a high level of motivated goal-setting in your life in general or in a specific endeavor, such as competitive sports, thinking at this higher horizon often needs a boost, if you have any sense that there would be value in tightening your focus. The beginning of a new cycle, such as a new year, provides a great excuse for stepping back from your activities and thinking at this horizon.

My wife and I go through a rather unsophisticated exercise in this regard at the end of every year. First we spend about a half hour taking an inventory of everything we accomplished and everything noteworthy that we did that year. Major projects completed, new places we traveled, significant events that we experienced—all are just dumped out into a long list. We discovered several years ago how well this stock-taking provides a refreshing sense of completion and acknowledgment. During the next half hour we simply ask ourselves what we would like to have on that list at the end of the following year, and capture those goals on another list.

Obviously setting goals and targets at this level makes sense for an enterprise, so that it can determine how to allocate its resources. Any organization's existence is dependent on creating and maintaining a viable relationship with the world within which it operates, and it must therefore maintain a sufficient focus to contain and direct its energies. It has to *produce* something. Having a commitment about a certain amount of production by a certain time will describe the requirements for its resources and structures. If it doesn't aim to achieve or sustain anything, or if it is pointed in too many different directions, it may be extremely difficult to keep it sufficiently intact to justify its existence.

Goals foster alignment, both internally for individuals and interactively for organizations. Even if you have a single, narrowly defined goal, identifying the scope and scale of how much to achieve by when is useful for establishing practical decision-making criteria. If your plan is to double the sales of a company, whether you expect that to happen within a year would make for very different plans and expectations going forward than if your target date was five years.

With that in mind, the most useful times to focus at thirty thousand feet would be at sufficiently consistent intervals to ensure that you can continue on a track of viable expansion, and whenever you sense that your energies for accomplishment are depleted or too scattered. If you know, for instance, that you should get your personal finances in order, setting a target of what you'd like to have true in that area twelve months from now will supply the motivation for you to get a handle on the situation (by capturing, clarifying, organizing, and reviewing it). This would be a good example of how a new perspective could facilitate control.

Playing the Game of the Bigger Game

It is well known that a common attribute of high-performing individuals and organizations is having a set of clear, written goals. The critical component here is actually concentrated focus, and written goals can certainly provide that.

The two most common situations I have experienced that call for a one-to-two-year reassessment are (a) when old goals have been overrun and haven't been reset, and (b) when commitment to a very ambitious long-term vision is having trouble getting connected to reality. In the first case, if you have achieved your previously set goals but haven't replaced them with sufficiently challenging and inviting new ones, it will seem as if you are stuck in a motorboat with the propeller still spinning but with no one's hand on the tiller. Your prior successes generated momentum that may still have thrust, but now it's directionless. You may feel as if you're trying to accomplish something, but you don't quite know what it is. You're all dressed up with nowhere to go.

In the latter case, you may have formulated a grand scheme, but you haven't grounded it in practicalities—lacking a strategy about how to do so. If you really wanted to become a successful fiction writer, what would you need to accomplish regarding this in the next year? If you do want to have sufficient assets to afford a certain lifestyle when you retire, what financial plans had you better set up within the next twenty-four months? If you want your organization to achieve a certain revenue and profit target to be able to attract a buyer five years from now, what goals would make sense in the shorter term?

The paradox of goals is, if they are so valuable, why is there often such resistance to the process? The real challenge goals present is simply that a commitment to any kind of long-term outcome assumes a willingness to abandon the familiarity of day-to-day existence and to risk a psychological jump into the unknown. What if I can't accomplish what I want? What if it's the wrong thing to pursue? What will I have to sacrifice? Your ability to hold and identify with images of positive futures for yourself will depend on the measure of confidence you have in your capacity to achieve what you desire, and your self-esteem may not yet be up to the task.

There are times when focusing on a highly ambitious goal may not be the wisest course of action, as it could easily cause you to feel *less* rather than *more* in control. Some subliminal part of you probably acknowledges the new and challenging things that await you if you do commit to something big and different in your life. If you're already feeling a bit shaky in your ability to manage your current reality, a goal that aims too high will probably be counterproductive. There have been periods during the growth of my own company when we weren't ready to focus on goals any farther ahead than simply getting the senior team and a working structure set up, which themselves would be a key foundation to have in place in order to allow us to set higher goals. And if you or your enterprise is in basic survival mode, because of cash flow or unexpected negative circumstances, all of your energies will be needed on much shorter horizons until those pressures are relieved.

Much of what I uncovered and developed in the GTD models was based on the fact that people couldn't appropriately focus on the bigger picture because of their inability to deal with the smaller stuff. There are times when that smaller stuff is simply so overwhelming that setting goals would be an artificial and burdensome exercise.

It could very well be that you don't need to have any more goals and direction than you currently have. Many successful people have professed to never having conscious goals and plans—they've just dealt with whatever opportunities seemed to show up in front of them. Despite their claims, I'm sure they had some sort of deeply rooted image of success or desire working that enabled them to perceive those opportunities and motivated them to take advantage of them. Still, a firm sense of direction or purpose does not have to be generated by, or tied to, more formalized kinds of thinking.

It is a tricky business to know when you should set goals and objectives in order to achieve a focus, and when you would be better off dealing with the acceptance and management of your current reality so you can later step into new directions and responsibilities with greater stability and clarity. Only you will know the answer to that, and only in the moment. The key to finding that answer is one of my core messages about how to make it all work—paying attention to what has your attention.

16 | Getting Perspective at Forty Thousand Feet: Vision

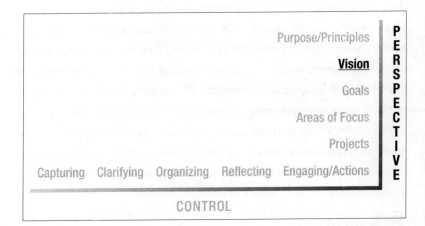

The future is not some place we are going, but one we are creating. The paths are not to be found, but made. And the activity of making them changes both the maker and their destination.

—John Schaar

Scope

The question that frames this horizon is: What would long-term success look, sound, and feel like? The vision involves focusing on issues that typically reflect or have impact, on multiyear time frames. For an individual, this could include lifestyle and career goals and directions. For an enterprise, it would encompass the nature of the company and what it intends to be doing in the world, at what level, as far into the future as it can imagine.

One rather prosaic way to pose this same question is, simply: What are your long-term goals—goals that stretch out further than two years? A more dynamic approach would be to ask: If you were *wildly successful* in the coming years, what do you imagine or see yourself doing or being?

"Long term" can certainly be a relative measure. What that means for a fourteen-year-old is very different from what it means for a retiree, and a long-term strategy for an aerospace company would likely be considerably different than it would for a software start-up or a grocery store. The frequency of the cycles of change that you or your enterprise is experiencing probably has a lot to do with the length of time you can envision in the future. If you are thinking about space exploration or city planning, it would be imperative to plan decades ahead. If you are considering how to build a consulting practice around open-source software, you'd probably be stretching it to imagine that you could trust anything further ahead than a couple of years.

Typical Formats

As was the case at thirty thousand feet, the environments and situations that are conducive to visioning often take the form of off-site meetings and conferences with executives, management teams, boards, or partners. The difference between the two levels may be the nature of focus and the degree of freedom given to an expanded brainstorming about possible futures beyond the operational planning level. Often outside consultants and facilitators are brought in to provide direction and structure to encourage participants to take ideas further than the normal and traditional bounds.

When I have coached forty-thousand-feet sessions, I have usually found it more productive to keep the discussion loose, flexible, and informal rather than to try to impose a rigid model on the proceedings. Each situation and configuration of people and circumstances is unique in terms of how far out into the future they can comfortably stretch and what form the ideas may take.

Sometimes the straightforward question, "So what do you see yourself doing five years from now?" is sufficient to elicit a stream of creative thinking and goal clarification. Giving an arbitrary set point in the future will often provide enough permission for the group to expand beyond its familiar context.

At other times it is best to simply ask, "What is the biggest and best thing you can imagine for yourself (or your organization)?" and, once that picture is brought forward, getting a best guess at how long it might take to achieve it.

As mentioned in the last chapter, though, this kind of scenario scripting can often be threatening to an individual or a group for numerous reasons, not the least of which is the relationship they may have to their success in their current situation. Visioning is too often imposed as a fruitful or necessary exercise in tenuous circumstances, either because an entity is forming, a major change in a company is in motion, or a crisis has forced a conversation about direction, focus, and motivation. Those are all tricky times in which to muster up the confidence to wear the mantle of great success, even if it's just in the imagination. It would seem easier and more productive to do positive visioning when things are flowing and operating smoothly, even though visioning may then be regarded as unnecessary boat-rocking—"if it ain't broke, don't fix it!"

In either case, these sessions benefit from the use of creative thinking techniques and models to break the ice, to move people out of their familiar patterns, and to grant permission to identify with the "what" of success before they have the "how." Consultants rely on countless versions of exercises to assist in this process, and "life coaching" has emerged as a specialized profession to help people craft where they want to go across the whole spectrum of life and work, and how they can get there.

"What-if" and "as-if" scenarios are common exercises. Having a team collaboratively write a major article in some well-known national or international publication, extolling the success the team or company has achieved, as if it has already happened, always produces interesting results. Though the assignment may sound somewhat artificial, "unrealistic," and even "hokey," I have often seen it generate a flow of productive decisions and directions that had an immediate impact.

For an individual, writing or crafting a script for an ideal future can serve the same purpose and have the same kind of positive effect. Over the years I have experienced innumerable instances in which people I have known (myself included) have simply written a list of all the things they would like to have in their ideal world—from quality of relationships, to living environments, aspects of career, health, and finances—and over time have watched them manifest.

A more detailed version of this kind of future thinking can take the form of writing out a more descriptive scenario, as if composing a short story about an ideal situation coming into being. If you are particularly visual, creating "treasure maps" can function the same way. Either drawing pictures and expressive icons or cutting and pasting pictures and text from magazines onto a collage can be wonderfully freeing, creative, and deeply motivating.

Below is a portion of a scenario I informally drew over a period of several days in November 1990. At the time it seemed to me that it would be useful to sit myself down and just imagine what I'd like my ideal life and lifestyle to include, so I gave myself permission to fantasize and capture whatever occurred to me. Twenty years later most of it has come to pass—at least in quality of experiences, if not in exact detail. Though most of it was purely a fantasy when I drafted it—that is, I had no idea how on earth I was going to be able to get from here to there—it affirmed and solidified a context deep inside me that opened my recognition and responsiveness to opportunities that were to cross my path, as well as aligning an internal identification with a unique positive future that encouraged me to take constructive risks I

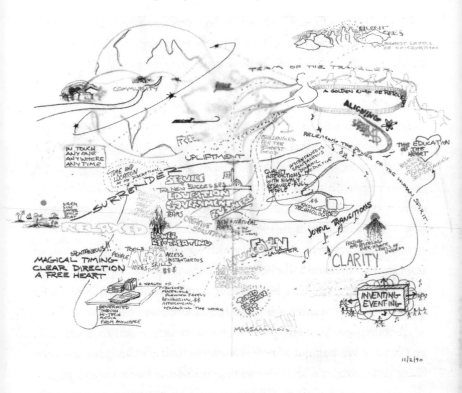

wouldn't have otherwise. (The blurred part of the drawing were not aesthetic choices—something spilled on it!)

When and How to Engage

As is true with the other more elevated Horizons of Focus, revisiting this level could be done on a regular basis as part of an ongoing commitment to keeping a vision active or whenever circumstances require a consideration of the overall situation from this perspective.

Many organizations include a long-term vision as part of their annual off-site planning session, and some may only have this discussion every two or three years. Often it will become clearer in focus with the passage of time, when it may need tweaking or recalibrating based on a greater amount of information, changing circumstances, and growth in maturity and experience of the players. There are also times when the identified future in play needs to be rethought because of challenges or opportunities that have arisen, which necessitate an updated version of the longer view that takes them into account.

In my own case, when my wife and I decided that we would be willing to allow our company to grow to keep up with the world's interest in and eagerness to utilize what we were offering, we had to get more specific about what that growth might look like. Bringing more people on board to help us then necessitated even more definition of the scope and scale of what we were committing to.

Obviously, any major transitional event in a life or in an enterprise can create a situation in which it will behoove you to update your vision of the future. Kids leaving the nest; death, divorce, or a new partner; an inheritance; a surprising job offer; an unexpected illness or disability—any and all of these should trigger vision rethinking. If you have a life partner who has a career, and she happens to come home one evening with the news that she's been given a major professional opportunity but it will require you to move to a country halfway around the world for at least two years, you will probably have a forty-thousand-feet dinner!

Changes in the world can obviously play a big role as well—major disruptions in political, military, organizational, environmental, and economic conditions have certainly caused many people and groups to shift their focus out of the day-to-day and back up into a consideration of broader issues. Companies that institute a voluntary retirement package to shrink their payroll create a perfect storm of challenge and opportunity for potential recipients, who now have the chance to rethink what they'd really like to be doing with their lives. Having personally been on Wall Street in New York on 9/11, I can affirm how intense and unexpected events can force a shift in perspective. For at least the next year I noticed most of the people in my world thinking much more consciously from forty-thousand-feet (and higher) perspectives. Coming face-to-face with our vulnerabilities and the impermanence of existence can certainly trigger a refocusing upward.

This section of your road map for life and work may only need a thorough conscious examination in unusual circumstances. It *could* be necessary at any time, however, and not only when transitional events occur, as mentioned above, but also if unresolved issues emerge regarding your shorter-term goals and objectives. Often the only way to get agreement and alignment about the near future is to get clarity on the longer one. And there are times that the only way to regain motivation and forward momentum is to regalvanize your visions.

The Future Is Now

The great secret about goals and visions is not the future they describe but the change in the present they engender. I've never been to the future—somehow my reality always remains firmly rooted in the present. But imagining that future unquestionably affects my perceptions and my comfort zones in the current moment, to some degree.

The true power in a long-range vision is the acceptance that holding that picture inside your consciousness permits you to imagine yourself doing something much grander than you would normally allow yourself. If I asked you to imagine how great things could be for you five years from now—what a Sunday afternoon might be like, for instance, with the kind of abundance, freedom, environment, influence, relationships, and opportunities you then had at hand—it's unlikely that you could do the same if I asked you to shorten the time frame to two weeks from now.

It is becoming more and more accepted that the pictures we hold in our minds about ourselves affect our neural patterns and self-image, which themselves are critical elements for determining what we perceive and how comfortable we feel about change. What's tricky is that your mind is inclined to hold only those images of yourself that in some way you feel you deserve or you're confident you could achieve. That tendency explains why goal-setting and visioning exercises are so often resisted. I have found that the image people hold of themselves and the goals they set have to be at least 51 percent credible to achieve stickiness in the psyche. If the goal lacks ambition, it won't represent a big enough change or challenge to be interesting and exciting; but if it's inaccessible, you will subtly undermine its power by implicitly affirming its lack of attainability.

Tremendous productivity can be generated, once a vision has been set, by reverse-engineering it back to short-term goals and objectives, for which you can then create projects that themselves trigger next actions. This is the most dramatic expression of the fundamental thinking process of GTD: What's the outcome? What's the next action? When a goal as visionary as "end world hunger" begins with practical next steps like "Call Johann about the soup kitchen proposal" and "Surf the Web for seminars on food distribution research," it can be quite energizing.

That said, it has been my experience that visions and long-term goals can create results simply by having them and focusing on them from time to time. Many of my own accomplishments originated as fantasies or ideas that I had had and held somewhere—an item on my Someday/Maybe list, an affirmation I repeated, or an element in some ideal scenario or treasure map I scripted. Even without being tied to the rigor and specificity of a project and next action, most of them at some point reached enough of a critical mass within me to cause me to finally feel uncomfortable about *not* moving on them, and I kicked them into gear.

So, in addition to linking forty-thousand-feet thinking into the more operational horizons where appropriate, it may be equally important to you to simply *have* a vision, not moving on it intentionally until it reaches enough of a crescendo that you then need to get going on it, in order to get it off your mind.

Although it's in our nature to be looking forward, the act of being conscious about how to put that focus on the bigger picture, and when it's necessary for achieving the appropriate perspective, provides a major key to sustainable success in business and life.

17 | Getting Perspective at Fifty Thousand Feet: Purpose and Principles

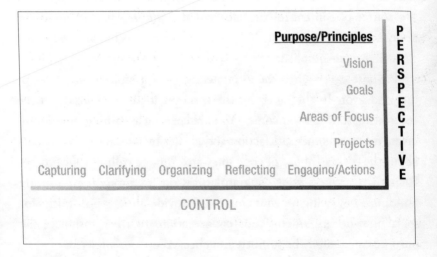

Nothing contributes so much to tranquilizing the mind as a steady purpose—a point on which the soul may fix its intellectual eye.
—Mary Wollstonecraft Shelley

It is an endless and frivolous pursuit to act by any other rule than the care of satisfying our own minds in what we do.
—Richard Steele

At the uppermost level of perspective we reach the fundamental questions: Why am I (are we)? and How am I (are we)? (The "how" in this case is not referring to any particular method, but rather the nature and quality of our being.)

The ultimate source of perspective rests at this horizon, which holds both purpose and principles at an equally lofty altitude. Purpose provides the ultimate intentionality for existence and direction; principles represent the core values to be maintained en route.

Purpose

SCOPE

The answer to the simple but remarkably potent question "Why?" is the source of content for this elevated viewpoint. What is the reason for this activity or pursuit? Why are we doing it? What are we hoping or trying to accomplish?

Purpose can refer to the ultimate goal—of a project, an action, or any endeavor. In this usage of the concept, it can be considered the motivating source of outcomes. You are creating a training program to create more customer satisfaction and loyalty by educating your clients about the successful use of your software. You are calling your brother Richard to express your congratulations on his promotion. You are building a new wing on your church to provide more opportunities for social networking among your congregation. In these instances the purpose can actually be fulfilled and checked off as completed.

Purpose can also in its deepest sense refer to the essence of something—its reason for being. In this usage it normally wouldn't refer to a task to be completed, but rather would function as the guiding definition and direction of the primary energies of an enterprise. Its fulfillment is achieved when the entity's focus, energies, and expression are all aligned with the stated reference. It is then "on purpose." If an organization's purpose is to provide the best products and services available within a certain defined arena, it can (and should) be fulfilling that intention, minute to minute. Purpose, in other words, is manifested continually.

One can have multiple simultaneous purposes and deeper levels of purpose than acknowledged. I have more than one reason for writing this book, and it never hurts to challenge myself by asking, "Okay, David, so why are you *really* writing this book?" Ultimately I take actions to complete projects in order to fulfill responsibilities that I have so that I can move myself forward to accomplish things that I do to make my vision come about, which will fulfill my purpose for being. In this frame of reference, the idea of purpose can be functional at and for many different horizons and levels of experience.

TYPICAL FORMATS

Determining, defining, or revisiting the purpose of an organization is one of those high-level events that is often correlated with the discussions and clarification of mission, vision, values, and long-term goals. Again, this typically takes place in the traditional off-site gatherings of the key leaders, owners, founders, or stakeholders of the enterprise. The output is usually in the form of a "mission statement" or "statement of purpose."

Down at other levels, any department, project, product, or process could recognize and affirm its own reason for existing: "We're doing this because . . . ," "We have brought ourselves together to . . . ," "The function of this software is . . . ," and so on.

On an individual basis, an equivalent personal statement of purpose would represent the highest criterion for direction and meaning. "I exist as a human being to . . ." On more mundane horizons, it could involve clarification of your purpose for having a family, planting a garden, serving as an officer of a local chamber of commerce, or organizing a bake sale for a local charity. Any endeavor will have a defining and guiding description of its purpose at whatever level it was brought into being, whether a party, a rest period, an exercise program, or music lessons.

Seldom are these outcomes and purposes expressed in concrete or formalized terms. Nor need they be, as long as the endeavors they serve flow smoothly and there are no conflicts that require a higher focus for their resolution. If everyone involved in a bake sale is comfortable with the prices being charged, there will probably never be a need to have a conversation about why it's being held. If there's disagreement about how much money should be made on each cake in the committee doing the planning, the level of focus may need to be bumped up a bit.

WHEN TO ENGAGE

You never need to know why you're doing something unless and until you do. What typically triggers the thinking at this level is a situation in which you are unclear about how and why you're involved or in which you have to make decisions about how to allocate limited resources. Purpose is the ultimate criterion for judgment about what's most important to do and how to evaluate your success. If you are clear that the purpose for having a large wedding reception is to create an environment in which it is comfortable for guests to express a connection and heartfelt emotions with people they care about and may not see regularly, then making decisions about the format and budget will be easier. And being able to feel great about the reception, after the fact, will be enhanced by how successfully it fulfilled its purpose. Did people actually take advantage of the environment created to share with one another?

At times it's healthy to consider having a discussion with yourself, and potentially others who have an investment in a given activity, about the deepest and most important level of purpose intended for it. The best time to at least start that dialogue is at the very beginning of the endeavor. Knowing your ultimate purpose will open the space to consider creative and original ideas about how to achieve it, as well as give you the parameters to evaluate options.

Another clue that it's time to visit fifty-thousand-feet level in your thinking is when there are differences and unresolved issues about the available resources for some designated event or enterprise. If you had an unlimited amount of time and money, there wouldn't be much pressure on you to be discretionary in how you spent them. It's when you have to start to make choices about how you spend a limited budget or (usually and more critically) a limited portion of your time that purpose starts to become a mandatory topic.

Should we acquire Acme Partners, SA? Should we consider allocating a larger percentage of our budget to research? Should we build a new facility in the San Francisco area?

Or, on a personal level: Should I get an advanced degree? Should I take advantage of this new career opportunity? Should we adopt a child now, at our age? Should I marry this person?

When you start an endeavor, or when all else associated with it fails, the best question to ask is, "Why am I (are we) doing this?" It's also the primary, fail-safe query to post whenever an increase in clarity, alignment, motivation, and forward motion is desired.

THE ULTIMATE (AND PATIENT) POWER OF PURPOSE

I need to state for the record that I firmly endorse the clarification of ultimate purpose as the primary criterion for setting priorities. If you don't know why you exist or where you are going, any road, indeed, will do. So if which road you're on matters at all to you, you need to know what you're about. Anytime and anywhere that you have the opportunity to regroup with yourself, or that your organization can retrench and evaluate the status quo from the highest level, it will probably be productive—in subtle but very important ways.

Too often, though, the admonition to discover and clarify life and organizational purpose has created inordinate pressure to have all the answers before there is sufficient commitment to getting involved and being fully engaged. It is true that getting your act together at the topmost level, and then focusing and organizing all your energies and resources in support of that unshakeable reference point, will be the most effective and productive model for getting the right things done and winning at the game of work and business of life.

But if you are not yet prepared to formulate and absorb that most subtle and sophisticated awareness of what you're about, and if you are still exploring and testing the deeper currents that may be fostering and running through your activities, attractions, and engagements, it's best to accept that fact. Any arbitrary and purely conceptual or theoretical conversations about these refined and very powerful levels of awareness can, at times, do as much disservice as benefit. If you or the people around you are not ready or capable of expressing, understanding, or integrating them, those are not explorations and processes to be forced.

Until you are ready to take on this responsibility, it's best to simply enjoy your ride. Learn from the rich field of experience you are generating for yourself. Focusing on your ultimate reason for existence is likely to trip up anyone with only a partially open consciousness, and in that context can quickly degenerate into naive navel-staring and insecure, self-absorbed romanticism. Big Picture reflections can serve as much as an escape as they can as an anchor point.

I have yet to come across a new organization that was confident enough that it could express, in full awareness, its mission and purpose and could state it clearly, any sooner than five years from its beginnings. Purpose is certainly there from the start, in the form of the "fire in the belly" of the founder(s) who had the commitment to bring it to life. But to express it in a tangible, conscious, and intellectually definable form is usually a long-term process requiring a depth of experience and a seasoned intention to understand and expand the DNA of what drives the enterprise. Similarly, if you truly discover why you're here, on this earth, in all of its phenomenal and sublime detail, at all the intricate levels of existence you're involved in, before you die, I will greet you as a true master and listen closely to everything you have to say.

But in my experience it's the "healthy skeptics" who are the people I most enjoy engaging. Their skepticism is such that they want to challenge the viability of any model or hypothesis so that they don't waste time with anything that can't prove itself quickly of its own efficacy. They typically have an eager willingness and openness to test out new ideas, models, and recommended best practices, to make sure they aren't missing anything that could serve them and what they're about.

Ask your kids why they think they're here. At times they may have the intuitive ability to cut through all the hype and mental static, because they're not yet programmed from years of relatively unconscious acculturation by it. They'll just give you a bracingly straight answer.

The "why?" question works everywhere, with everyone, anytime. If it doesn't, the discussion itself is probably not worth wasting time on. And, there's no pressure to resolve the issue quickly, for the answer to that question usually has nothing to do with time.

Principles

SCOPE

Standing at an equal level with the purpose in determining your priorities and investments are the values you hold. Your purpose for taking a course in Italian may be to expand your intellectual and cultural bandwidth, but your standards about what you hope to experience in the process will provide a parallel measure for whether you remain involved. Is it fun? Am I learning and growing at the pace I want? Is it worth the money I'm paying for it?

What I'm identifying at this top level of "principles" are the criteria that run deep for you or an enterprise that represents the core standards. We all have principles that guide us through our lives, emotional, intellectual, physical, or spiritual reference points that influence what we'll tolerate and what we won't.

If I asked you, "What would have to be true about a situation for you not to really care where you worked or what you were doing?" what would your answers be? Whatever they were, they would represent what you consider the core values about your work and work style. I could pose similar questions for other areas of your life, such as, "You wouldn't care where you live as long as . . . ?" Or even, "You wouldn't care who you married as long as . . . ?" If you were willing to be direct in your focus and honest in your answers, you'd have begun to identify your touchstones at this horizon.

Applied professionally and organizationally, this level would address the behaviors that you have defined as critical for an enterprise's success. What level of customer service, quality control, caring, and complete communication do you consider the standards for excellence in your company? Whether they're referred to as values, standards, guiding principles, or codes of conduct, organizations may have as few as three and as many as thirty, and they may include such objectives as exceeding customer expectations, supporting the growth of employees, providing increasing value to all stakeholders, operating within the laws of the land, contributing to the communities within which it does business, and so on. I can still remember from my years in the Boy Scouts that organization's famous principles, extolling its members to be "trustworthy, loyal, helpful, friendly, courteous, kind, obedient, cheerful, thrifty, brave, clean, and reverent." In our own company we frame the question about our values this way: We are at our best when what's true? We've come up with two dozen answers, including:

- We build vital, ongoing, expanding relationships.
- We operate in a highly productive and efficient way.
- We communicate richly with open systems, updates, questions, clarifications, and ideas.

At the highest levels, focusing on principles would address the nature of the company and its values, and your relationship to them. It would also reflect your personal comfort with the behaviors of the key people with whom you must engage. The primary reason, statistically, that people change jobs is not the nature of the work itself but the nature of their boss's behavior. It's not that they simply don't like their boss—employees can actually work constructively with managers with whom they don't resonate personally—but that they experience their behaviors and standards as being at odds with their own deepest values.

If you were to create your own list of the core values, you might have as many as ten or twenty:

- Being honest
- Consistently improving yourself
- Being supportive of people you are close to
- Being of service to your community
- Conducting your affairs with integrity
- Giving back of your resources to those who are in need
- Staying connected to your spiritual source

TYPICAL FORMATS

Visiting this part of the highest horizon usually takes place in association with purpose and mission clarification and in the company of the key leaders of an enterprise. The results of those discussions are often published as a list and distributed within the company. On a more operational level, these values might be used by project teams and groups as guidelines for their particular area or activity.

Organizations that employ "360-degree feedback" processes (each person evaluated by everyone with whom they work directly) will often include survey questions that evaluate an individual's expression of key success behaviors, as determined by the leaders. "How well does this person keep his agreements?" would be an example of an assessment motivated by company principles.

On the personal side, you might compose a set of personal affirmations or a personal credo as a document for review and inspiration. I have maintained a set of thirty or so self-image scripts since the early 1980s, when I discovered their value in reinforcing deeper patterns of my thought and behavior. "I freely and spontaneously take time to enjoy the simple and profound pleasures of life," for instance.

Families and other close-knit groups such as membership and social clubs may create a set of "rules of engagement" for themselves, to affirm and motivate collaboration, clarify expectations, and prevent misunderstandings and unnecessary conflicts later on.

WHEN TO ENGAGE

Discussions about principles can be extremely useful if conducted at the beginning of an enterprise or project, especially if the people involved are not familiar with one another, or when it would make sense for the mode of operating together to be clarified. Such conversations are also helpful to communicate the expectations and standards of the leadership and the culture when new people join an existing endeavor.

When my business consisted solely of my wife and myself, there wasn't really any need to objectify what was important to us—we had by then been friends, business colleagues, and then a married couple for many years, so there weren't many unknowns with respect to our personal and professional operating guidelines. If clients called with a request, our standard was to respond almost immediately and pay close attention to everything involved in the relationship to ensure that we could keep these people in our network as long as they were interested in being there. When we began to hire other people, however, we realized that it would be useful for us to let them know what we thought and felt about how we did our work, so there wouldn't be any surprises later on in terms of the behaviors we appreciated and those that made us very uncomfortable. I have been in too many situations over the years in which topics like this were never discussed, and the mismatch of standards became apparent only after conflicts developed later on, when it was too late to navigate and negotiate them easily.

It's always productive to at least raise questions about values and rules of engagement as relationships are forming. When organizations or teams need to merge, when strategic partnerships are being negotiated, when you hire a new assistant, and even when your niece and nephew are coming to stay with you for the summer, the front end is the ideal time to broach the subject, with talking points like:

- "What we consider really important in our day-to-day activities are . . ."
- "What I want you to know about how I work is . . ."
- "What would most bother us in this alliance would be . . ."

Once at an annual off-site planning meeting I saw a senior executive, toward the end of a presentation to his divisional managers, display a slide titled, "Here's what makes me cranky!" It listed quite a number of behaviors that he considered counterproductive and capable of undermining their ability to deal as members of a team with the challenging business environment they were facing. It would have been nice had he produced another slide to balance the discussion— "And here's what really makes me happy!"—but I credit him for at least raising the issues and letting people know what he personally considered off course.

Another company with which I worked considered its three top company principles so critical to its success that it actually had a human resource manager whose full-time job it was to ensure that those standards were maintained in the culture. Every employee was evaluated consistently on his compliance. One of the values was "creating customer delight." How would everyone in your organization fare if, in their next review, they were given a score and then a raise or a demotion based on that criterion?

In general, an excellent time to refer to this section of the road map is when it is critical to define the parameters of activities that ensure aligned and effective functioning—for individuals, groups, and even whole cultures. This could cover topics ranging from how frequently everyone agrees to check his e-mail to the point at which a country should draft a Bill of Rights.

The Principles level will also be relevant when disagreements and inappropriate behaviors show up. Because it is human nature to assume everyone around you shares your values, you often become aware of what your own values are only when someone else violates them. The more an awareness of principles is acknowledged and embraced by everyone at the early stages of relationship-building, the easier it will be to manage those developing and challenging situations to resolution and closure, to deal with them before they become too toxic.

As a general rule, the more you explore and identify what you personally consider the most essential factors and features of your life, the more solid your reference point for the times when you have to make tough choices. Is this decision really in keeping with my purpose? Does it line up with what I consider really important? That's the kind of perspective that provides the greatest ballast for staying in control in deep seas and rough water.

18 | Getting Perspective: Gracie's Gardens Revisited

While any one of the six horizons I have described in the previous chapters could call out for quite a bit more development, I'll be bold enough to assert that I've covered all the fundamental bases—all the levels of thinking, conversations, and decisions that should help bring perspective to, and set priorities for, any endeavor, from preparing a nice dinner to dealing with a subculture within a new country that now wants its own country. No effective framework will ever get any simpler than the continuum of purposes/principles, vision, goals, areas of focus, projects, and next actions. Anything more complex will only obfuscate the holistic nature of experience and will probably give improper emphasis to horizons that at the time are little more than mirages.

Always keep it as simple as possible, but no simpler.

Focus for the Business

Let's return to our friend Ron and his (hypothetical) situation of inheriting an out-of-control small business from his great-aunt Gracie. Once he has gotten under control—first the enterprise itself and consequently his own life, incorporating the new reality of his ownership—what comes next? The balance of the self-management equation involves focus.

Let's assume that Ron has read and taken to heart the contents of the last six chapters of perspective building, and has integrated their lessons into his thinking and conclusions about the business. Perhaps a weekend away with the key stakeholders of Gracie's Gardens would produce something akin to the following document.

Gracie's Gardens—Overview of the Business

Purpose

To provide the highest-quality landscape and garden materials to delighted retail and wholesale customers.

Principles

Strong and lasting customer relationships
Environmentally friendly products
Well-supported staff
Profitable and viable business

Vision

Recognized as the #1 garden and landscaping store within the tri-county district. A fun, interesting, creative, informative place to browse and shop, attracting and serving discriminating clientele who can spend discretionary time and money on an ongoing basis. Known as the "go-to" place for people who really know about plants and garden equipment. Profitable expansion to other locations.

Goals

In 12 months: 15% sales growth; 20% profitability; wholesale business established and in the black; expanded retail space; senior team in place (sales manager, office manager, controller, operations manager).

Areas of Focus

Executive; administration; PR/marketing; sales; finance; retail operations; wholesale operations; landscaping services and education.

Projects

Set up wholesale division
Get the books in order
Hire a head of Sales
Finalize Acme Landscaping contract
Fix/upgrade the HVAC system
Launch customer VIP program

Next Actions

Draft plan for wholesale division
E-mail Sandy/Tom re: bookkeeper recommendations
Call Brandon re: lunch meeting
Review Acme purchasing history
Surf/check out competitive Web advertising
Call Chris re: Italy trip

Gaining Personal Perspective

After an intense but highly productive session with himself and with the Gracie's Gardens staff and investors, Ron heads back home, where he feels himself alternately overwhelmed, inspired, and unfocused. Now that he's got Gracie's Gardens lined up for the foreseeable future, he begins to apply the six Horizons of Focus to his personal situation. He takes an entire day, with his life partner and a personal coach, to determine what's true for him, now, about . . .

PURPOSE

To experience a fulfilling life expression, adding ever-increasing value to myself and others.

VISION

Traveling frequently to interesting, beautiful places. Reach my perfect weight, with great energy, and a regular exercise program in place. Personal net worth allowing me freedom and discretion with my time and resources. Have sold Gracie's Gardens for a sizable profit to highly responsible new owners who continue to grow and upgrade the brand and business.

GOALS

- Get Gracie's Gardens' senior team set up and functioning well
- Get long-term investment strategy in place
- Get conversational in Spanish
- Renovate the kitchen/den

AREAS OF FOCUS

Career; health; spiritual; family; personal development; household; creative expression; service; assets; fun/recreation.

PRINCIPLES

- Honesty and directness, tempered with sensitivity to others
- Caring support for family and those close to me
- Continual self-observation, understanding, and growth
- Balanced and sustainable lifestyle.

PROJECTS

- Finalize Gracie's Gardens meeting/planning off-site
- Get Spanish instruction CDs set up on iPod
- Hire architect for the renovation
- Take Mexico vacation
- R&D workout gyms in the area.

NEXT ACTIONS
- Call Susan re: architect they used
- Order Spanish program/Web
- Draft meeting agenda for the off-site
- Take bike in for repair
- Surf Web re: current investment books
- Call Jonathan—happy birthday

Captain and Commander

If there was, indeed, a Ron Taylor, who had, indeed, inherited a Gracie's Gardens, and he had walked himself and his enterprises through the five stages of getting control and the six Horizons of Focus, you'd probably meet a guy who would be maximally available to you, in whatever context you met him.

He would have captured, clarified, and organized everything that he had accepted into his universe. He would have matured his thinking about why he was doing what he was doing, within a specific set of parameters, with a vision that he was realizing through goals that were firmly in place. He would have structured his environment such that each important function could be maintained appropriately, and all the right people could be trusted to be moving forward on all the right projects, with all the current actions determined and embedded with the right people. He would have his personal actions defined and organized in such a way that all of his individual responsibilities were appropriately clarified, operationalized, and in play within his systems.

If you met a real person in such a situation, you would likely experience someone focused, relaxed, in control, clear, and positively engaged in the multiple levels of his life.

19 | Making It All Work—in the Real World

The world isn't interested in the storms you encountered, but whether or not you brought in the ship.

—Raul Armesto

What does the process this book has proposed really look, sound, and feel like in the day-to-day world? The Gracie's Gardens scenario is obviously a rather rarified distillation of what might actually take place in such circumstances. Models are always nice and orderly, and yet our experience of the real world is seldom so. We all live within much more richness and complexity (and mess) than any case study or fable or allegory can encompass. As you're reading or listening to this, the background of your current world will likely feel more ambiguous, unclear, and in motion than what I seem to be describing. My own often does. But the forms I've described here are valuable stable reference points that can be used for facilitating a sense not only of coherence but of progress.

I have attempted to describe here each of the basic stages of gaining control and achieving perspective in a sequence that most closely matches how, in my own experience, the full spectrum of both are most easily achieved. You can hardly go wrong by capturing, clarifying, and organizing whatever has your attention; reviewing it all with an eye on all the horizons of your commitments; and taking the consequent action that emerges as the best course to take in the moment. As a complete and coordinated set of behaviors and thinking, it will help you achieve and maintain the role of Captain and Commander in life and work.

Tricky Business

As you probably have realized, though, staying in that balanced, relaxed, and focused place is a tricky business, given the complexity of experience, the rapidity of change, and the volume of data that comes across the transom. When confronted with all that, parts of this ideal pattern of self-management can lose their integrity and stability rather quickly. You can start your day a half beat ahead, but after three intense phone calls, one unexpected problem with a major project, biting a hard piece of crust that loosened a cap on your tooth, and a morning's worth of e-mails, you could find yourself having to take steps to shore up the loose pieces and reshape your focus for the afternoon. Or your significant other may have been given a career opportunity that will require you to change jobs, forcing you to rethink several horizons in order to regain balance. Or you see a puppy for sale. Or get an unexpected promotion. Or find out you're pregnant.

Winning at the game of work and the business of life is not maintaining everything in perfect order but rather having sufficient familiarity with the use of the road map of the horizontal and vertical aspects of experience to be able to quickly gain coherence and reorient yourself for the next round when you're faced with disruption.

Do you know when you need to process e-mail and when to ignore it? When should you have a staff meeting, with what agenda, and when would it be a waste of time? When do you need to take a walk with your kids, and when should you take a walk with yourself instead? When do you review and update all your project notes instead of continuing to draft a long proposal? Everyone makes such decisions all the time—thousands a day, in fact. Every time you think about one subject, you give it more importance than you would thinking about anything else. The trick to making informed and intelligent choices is to lay out the appropriate pathways and trail markers that guide your focus and actions along the routes that serve you the best.

Planning for Inconsistency

If you're like me, you're not going to experience yourself as unwaveringly intelligent, aware, and inspired. Sometimes you'll be "on," and sometimes you're going to be rather thick, obtuse, and reactionary. The problem is, when you are bright and motivated you tend to lose sense of time, and the heightened experience feels as if it could go on forever. Really smart people know, however, that they won't always have access to that capability. They use that awareness to build in processes and structures that enable them to do smart things when they aren't in smart mode. It's the less intelligent consciousness that doesn't plan for periods of less intelligence.

What compounds the challenges of the self-management game is that often the most effective thing to do feels like the last thing you're capable of doing. When you most need to plan is when you least think you have the time. When you most need to relax is when you feel most pressured to push hard. And when you most need to deal with cleaning up the minutiae of your life is when you feel most compelled to try to stay focused on something "more strategic."

Because reality seldom cooperates by being attuned to your mood at any given time, it's a great idea to have some fundamental structures at hand, simple to apply, that you can easily use to integrate the various aspects of control and perspective to bring the inner and outer worlds into balance.

Employing Tools and Tricks—Working a System

There's nothing like having outstanding tools, comfortable environments, and simple behavioral tricks to turbocharge your productivity. It's easier to win a game and conduct successful business with proper gear, a conducive atmosphere, and some smart habits and rituals that support the best practices.

In other words, you need a good system. A friend of mine, head of quality and research for a major clothing company, told me that their studies have proven that the vast majority of all performance improvement is systemic. Additional motivation and intelligence make only a negligible difference in the long run. Almost all of the increase is a direct result of the quality of the tools and the processes adopted. Commenting on the value of the GTD methods, his point of view was that although the upgrades in organizational systems improve the mechanical procedures, GTD was the first process improvement for productive thinking.

I have to agree. Executive thinking is a process, one that everyone (not just executives) must utilize to get things done. And that process can be sharpened and streamlined once it's recognized and understood.

Recently one of the largest organizations in the world began a series of pilot programs implementing GTD for its leadership ranks, including their direct teams and assistants. By simply introducing some of the key best practices for getting control, with special emphasis on e-mail, meeting, and work flow management, they were able to free up a significant amount of time during the day as well as greatly enhance the quality of decision-making, planning, and creative thinking. No one became any smarter as a result of the training (although they felt they had more access to their intelligence) or worked any harder. They merely eliminated the attention-draining elements of unprocessed "stuff" by installing the kind of capturing, clarifying, and organizing behaviors that are part of the GTD system.

As simple and elegant as these control and perspective elements may appear, and as elementary a habit as it may seem to execute them consistently, in actual practice it may not be quite that easy. Indeed, although the best game plan for winning at work and business plan for the business of life is a subtle and internal thought process, what helps tremendously is having the best structures in place that support the optimal thinking and focusing practices.

Constructing Your System

Over the course of many years of experience we have noticed that there are some key elements that make a significant difference in the ease with which these processes can be worked. Implementing each of them will go a long way toward reducing the *unconscious resistance* to acquiring these new habits. When you are in the heat of battle (like mid-morning during a busy day at work or when you are trying to keep track of and manage a three-year-old and a six-year-old simultaneously), you will tend to avoid any process behavior that requires too much thought or conscious discipline. The better the quality, accessibility, and usability of your personal management hardware and space for thinking and organizing, the more likely you will be to take advantage of them to get control and focus.

ENSURE YOU HAVE GREAT CAPTURING TOOLS

Do whatever it takes to make it easy, fun, and an ingrained habit to grab and objectify all the ideas, information, and commitments that stream through your head. Of all the changes in behavior required for the majority of adults with whom I have worked over the years, the most important and the most challenging has been learning to capture everything that needs processing later on into some medium that can be managed procedurally. That change in habit, if you haven't made it already, will have incredible consequences, for it serves as the gateway for the entire set of these best practices.

Do you have something available to you, and always at hand, on or in which you can write or record anything that might be valuable or necessary at a later point in time? If not, I suggest you find a notepad with a pen or a pocket digital recorder that you can incorporate into your personal always-with-you gear. Place notepads at every telephone location in your home and office. Keep a notepad available with a fresh page staring at you while you are at your desk, whether at home or at work. Set up whiteboards wherever you spend time thinking, and wherever you meet with others. Consider purchasing mind-mapping, outlining, and other free-form brainstorming software. Look into transcription services that will turn telephone messages into e-mail. And by all means, place a physical in-basket that looks and feels great directly in front of you at every workstation you use as well as at home. Keep a plastic or vinyl file folder in your briefcase or satchel dedicated solely to the capture function.

There is no equipment in my life that is as important for keeping my head clear and things organized as my tear-off writing pad, my in-basket, my traveling notepad wallet, and my red "IN" folder that goes with me in any briefcase.

My habit of keeping those buckets airtight—not letting anything stray outside of them—remains one of my most critical techniques of control. The older I get, the more frequently I have good ideas in places other than where I'd actually be implementing them (that's sophistication, not senility!). I come up with topics that might be relevant to a major project six months away when I'm having coffee during a break from a seminar. I'll be in a project meeting and think about something creative to pick up at the store for a dinner we're having with guests in a couple of days. Trusting that anything captured in those contexts will invariably be dealt with in an appropriate way at the right time is wonderfully freeing.

My experience is that the more senior and responsible you become, professionally and personally, the more your good ideas about your work will not occur at work, just as the best ideas about your family and creative life won't happen while you're engaged directly in those arenas. As your responsibilities increase, so will your need to hold a specific kind of focus as you're involved in fulfilling them.

You won't have room to handle much more than what you're already committed to handling while you're "in the trenches." The really valuable, creative content will often materialize in the strangest and most serendipitous places and times. Having great personal habits and tools for hooking those thoughts when they appear and responding to them quickly is a hallmark of the Captain and Commander experience.

SET UP YOUR CALENDAR AND ACTION LIST MANAGER

You probably already have a good working calendar. Make sure that you trust it and that all its relevant protocols are clear to whoever has access to and authority for managing your schedule.

If you haven't already done so, decide where to locate your lists of action reminders—phone calls, errands, computer-based actions, things to do at home, things you're waiting on from others, and so on. These groupings can easily be managed in file folders, pages in a loose-leaf notebook, or categories of actions or folders in a software application. If you are completely new to this idea but want to at least try it out, I suggest using something simple that you're already comfortable with to organize these reminders.

SET UP AD HOC LIST FUNCTIONALITY

You'll want to have the capability to create and store an infinite number of lists that will be quickly accessible. If you decide to capture ideas within each of the Horizons of Focus, for instance—goals, annual plans, long-term vision components, personal values, and so on—you will want to be able to keep them organized in an easily retrievable way.

A paper-based planner works well for these kinds of ad hoc lists. You can also utilize the functions of various software applications for free-form organizing—the Notes function with Microsoft Outlook or the Personal Journal database in Lotus Notes, for instance. Anything that enables you to create a topic and organize items within it would be fine.

SET UP A FUNCTIONING REFERENCE SYSTEM

Because the volume of both digital and paper-based reference information is so great, it is critical that you are comfortable with being able to park miscellaneous data. If you don't have this kind of system set up and functioning, a lot of "stuff" will tend to mount up, making it difficult to keep other important categories of reminders and data cleanly organized and discrete.

STRUCTURE EFFECTIVE PERSONAL OFFICE, HOME, AND TRANSIT WORKSTATIONS

One of the most important investments you can make for winning at the game of work and the business of life is a well-crafted workstation at which you can think and manage your affairs. You need such a place at your office and at home (if that's different from where you work), as well as a compact version of it you can take with you anywhere, if you like or need to stay focused, organized, and productive while you're traveling or in transit.

There is hardly a better single motivating factor for getting yourself in control and thinking creatively than having an attractive and highly functional space within which that kind of activity can readily occur. Your workplaces should give you the sense that you are in the cockpit of a plane, with easy access to all your processing and communication tools, work reminders, support and reference information, and productive thinking equipment. If you don't have such a trusted place, or yours is messy (in your terms) or unattractive, you'll spend an inordinate amount of time reorganizing instead of actually being able to *use* it as soon as you step into that environment. You need to be able to "hit the road running."

You should also set aside your own space, both at work and at home, which you can structure and control without having to tolerate someone else's interference in your flow. You don't need a large volume of room within which to function, but it needs to be your own.

Of course you will greatly expand your freedom and opportunities to stay focused and in control if you have access to a virtual office, that is, a container and set of tools that can serve as a portable traveling desk. A good briefcase, pack, or satchel is indispensable in this regard. I have several of different styles and capacities, to match the particular needs I may have in different locations at different times.

POPULATING THE SYSTEM

It's one thing to have all the structures and gear in place, and quite another to actually have them serve their highest function of allowing you to offload from your psyche the job of remembering and reminding. The degree to which your system is incomplete is the degree to which your mind will have to retain the lower-level job of keeping track of commitments and information.

Complete Mind Sweeps

If you are just starting to implement my recommended best practices, one of the first things to do is to complete the capture of whatever may still be resident in your head and lurking in the nooks and crannies of your environment. You will want to do thorough site walkarounds, where you live and where you work, gathering reminders of all the things you notice that have your attention and need something done about them.

Until it becomes an ingrained habit, use something to jog loose whatever may be residing in your mind that needs to be externalized. The Incompletion Trigger list, Appendix i, can be a useful aid in this regard. Having great capturing tools is an important first step, but getting the rock-solid habit of *using* them consistently is what makes them valuable. If in the course of reading or listening to this book you have had things pop into your mind, I hope you've already been using something to ensure that those ideas are not lost.

IDENTIFY PROJECTS AND ACTIONS TO IMPROVE YOUR SYSTEM

Is there anything still to be done to enhance your systems? Some of the best projects and actions to be identified are those that support the improvement of your own processes. If you have a commitment to upgrade any of them, make sure you have specified the project—perhaps something like, "Finalize personal management system setup." Keep that as an open item on your Projects list, evaluate it regularly, and ensure that you keep the appropriate actions moving forward until you've reached the point at which you're satisfied.

INCORPORATE TIME FOR PROCESSING

Working your process takes time. As I described in chapter 6 on clarifying, it usually requires an hour a day just to stay current with the typical volume of incoming information. That's a highly productive expenditure of time, during which you'll be thinking, making decisions, completing short actions, routing data, communicating, and defining and organizing new work. But it's not the kind of activity you can do *while* you're working on longer tasks or in meetings. Though many executives find it useful to leave the first hour or so of the morning open for it, processing time is something that you may not find easy to block out. Some people have a stable enough work environment to allow for clearing the decks first thing in the morning and last thing in the evening, but you may simply have to clean up your in-basket "between the lines"—whenever you can as you move through your day.

The critical factor is to be aware that it will take time. If you allow yourself to be booked in meetings through an entire day, you will fall at least an hour behind in your processing. There's nothing inherently wrong with that, as long as you realize that you will have to "pay the piper" sometime soon. Many, however, don't seem to realize or accept this reality and then operate in a constant state of frustration over having to make up the lost time. That's like complaining that taking a shower eats into your day! People who get accustomed to the true amount of time and energy required for these procedures begin to incorporate it into the stride of their life and work, instead of railing against it.

BUILD IN THE WEEKLY OPERATIONAL REVIEW

Whereas daily processing is seldom an activity you can nail down in a hard-and-fast time frame, the Weekly Review is, and probably should be scheduled on your calendar if it's not already a recurring event. This once-a-week exercise, which allows you to regroup and refresh your world, is such a critical factor in making everything work that whatever you can do to structure the time and focus it demands will pay off exponentially.*

I would recommend scheduling a two-hour block of time. You'll make good use of it, I'm certain, even if you don't need the entire amount for the Weekly Review. Trusting that you have a slot of time will allow you to be more relaxed during the week, knowing that you have a window available in which you'll be able to catch up.

CREATING ELEVATED HORIZON EVENTS

For the most part, the discussions, conversations, and decisions that are part of twenty-to-fifty-thousand-feet perspective-building will need to be scheduled, if they are to receive sufficient focus. Departmental reviews of your annual plans, going "off-site" with your life partner to a nice place to talk about some of your lifestyle goals, and even having a good job review with your boss—few of these kinds of conversations will ever happen extemporaneously. They require a commitment and focus, and they should be planned and scheduled.

If you need or want more perspective from any of the higher altitudes, decide what format it should take and who should be involved, and make time in your schedule.

WORKING THE SYSTEM

The third leg of the stool, after setting up your system and populating it with the appropriate contents, is, of course, to actually *use* it. The ultimate purpose of any kind of structures like these is to facilitate your engagement with the flows of life and work.

---

* Use the checklist in Appendix v to facilitate this exercise.

How long you can let items that have potential meaning and value to you lie fallow and still remain in control and appropriately focused is obviously up to you, and also somewhat dependent on the unique circumstances you're in. The critical factor is how comfortable you are that you can get current quickly and completely, whenever you decide to. That's why GTD has made such comfort possible—not that you should work more intensely or more quickly, but that you know you could, successfully, if the situation demanded it. It's the lurking, gnawing sense of anxiety that you could not get control of what's mounted up in your game of life and work that creates the sense of losing.

The following practices will help instill this confidence factor for you.

Use and Empty Your In-baskets

This practice should be self-evident by now (if it wasn't to begin with)—you've got to *use* your in-baskets for them to create control and relief. That doesn't mean just putting things *in* them—you've also got to get them all *out* again. One of the best standards to reinforce until it becomes automatic is getting all your collection buckets empty—e-mail and paper as well as your voice mail and answering machines. A great target is to reach to zero with all your input every twenty-four to forty-eight hours. Bigger pileups will always happen, but those should be the exception, not the rule.

Do Weekly Reviews

It bears repeating that the best tactic for managing what has your attention is that every-few-days review and catch-up. Whatever it takes to trigger that behavior for you, consistently, will be one of the best process improvements you can implement for the rest of your life.

Reassess and Refresh Your System Consistently

Everything gets out of date. Your world changes, your responsibilities shift, you get better at some things, other things become less fun or interesting . . . ad infinitum. The more you can trust that you will be revisiting and potentially overhauling how you're doing whatever you're doing, the more freedom it will give you to experiment and be a little extravagant with what you think you can and want to manage.

This can be another review and recalibration you might want to build in on a regular basis: purging your filing system, rethinking how you're managing lists, new tools and technology you might want to try out now.

One great trick to accomplish this is to move, regularly—office, home, computer system, and so on. Whenever you have to uproot and then reconfigure your operations for a new environment—physical or digital—you'll have a great opportunity and sometimes a real necessity to reconfigure your data and systems. If you don't have the luxury (?) of doing that on some consistent basis, then it would be good to create, or at least be very open to, some version of a re-thinking of your personal systems at regular intervals. This is an especially good arena in which to practice the core admonition: pay attention to what has your attention. When you find yourself being subtly distracted by the outdatedness of your files, the mess in your storage areas, the inaccessibility of your computer data, the disarray of your tools in the shed—that's the time to create a new project and a next action about getting your structures up-to-date.

Every time I eliminate something problematic from any area, something cool soon shows up to fill the space—psychologically as well as physically. I've also discovered that it doesn't really matter how much you decide to keep around, but rather how clear you are about exactly what everything is and whether it still belongs there.

So, What . . . ?

The procedures I've been describing for setting up, populating, and working your personal system are, as you've probably noticed, commonsense and to some degree familiar to you. I hope, however, that the discussions about getting control and perspective have given you a broader context within which to understand the utility of implementing these structures and behaviors, and motivation to fine-tune yours accordingly. The key is to be able to have them functioning without undue impediments when you need to return to Captain and Commander mode.

IF YOU'RE NOT FEELING IN CONTROL . . .

How do you decide whether to collect stuff, process it, organize it, review it, or just do something? Which is most important? This comes back again to the key concept of this book: What most has your attention? Is any one of these five stages more critical than another? Because they all work together holistically, there's no particular priority in general—only in the specific circumstance can you ask, "What is the weakest link in the chain?" You may have a lot of unprocessed stuff piled up in your in-basket, but there may be some action you should be taking that's more important than getting IN to empty. At times organizing more effectively or differently will take precedence. And certainly there are instances in which the priority is to step back and review the landscape.

If you're not sure which of these processes you should pursue in the moment, I'd recommend cleaning up your in-baskets and reducing your backlog toward zero. There are several good reasons for this choice. First, it helps clean up resident stuff in your head so you can think more clearly. Second, it ensures that all the options about what you could be doing are evident in front of you. Third, it serves as preventive maintenance so that you can be ready for new stuff coming toward you that you can't foresee. And last, it's usually rather fun and freeing to be playing a part of the game that you know you can win, cleaning up, making progress, and generating creative and productive ideas along the way.

. . . AND IF YOU NEED A FOCUS

Each of the six horizons I have identified has its own scope, content, formats, and levels of involvement. I also described some of the most typical circumstances in which you would be likely to visit each one. Just as the practices for achieving control all exist in relationship to one another, with no one any more critical than another in principle, the one that needs your attention most is probably the most important.

If you feel that the changes in your work situation require you to shift the focus of your job, but you're not sure that you and your boss see eye-to-eye about your new priorities, then having that conversation and negotiation at twenty thousand feet may be the most strategic course for you to follow. If you've just moved into a new job, determining the current projects in motion and identifying your own in order to get onto cruise control (ten thousand feet) might be the top priority. If you just moved into a new house and things are in a relative state of turmoil, focusing on the runway with your have-tos on your calendar and your list of things to pick up at the hardware store could be your best focus. And if you've been challenged with a major life situation that forces you to make some significant decisions and perhaps difficult choices between commitments to family and to your own personal and professional growth, you might have to reach into your core values and purpose at fifty thousand feet to get more direction and comfort about what to do.

The key to winning the perspective game is to be able to shift horizons and link the results of your discoveries at one level to any of the others as required. Is the vision that you are moving toward in terms of lifestyle in alignment with your purpose and values? Do you have the right projects in play to move yourself toward it effectively? Does the project you developed have a next action associated with it? Does it support your achieving your goals for this year?

At some point you will have to deal with each of these levels directly. Life simply won't leave you alone. If you try to prevent change, you will be attempting to push a large river backward. The nature of many of these changes will undoubtedly force you to have to shift perspective to make sense of them and then navigate accordingly. Whether you win the lottery or lose a limb, find yourself totally taken with oil painting or nearly overcome by the demands of an elderly parent, you will have to recalibrate your focus. If you are winning at the game of work and the business of life, you'll be prepared for any of these shifts, when and where they happen.

That preparation can take the form of engaging with each of these levels to some degree before you have to. In my experience, there are three ways to be involved with each altitude, and the more comfortable and familiar you are with each, the more capable you'll be of using the horizons as a practical and effective road map:

- Identifying and clarifying your current commitments
- Reviewing and reminding yourself *about* the commitments
- *Changing* the commitments.

You might give yourself permission to create separate documents for each of these horizons. Don't agonize about the "right" format—just start allowing yourself to capture what shows up for you when you place your attention at each level. What do you want to have true by the end of the next year or two? What are some of the features of your ideal lifestyle five years from now? What are the most important values you hold for yourself? What do you think you are here on the planet to accomplish?

Perhaps you have already answered one or more of these questions for yourself or your organization. If so, you might want to find a way to integrate them into an overview along with all the other frameworks, to gain additional perspective from their relationships to one another. But if you haven't ever spent quality time alone with yourself (or, with your key partners in life) considering some of them, I suggest you give it a try. It's easy to resist this exercise, for all the reasons that we find such things often out of our comfort zone. My recommendation is to consider this merely a practice run or an exploration of possibilities, not a hard-and-fast commitment that has to be "right." As you lay track down these avenues of thinking, the process itself will start to come easier and easier, and you will be more capable of bringing these parts of your road map to bear when necessary.

In addition to creating these documents, consider building in some sort of regular review of them. You might put on your calendar or in a tickler system a reminder to review your annual goals every one to three months. I put my vision treasure maps in my tickler file for a random assessment every few months, so it gives me an opportunity to visualize and affirm those pictures consciously when I see them again. I do the same thing with my purpose and some of my most important and inspirational value statements, so I get to confront them unexpectedly, which causes me to pay more attention to them than some automatic procedure would.

And finally, you should be flexible enough with this kind of focus to be able to change any of the contents as you yourself change. Having them all close by in some overview, as I do, will make it easier to remind yourself when it may be time to recast your job description, update your longer-term goals, and spend some time adding some new components to your visions of success.

GETTING BACK TO "ON"

These procedures are designed to be incorporated into your life to get whatever you can *off* your mind. This achievable "mind like water" state doesn't mean that nothing is going on or that there is total silence. If you are conscious, you will always be focused on something. I've discovered, though, that when all the noise has stopped, what's left that is pulling or attracting the attention is the best place to put it. It's like transforming a cacophony into a clear melody—it's much easier to follow with an experience of flow and fulfillment.

20 | In closing . . .

Those who face that which is actually before them, unburdened by the past, undistracted by the future, these are they who live, who make the best use of their lives; these are those who have found the secret of contentment.

—Alban Goodier

If it's true that life is a journey and not a destination, then making it all work is simply about getting your act together and taking it on the road. In other words, acquire and demonstrate coherence and direction, control, and perspective. Those are not answers or final solutions—they are the application of a process. The *way* you are in the game is how you win, not the final score.

But if the ultimate challenge is to be "on"—positively and constructively experiencing and expressing yourself in work and life—is there something concrete and specific you can learn and apply to achieve that result? Hopefully after reading or listening to this book, you can answer in the affirmative. There are optimal ways to engage with the stream of life's experiences and inputs and to direct your intentions, and though those techniques are understandable and universally applicable for everyone, they don't occur automatically.

Awareness and appropriate application of systemic approaches can improve dramatically how well you do, but the processes must work, and you must work them.

In these pages I have deconstructed the separate stages and aspects of how we actually gain control and achieve perspective, in order to illuminate and explore the potentially relevant details and emphasize the necessity for different tools, approaches, and techniques required at different times for different circumstances. But in truth the way we experience life and work is a lot more of a scramble than a neat set of ordered procedures to follow.

Though I am familiar with all of the stages of control and Horizons of Focus, I am rarely in a situation in which I have either the time or awareness to think about them consciously. I'm just trying to pay attention to what most has my attention and resolve it, as easily and quickly as I can, so I can reclaim clear space in my head. Having trained myself in these models, however, gives me the confidence that I can apply the right set of behaviors and thinking to match the situation.

The reason to work through this material with some rigor is so that you will know you have the ability to apply the right tool and approach when desired or required. If you know you can lead a discussion with your team or family about long-term goals but still feel like your e-mail is unmanageable, you will be limited in your psychic resources. If you know how to execute well on specific tasks, but are still unclear how to present your boss with your suggestions for strategic improvements in your area, you won't be able to always know how to experience the state of Captain and Commander.

The good news is that any and all of these challenges and opportunities can be addressed with the five stages of control and the six Horizons of Focus. I will repeat myself here in saying that, though I would love to have made it simpler, I can't, and anything more complex wouldn't be universally applicable. I've done my best to avoid making it simpler than it should be or more complex than it need be.

Interestingly, to validate this book's subtitle, when these principles are implemented from a practical perspective, a majority of people lighten up tremendously about their work and their job, and they get a lot more businesslike about the rest of their life. That doesn't mean that they become unfocused and flaky from nine to five, or that they turn into cold, mechanical machines about their home and family life. They just realize that it's all essentially the same thing, restoring the fun to the game of work and greater freedom and control in their more personal world.

I hope that what I have shared in these pages has served to highlight the specific things you can do that will be timeless in their usefulness and rich in their reward. I doubt I've shared much of anything that you didn't already know, in some way. But I think that when something resonates with the truth, it will continue to spark deeper levels of awareness each time you engage with it. I can attest that in the process of writing this book I have dramatically deepened my own experience and awareness of these processes. I remain a fellow student.

A university executive described his experience with this material like this:

> I'm sure I'm not done, because just when I expect to react that I've mastered this, I come away somehow feeling I've gotten a better understanding by listening again. And I am generally a quick study! But I am finding myself hearing things, and understanding things at a deeper level, each time I listen. It is also interesting how my focus as to what is most relevant for me keeps changing—as I get a deeper grasp of one aspect, another one takes on deeper relevance I hadn't caught before. It is quite an amazing experience. I do recall you saying this could happen, but I wasn't expecting it to unfold quite as dramatically as this.

That's encouragement to read, review, and experience the contents of this book again, at another appropriate time in the future.

Test this material out. Insert it into whichever environments and situations call for more control and perspective. Teach these principles and techniques to your kids. Bring these principles into your town meetings and your boardroom. Nudge your life partner, your boss, or your secretary with them. Integrate these ideas into your everyday conversation and vocabulary.

> "What's most got your attention?"
> "What do you want to have happen about that?"
> "What's the next action that would move this forward?"
> "What *really* matters to you, which has you interested in this?"
> "What do you need to keep track of, about this? Where's the best place to park that?"
> . . . and so forth.

Please share what you experience and learn from engaging with *Making It All Work*. We're in this together, and the more we can validate and reinforce the implementation of these best practices, the easier it will be for each of us to participate in our world ever more constructively. It will be more fun to turn on the computer, run a staff meeting, catch up with the kids, draft a proposal, and walk down the street. And because winning at all this is merely a matter of approach, it's always close at hand, as is celebration.

Appendixes

Appendix i

INCOMPLETION TRIGGER LIST

What do you have attention on?
Professional

Projects started, not completed

Projects that need to be started

"Look into" projects

**Commitments/promises
to others**
boss, partners, colleagues, subordinates, others in organization, other professionals, customers, other organizations

Communications to make/get
calls, e-mails, voice mails, faxes, letters, memos

Writing to finish/submit
reports, evaluations, reviews, proposals, articles, marketing material, instructions, summaries, minutes, rewrites and edits, status reporting, conversation and communication tracking

Meetings
upcoming, need to be set or requested, need to be de-briefed

Read/review
books, periodicals, articles

Financial
cash, budget, balance sheet, P&L, forecasting, credit line, payables, receivables, petty cash, banks, investors, asset management

Planning/organizing
goals, targets, objectives, business plans, marketing plans, financial plans, upcoming events, presentations, meetings, conferences, travel, vacation

Organization development
org chart, restructuring, lines of authority, job descriptions, facilities, new systems, change initiatives, leadership, succession planning, culture

Administration
legal issues, insurance, personnel, staffing, policies/procedures, training

Staff
hiring, firing, reviews, staff development, communication, morale, feedback, compensation

Systems
phones, computers, software, databases, office equipment, printers, faxes, filing, storage, furniture, fixtures, decorations, supplies, business cards, stationery, personal organizers

Sales
customers, prospects, leads, sales process, training, relationship building, reporting, relationship tracking, customer service

Marketing/promotion
campaigns, materials, public relations

Waiting for
information, delegated projects/tasks, pieces of projects, replies to communications, responses to proposals, answers to questions, submitted items for response/reimbursement, tickets, external actions needed to happen to continue or complete projects . . . (decisions, changes, implementations, etc.), things ordered

Professional development
training, seminars, things to learn, things to find out, skills to develop or practice, books to read, research, formal education (licensing, degrees), career research, resume

Wardrobe
professional

INCOMPLETION TRIGGER LIST

What do you have attention on?
Personal

Projects started, not completed

Projects that need to be started

Projects - other organizations
service, community, volunteer, spiritual organization

Commitments/promises to others
spouse, partner, children, parents, family, friends, professionals

Communications to make/get
calls, e-mails, faxes, cards, letters, thank-yous

Upcoming events
birthdays, anniversaries, weddings, graduations, outings, holidays, vacation, travel, dinners, parties, receptions, cultural events, sporting events

Family
projects/activities with spouse, partner, children, parents, relatives

Administration
home office supplies, equipment, phones, answering machines, computers, internet, TV, DVD, appliances, entertainment, filing, storage, tools

Leisure
books, music, videos, travel, places to visit, people to visit, web surfing, photography, sports equipment, hobbies, cooking, recreation

Financial
bills, banks, investments, loans, taxes, budget, insurance, mortgage, accountants

Legal
wills, trusts, estate, legal affairs

Waiting for
mail order, repairs, reimbursements, loaned items, information, rsvp's

Home/household
real estate, repairs, construction, remodeling, landlords, heating and A/C, plumbing, electricity, roofs, landscaping, driveways, garages, walls, floors, ceilings, decor, furniture, utilities, appliances, lights and wiring, kitchen stuff, laundry, places to purge, cleaning, organizing, storage areas

Health
support and maintenance, doctors, dentist, optometrist, specialists, checkups, diet, food, exercise

Personal development
classes, seminars, education, coaching, career, creative expressions

Transportation
autos, bikes, motorcycles, maintenance, repair, commuting, tickets, reservations

Clothes
professional, casual, formal, sports, accessories, luggage, repairs, tailoring

Pets
health, training, supplies

Errands
hardware store, pharmacy, department stores, bank, cleaners, stationers, malls, gifts, office supply, groceries

Community
neighborhood, neighbors, service work, schools, civic involvements

Appendix ii

NATURAL PLANNING MODEL®

1. Purpose/Guiding Principles

- Why is this being done? What would "on purpose" really mean?
- What are the key standards to hold in making decisions and acting on this project? What rules do we play by?
- The purpose and principles are the guiding criteria for making decisions on the project.

2. Mission/Vision/Goal/Successful Outcome

- What would it be like if it were totally successful? How would I know?
- What would that success look or feel like for each of the parties with an interest?

3. Brainstorming

- What are all the things that occur to me about this? What is the current reality? What do I know? What do I not know? What ought I consider? What haven't I considered? etc. (see Project Planning Trigger List).
- Be complete, open, nonjudgmental, and resist critical analysis.
- View from all sides.

4. Organizing

- Identify components (subprojects), sequences, and/or priorities.
- What needs to happen to make the whole thing happen?
- Create outlines, bulleted lists, or organizing charts, as needed for review and control.

5. Next Actions

- Determine next actions on current independent components. (What should be done next, and who will do it?)
- If more planning is required, determine the next action to get that to happen.

Shift the level of focus on the project as follows if needed:
If your project needs more clarity, raise the level of your focus.
If your project needs more to be happening, lower the level of your focus.

How much planning is required?
If the project is off your mind, planning is sufficient.
If it's still on your mind, then more is needed.

Appendix iii

PROJECT PLANNING TRIGGER LIST

Resources
Whose input do you need?
Whose input could you use?
Has anything like this been done before?
What mistakes can you learn from?
What successes can you learn from?
What resources do you have?
What resources might you need?

Executive issues
How does this relate to the strategic plan?
How does it relate to other priorities, directions, goals?
How will this affect your competitive position?

Administration
Who's accountable for this project's success?
Lines of communication
Methods of reporting
What structures do you need?
What planning is still likely to be required?
What regrouping will you need? How often?
What people do you need?
Current staffing?
Hiring?
Subcontractors, consultants?
How do you get involvement?
What skills are required?
Who needs to know how to do what?
What training do you need?
How do you get it?
What other communication do you need?
Who needs to be informed as you go along?
What policies/procedures are affected?
What about morale? Fun?

Finance
What will this cost?
How do you get it?
What might affect the cost?
Might you need additional financing?

What are the potential payoffs (profit)?
Who signs the checks?

Operations
What is the timing?
Hard deadlines?
What might affect timing?
Who's going to do the work?
How do you ensure complete delivery?

Quality
How will you monitor the progress?
How will you know if the project is on course?
What data do you need, when?
What reports, to whom, when?

Politics
Whose buy-in do you need?
How can you get it?

Stakeholders' Considerations
Board
Stockholders
Employees
Vendors
Customers
Community

Legal
Issues?
Regulations?

Space/Facilities/Equipment
What requires room?
How do you get it?
What tools do you need? When?
Phones/computers

Research
What might you need to know?

Public Relations

Is there value in others knowing about this?

How do you do that?

Risks

What could happen?

Could you handle it?

Creative thinking . . .

Who would have concern about the success of this project?

What would they say, ask, or input that you haven't done yet?

What's the worst idea you can imagine about doing this project?

(What is therefore the best idea, which is its opposite?)

What is the most outrageous thing you can think of about this project?

What would make this project unique?

What haven't you asked yourself about this yet?

Appendix iv

1. Collect

- Capture anything and everything that has your attention in leakproof external "buckets" (your in-baskets, e-mail, notebooks, voice mail, etc.). Get them out of your short-term memory (use the Incompletion Trigger Lists to keep yourself "downloaded").
- Have as few of these collectors as you can and as many as you need.
- Empty them regularly, by processing and organizing (see below).

2. Process

- Process the items you have collected (decide what each thing means, specifically).
- If it is not actionable, toss it, "tickle" it for possible later action, or file it as reference.
- If it is actionable, decide the very next physical action: do it (if less than two minutes); delegate it (and track it on a "waiting for" list), or defer it (put it on an action-reminder list or in an action folder). If one action will not close the loop, then identify the commitment as a project and put it on a reminder list of projects.

3. Organize

- Group the results of processing your input into appropriately retrievable and reviewable categories. The four key action categories are:

  Projects (projects you have a commitment to finish)

  Calendar (actions that must occur on a specific day or at a specific time)

  Next Actions (actions to be done as soon as possible)

  Waiting For (projects and actions others are supposed to be doing and which you care about)

- Add subcategories of these lists if it makes them easier to use (Calls, Errands, At Home, At Computer, etc.).
- Add lists of longer-horizon goals and values that influence you.
- Add checklists that may be useful as needed (job description, event-trigger lists, org charts, etc.).
- Maintain a general-reference filing system for information and materials that have no action but which may need to be retrieved.
- Maintain an "on-hold" system for triggers of possible actions at later dates (Someday/Maybe lists, calendar, tickler).
- Maintain support information files for projects as needed (can be kept in reference system or in pending area).

4. Review

- Review calendar and action lists daily (or whenever you could possibly do any of them).

- Conduct a customized weekly review to get clean, get current, and get creative (see Weekly Review).

- Review the longer-horizon lists of goals, values, and visions as often as required to keep your project list complete and current.

5. Do

- Make choices about your actions based on what you can do (context), how much time you have, how much energy you have, and then your priorities.

- Stay flexible by maintaining a "total life" action reminder system, always accessible for review, trusting your intuition in moment-to-moment decision-making.

- Choose to:

  1- do work you have previously defined or

  2- do ad hoc work as it appears or

  3- take time to define your work

  (You must sufficiently process and organize to trust your evaluation of the priority of the ad hoc.)

- Ensure the best intuitive choices by consistent regular focus on priorities. ("What is the value to me of doing X instead of doing Y?") Revisit and recalibrate your commitments at appropriate intervals for the various levels of life and work (see Horizons of Focus):

- **Runway** - current actions (daily)

- **10,000 ft.** - current projects (weekly)

- **20,000 ft.** - current responsibilities (monthly)

- **30,000 ft.** - 1–2 year goals (quarterly)

- **40,000 ft.** - 3–5 year goals (annually)

- **50,000 ft.** - career, purpose, lifestyle (annually +)

Appendix v

THE WEEKLY REVIEW

Get Clear

Collect Loose Papers and Materials
Gather all accumulated business cards, receipts, and miscellaneous paper-based materials into your in-basket.

Get "IN" to zero
Process completely all outstanding paper materials, journal and meeting notes, voice mails, dictation, and e-mails.

Empty Your Head
Put in writing and process any uncaptured new projects, action items, waiting-fors, someday/maybes, etc.

Get Current

Review Action Lists
Mark off completed actions. Review for reminders of further action steps to record.

Review Previous Calendar Data
Review past calendar in detail for remaining action items, reference data, etc., and transfer into the active system.

Review Upcoming Calendar
Review upcoming calendar events (long- and short-term). Capture actions triggered.

Review Waiting-For List
Record appropriate actions for any needed follow-up. Check off received ones.

Review Project (and Larger Outcome) Lists
Evaluate status of projects, goals, and outcomes one by one, ensuring at least one current action item on each. Browse through project plans, support material, and any other work-in-progress material to trigger new actions, completions, waiting-fors, etc.

Review Any Relevant Checklists
Use as a trigger for any new actions.

Get Creative

Review Someday/Maybe List
Review for any projects which may now have become active and transfer to "Projects." Delete items no longer of interest.

Be Creative and Courageous
Any new, wonderful, harebrained, creative, thought-provoking, risk-taking ideas to add into your system?

WORK FLOW PROCESSING & ORGANIZING

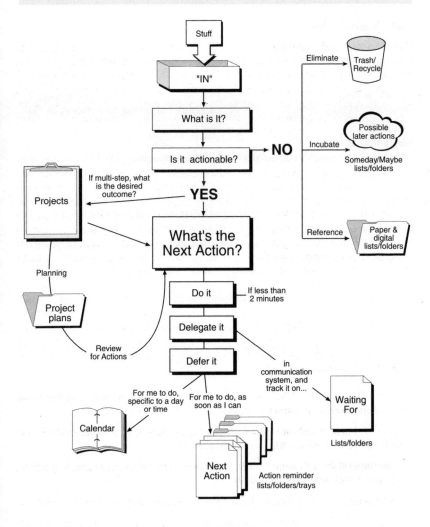

Appendix vii

The Altitude Map

"Work" is defined and managed from at least six different horizons, corresponding to different altitudes of perspective. These range from core intention—the understanding of the purpose and values of an undertaking, enterprise, or life—to the most mundane—the next physical actions required to move them forward. Clarity is enhanced and distraction reduced when the multiple levels with which you are engaged have been assessed and the commitments emerging from each one have been appropriately identified, captured, and implemented. Alignment of the various levels produces maximum productivity.

Priorities are determined from the top down—i.e., your purpose and values will drive your vision of the purpose being fulfilled, which will create goals and objectives, which will frame areas of focus and responsibility. All of those will generate projects, which will require actions to get them done. Each horizon is equally important to clarify, however, to get things done, and the content of your thinking and commitments will be different on each level. A key driver for your life may be to assist others in achieving their dreams (purpose), which you will express by becoming a world-class athlete and spokesperson (vision), for which you will achieve a starting line-up position on a national team (goal). To do all this you need to maintain a rigorous training program (area of focus). You realize you want to get a new personal trainer (project), for which you need to call your college coach (next action) to get his recommendation.

An altitude map can be used to identify which conversation, at what horizon, with yourself and others, might have the most value, at any point in time. It could be at any level or include a combination of them. You may know the long-term goal but have yet to identify the projects needed. You may know the vision but not the actions and who's doing them. Et cetera. Keeping your thinking current at all horizons is a dynamic process. As your world and your awareness of it change, so must these arenas of your focus be continually updated.

Following is a general list of the levels of focus, with typical formats and suggested frequencies of visitation. (Samples given from a hypothetical business - Gracie's Gardens)

50,000 ft. - Purpose and core values. Ultimate intention for something and the standards for its success. Why are we doing this? What are the critical behaviors?

> **Formats:** Off-sites with partners, board, team, family; initial discussions for launching projects, meetings, whole enterprises; life planning

> **Frequency:** Whenever additional clarity, direction, alignment, and motivation are needed

> *(Gracie's Gardens: "Provide the highest-quality landscape and garden materials to delighted retail and wholesale customers"; "Strong and lasting customer relations; environmentally friendly products; well-supported staff"; etc.)*

40,000 ft. – Vision. What it will look, sound, feel like with successful implementation. Long-term outcomes and ideal scenarios.

Formats: Off-sites with partners, board, team, family; initial discussions for launching projects, meetings, whole enterprises; life planning; annual revisiting of enterprise direction; ideal scene development; personal treasure maps

Frequency: Whenever additional clarity, direction, alignment, and motivation are needed

(Gracie's Gardens: "Recognized as the #1 garden and landscaping store in the tricounty district; a fun, interesting, creative, informative place to browse and shop, attracting discriminating clientele who love to spend time and money on an on-going basis;" etc.)

30,000 ft. – Goals and objectives. What do we want and need to accomplish, specifically, within the next 12–24 months, to make the vision happen?

Formats: Off-sites with partners, board, team, family; strategic planning; annual goal-setting and broad planning sessions; life and family planning

Frequency: Annually; quarterly reviews and recalibrations

(Gracie's Gardens: "By year-end, 15% sales growth, 20% profitability, wholesale business established and in the black," etc.)

20,000 ft. — Areas of focus and responsibility. Important spheres of work and life to be maintained at standards to "keep the engines running."

Formats: Job descriptions; organization charts; employee manuals; personal lifestyle checklists; family responsibility designations; project checklists

Frequency: Performance reviews; monthly personal check-in's; whenever job or life changes require reassessment of responsibilities

(Gracie's Gardens: "Executive, administration, PR/marketing, sales, finance, wholesale operations, retail operations," etc.)

10,000 ft. – Projects. Outcomes we want to achieve that require more than one action and which can be completed within a year.

Formats: Overview list of all projects; project plans (defined subprojects)

Frequency: Weekly review; whenever next-action contents are not current

(Gracie's Gardens: "Set up wholesale division, get the books current, hire director of marketing, finalize Acme contract, upgrade HVAC system," etc.)

Runway – Actions. Next physical, visible actions to take on any project or other outcome; any single action to take about anything

Formats: Calendar, action lists (e.g. calls, errands, at home, at office, talk to boss about . . .); action folders or bins (e.g. read/review, bills to pay)

Frequency: Multiple times daily; whenever a question about what to do next

(Gracie's Gardens: "Draft plan for wholesale division, e-mail Sandy re: bookkeeper recommendations, call Brandon re: lunch meeting, review Acme purchasing history, surf web for competition ads" etc.)

Index

Acheson, Dean, 175–76
Action, taking
    action list, 141–43, 272
    evaluating need for, 112–14
    keeping things current, 163–64
    on low energy, 147
    movement, and sense of control, 191–92
    next action lists, items on, 144–48
    precursors to, 33–34
    projects, 217–26
    Someday/Maybe items, 121–24
    and thinking process, 114–15
Action list, organizing, 141–43, 272
Ad hoc work, 186–88
    forms of, 186–87
Affirmations, 139, 248, 257
Agendas list, 145–46
Altitude map. *See* Horizons of Focus
Anywhere list, 145
Appointments, calendar, use of, 143–44
Areas of Focus, 227–34, 300
    checklists, use of, 230–31
    Gracie's Gardens, case example, 263,
      264
    relevant categories in, 229
    scope of, 228–29
    strategic approach to, 232–34
    time to engage in, 231–32

Attention
    broken. *See* Distractions
    concentration, 38–39
    creative thinking, 47
    extended mind, 46–48
    finishing thinking, 44–45
    focus and GTD method, 33–34
    placeholders, using, 46–47
    starting point for, 72–75
    what has your attention, 72–75, 278

Balance, life/work balance fallacy, 58–59,
    225
Bookmarking, as capturing activity,
    95–96
Brainstorming
    as capturing activity, 88–89, 109–10
    forms of, 88
"Bright bauble" syndrome, 68

Calendars
    calendared later starts, 150–51
    and finishing thinking, 44–45
    and flow of creative thinking, 47–48
    not used, problem of, 42–43
    reviewing, 220–21
    use in personal system, 272
    using, scope of, 143–44

Captain and Commander, 69–71
  barriers to mode, 74
  characteristics of, 69–70, 185
  of Gracie's Gardens, 265
  negative aspects of, 70–71
Capturing phase, 76–102
  and bookmarking, 95–96
  and brainstorming, 88–89
  cleaning up, 89–90
  definition and scope of, 77–78
  focus/responsibility, areas of, 82
  goals and objectives, 83
  Gracie's Gardens, case example, 194–95,
    196–97
  group capturing, 78, 90–91
  habit, acquiring and practicing, 91–94
  and journal writing, 87
  mind sweep, 78–80
  and note-taking, 95–98, 101, 270–71
  project-level, 81
  purposes and principles, 84–86
  as solution to interruptions, 94–95
  successful, practices for, 99–101
  vision, 84
  whiteboards for, 98–99, 271
Change, and stress, 21
Checklists, for Areas of Focus, 230–31
Clarifying phase, 103–27
  action, evaluating need for, 112–14
  action focus, 114–15, 118–19
  clarifying questions, 111–12
  definition and scope of, 104
  Gracie's Gardens, case example, 195, 197
  in-basket, clearing, 110–11
  no action, areas for, 120–24
  outcome focusing, 115–18
  stuff, dealing with, 106–10
  and thinking process, 104–5, 125–27
Cleaning up, as capturing activity, 89–90
Clearing, and getting control, 73
Collaboration, group capturing, 78, 90–91
Collect, Mastering Work Flow model, 293
Computer list, 145
Concentration, importance of, 38
Context, engaging phase, 182–83
Control, gaining
  capturing phase, 76–102
  clarifying phase, 103–27
  and clearing, 73

connection to perspective, 60–61, 165,
    201–3, 214–15
  engaging phase, 170–92
  Gracie's Gardens, case example, 192–99
  hardwiring for, 171–72
  movement, and sense of control, 191–92
  organizing phase, 128–60
  reflecting phase, 161–69
  self-management matrix, 61–72
Crazy Maker/Visionary, 67–69
  and capturing, 108–9
  characteristics of, 67–70
  positive aspects of, 68–69
Creative thinking
  get creative review, 221
  and GTD method, 37
  treasure maps exercise, 244–45
  and use of calendar, 47
  and visioning, 243–45
  what-if/as-if scenarios, 244
Crisis, and Victim/Responder, 64–65

Deadlines, 83
Decision-making
  and meaning, 105–6
  next action decisions, 210–11
  and thinking process, 104–5, 125–27
  variable affecting, 179–80
Delegation
  definition and scope of, 177–78
  Do, Delegate, or Defer (3Ds), 177–79
Disorganization
  and emergency scanning mode, 189
  as energy drain, 129
  and loss of control, 157–58
  signs of, 130–31
  and support material, 152
Distractions
  "bright bauble" syndrome, 68
  causes of, 39
  and Crazy Maker/Visionary, 67–69
  and interruptions, 77–78
  and mismanaged commitments, 39–41
  self-agreements, broken, 41–44
  solutions to, 36–37, 73–74
Do, Mastering Work Flow model, 294
Do, Delegate, or Defer (3Ds), 177–79
Drag, elimination of, 19
Drucker, Peter, 57

Energy
    and actions to take, 184–85
    disorganization as drain of, 129
Engaging phase, 170–92
    action/movement, taking, 191–92
    actions, options for, 185–89
    and context, 182–83
    decision-making, variables in, 179–80
    definition and scope of, 170–72
    delegation, 177–79
    and energy level, 184–85
    Gracie's Gardens, case example, 196, 197
    limiting factors, 182–85
    next action decisions, 172–77
    priorities, 189–91
    strategic aspects, 180–82
    time factors, 183–84
Errands list, 145
Execution, and next actions, 213–14
Extended mind, 46–48, 221–22

Family weekly review, 224–25
Fifty-thousand-feet thinking, 56, 84–86,
        181
    purpose and principles, 249–60, 299
Focus
    and GTD method, 33–34, 52–53
    Horizons of Focus. See Areas of Focus,
        300
    reminders, organizing, 140
    twenty-thousand-feet thinking, 82
    See also Attention
Forgetting, 96
Forty-thousand-feet thinking, 84, 181, 208
    vision, 241–48, 299–300
Future, focus on
    Someday/Maybe items, 121–24, 149–50
    See also Goals and objectives; Vision

Get clear review, 220
Get current review, 220
Getting Things Done approach. See GTD
        method
Goals and objectives, 235–40
    formats for, 236
    Gracie's Gardens, case example, 262,
        264
    Horizons of Focus, 55–56, 83, 300
    long-term. See Vision

organizing, 140
    reassessment of, 238–40
    resistance to, 239–40
    scope of, 235–36
    taking-stock, value of, 237
    time to engage in, 237–38
    written, 238
Gracie's Gardens
    Captain and Commander of, 265
    gaining control, 192–99
    gaining perspective, 261–65
Group activities. See Collaboration
GTD method
    definition and scope of, 26–27
    expansion of, 4–9, 32–33
    focus as core of, 33–34, 52–53
    goals of users, 50–51
    Gracie's Gardens, case example, 192–99,
        261–65
    high-tech business use of, 16–17
    holy grail of, 110, 203
    Horizons of Focus, 30–32
    intuitive aspects of, 23–25
    learning of, 22–23
    logic of, 37–46
    Mastering Work Flow model, 28
    and mental intelligence, 34–37
    Natural Planning model, 28–30
    phases of. See Control, gaining;
        Perspective
    popularity, factors in, 14–25
    proponents of approach, 3–4, 8, 16–18,
        93–94, 269
    setting up system for. See GTD system
    as system-independent approach, 17, 20
    See also specific elements of method
GTD system, 269–82
    ad hoc lists, organizing, 272
    calendar, 272
    capturing tools in, 270–72
    control, gaining, 279
    focus, gaining, 279–80
    horizon events, 276
    in-basket, 277
    mind sweep, 274
    moving, effects of, 278
    office space and workstation, 273–74
    perspective, maintaining, 280–82
    projects, identifying, 275–76

GTD system (*cont.*)
  reference system, 273
  reminders/lists in, 272
  time management, 275
  weekly review, 276, 277

Home list, 145
Horizons of Focus, 299–300
  definition and scope of, 30–32
  focus and responsibility, areas of,
    227–34, 300
  and gaining perspective, 203–4
  goals and objectives, 235–40, 300
  projects, 217–26, 300
  purpose and core values, 299
  runway and next actions, 210–15, 300
  stages of, 31
  vision, 299–300

Ideas, generating. *See* Capturing
In-basket, emptying, 110–11, 277
Incompletion Trigger List, 274, 287–88
  and mind sweep, 80
Inconsistency, inevitability of, 268
Interruptions
  capturing as solution to, 94–95
  normal distractions, 77–78
  reactions to, 187–88
Intuition, and GTD method, 23–25

Job description, reviewing, 82
Journal writing
  as capturing activity, 87
  software for, 272
  types of, 87

Knowledge work, defining, difficulty of,
    57

Laptop, for capturing, 98
Life coaching, 243
Life/work balance, fallacy of, 58–59, 225
Lists
  action list, 141–43, 272
  for ideal future, 244
  Incompletion Trigger List, 80, 274,
    287–88
  next action lists, 144–48
  Project Planning Trigger List, 291–92

Projects list, 218–19
  resistance to use, 167
Long-term
  as relative measure, 242
  See also Vision
Low energy, action, taking on, 147

Maps, usefulness of, 53–54
Maslow, Abraham, 205–6
Mastering Work Flow model
  definition and scope of, 28
  stages of, 28, 293–94
Meaning
  and decision-making, 105–6
  and organizing, 133–35
  and stuff, 120–21
Memory, capacity of, 40
Mental intelligence, 34–37
  and attention, 36–37
  concentration, 38–39
  creative thinking, 37, 47–48
  extended mind, 46–48, 221–22
  finishing thinking, 44–45
  "mind like water" concept, 37–38, 44,
    84, 282
  perspective, maintaining, 45–46
Micromanager/Implementer, 65–67
  and capturing, 108–9
  characteristics of, 65–66, 69–70, 92
  positive aspects of, 66–67
"Mind like water" concept, 37–38, 44, 84,
    282
Mind-mapping software, 88, 95, 99
Mind sweep
  brainstorming as, 88–89
  elements of, 78–80, 274
Mission statement, statement of purpose,
    251–52

Natural Planning model
  definition and scope of, 28–30
  stages of, 29, 289
Next actions
  decision-making about, 172–77, 210–11
  and delegation, 177–78
  development of concept, 174–75
  and execution, 213–14
  Gracie's Gardens, case example, 263, 265
  lists, 144–48

possible scope of, 210
and priorities, 211–12
time to engage in, 210–11
Note-taking, as capturing activity, 95–98,
   101, 270–71

Objectives. *See* Goals and objectives
Observation, value of, 87
Office list, 145
Organizing, 128–60
   and action, 141–48
   calendar, using, 143–44
   calendared later starts, 150–51
   categories for, 136–37, 159
   definition and scope of, 130–33
   Gracie's Gardens, case example, 195, 197
   Mastering Work Flow model, 293
   and meaning, 133–35
   next action lists, 144–48
   organizer as therapist, 105–6
   and outcomes, 137–41
   reference information, 153–55
   Someday/Maybe items, 149–50
   support material, 151–53
   tools, 134–35, 168–69
   trash, 156–58
Outcomes
   and organizing, 137–41
   of others, tracking, 141
   of projects, 218
Outcome thinking, 115–18
   resistance to, 116–17
Overcapture, 100

Personal organizer, as therapist, 105–6
Perspective
   Areas of Focus, 227–34
   connection to control, 60–61, 165,
      201–3, 214–15
   goals and objectives, 235–40
   Gracie's Gardens, case example,
      261–65
   and Horizons of Focus, 203–4, 207–8
   maintaining, 45–46, 50, 55
   next actions, 210–15
   projects, 217–26
   reflecting for, 164–66
   self-management matrix, 61–72
Predefined work, forms of, 186

Principles, 255–60
   affirmations, organizing, 139
   definition and scope of, 255–57
   discussions, time to engage in, 258–60
   examples of, 256–57
   fifty-thousand-feet thinking, 84–86
   Gracie's Gardens, case example, 262,
      264
   360-degree feedback, 257–58
Priorities, 189–91
   bottom-up thinking about, 181
   importance of, 190–91
   and next actions, 211–12
   and purpose in life, 253
Problems, ten-thousand-feet thinking, 81
Process, Mastering Work Flow model, 293
Processing. *See* Clarifying phase
Projects
   definition and scope of, 217
   Gracie's Gardens, case example, 263,
      264
   Horizons of Focus, 300
   materials, organizing, 140–41
   outcome words related to, 218
   overview index for, 218
   problems as, 81
   process projects, 117
   project-level thinking, power of, 222–26
   Project Planning Trigger List, 291–92
   Projects list, 218–19
   reviews, types of, 219–22
   ten-thousand-feet thinking, 81
   time to engage in, 219–22
Purpose in life, 250–55
   definition and scope of, 250–51
   fifty-thousand-feet thinking, 84–86
   formulating, power of, 253–55
   Gracie's Gardens, case example, 262,
      263
   Horizons of Focus, 299
   and priorities, 253
   statements of, 138-139, 251–52
   time to engage in, 252–53

Read/review list, 146
Reference information
   clarifying, 124
   controlling amount of, 155
   forms of, 153–54

Reference information (*cont.*)
    organizing, 153–55, 201, 273
    read/review, on next action list, 146
    support material, 151–53
Reflecting phase, 161–69
    Gracie's Gardens, case example, 195–96,
        197
    mental activity during, 165–68, 192
    for perspective taking, 164–66
    to update systems, 163–64
Relationship-building, and principles,
    259–60
Reminders
    organizing, 148–51, 183
    use in personal system, 272
Responsibility
    Horizons of Focus, 300
    twenty-thousand-feet thinking, 82
Reviewing. *See* Reflecting phase
Reviews, 219–22
    of calendar, 220–21
    family weekly review, 224–25
    get clear review, 220
    get creative review, 221
    get current review, 220
    Mastering Work Flow model, 294
    weekly review, 219–22, 276
Runway
    complexity of, 212–13
    managing, success factors, 213–14
    and priorities, 211–12
    scope of, 210
    time to engage in, 210–11
    See also Next actions

Self-agreements, broken, 41–44
Self-management
    control and perspective, degrees of. *See*
        Self-management matrix
    starting point for, 72–75
Self-management matrix, 61–72, 205–7
    Captain and Commander in, 69–71
    Crazy Maker/Visionary in, 67–69
    as fluid/situational/relative, 71–72
    Micromanager/Implementer in,
        65–67
    overlapping profiles, 71–72
    Victim/Responder in, 62–65
Situational awareness, 223

Software
    mind mapping, 88, 95, 99
    for organizing, 272
Someday/Maybe items
    affirmations on, 248
    and clarifying phase, 121–24
    and organizing phase, 149–50
Statement of purpose, 251–52
Strategic plans
    and Areas of Focus, 232–34
    engaging phase, 180–82
    Horizons of Focus, 83
Stream of consciousness, 100
Stress
    and change, 21
    and disorganization, 129–31, 157–58,
        189
Structure, overstructure and
        micromanager, 65–66
Stuff, 106–10
    backlog cleanups, 187–88
    dealing with, 108–11, 115. *See also*
        Organizing
    empty in-basket, 110–11
    forms of, 107, 134
    for future reference, 124
    as meaningless, 120–21
Stuster, Jack, 176
Support material
    forms of, 152
    organizing, 151–53
Survival mode, 205–6

Technology business, GTD method, use
        of, 16–17
Telephone, call list, 145, 147
Ten-thousand-feet thinking, 81, 181,
        208
    projects, 217–26, 300
Thirty-thousand-feet thinking, 55–56, 83,
        181, 208
    goals and objectives, 235–40, 300
360-degree feedback, 257–58
Time factors, engaging phase, 183–84
Time management
    and daily GTD system, 275
    failure, reasons for, 66, 109, 134–35
    overly structured tools, 66
    and self-management, 21–22

Trash
  and stuff, 120
  systematic approach to, 124, 156–58
Treasure maps exercise, 244–45, 282
Twenty-thousand-feet thinking, 56, 82,
    117, 181, 208
  focus, areas of, 227–34, 300

Victim/Responder, 62–65
  characteristics of, 62–63
  positive aspects of, 64–65
Vision, 241–48
  creative thinking models, 243–45
  future, connection to present, 247–48
  Gracie's Gardens, case example, 262,
    264
  Horizons of Focus, 84, 299–300
  images of, organizing, 139–40
  mental imprinting of, 247–48
  reverse-engineering of, 248
  scope of, 241–42

  time to engage in, 245–47
  updating/reassessing, 246–47

Waiting for list, 146
Weekly Review, 276, 277
  elements of, 219–22, 295
What-if/as-if thinking exercises, 244
Whiteboards, for capturing, 98–99,
    271
Work
  ad hoc, 186–88
  defining and GTD, 188–89
  definition and scope of, 56–58
  life/work balance fallacy, 58–59, 225
  predefined, 186
Work flow
  Mastering Work Flow model, 28,
    293–94
  processing and organizing diagram, 112,
    297
Workstation, 273–74

GTD-Q—What is Yours?

Take the free GTD-Q assessment and discover where *you* are right now on the **control** and **perspective** matrix!

Visit www.gtdiq.com and in less than five minutes you can get valuable feedback and specific recommendations, tailored to your assessment score, for the best techniques to move you further into "Captain and Commander" mode.

You can take this assessment anytime, at no cost, and as often as you like. Notice what changes and what remains consistent in your scores over time. The **GTD-Q** tool and its related support and educational materials is a success builder that will continue to assist you at the game of work and the business of life. If you have interest in implementing any of the powerful ideas and practical techniques in *Making It All Work,* **GTDIQ. COM** is a great place to start!

Go to **GTDIQ.com** and follow the simple instructions for your free GTD-Q assessment. Your results will be available immediately.

David Allen is the bestselling author of *Getting Things Done* and *Ready for Anything*. He is chairman and founder of the David Allen Company, a global management and consulting company, widely recognised as the world's leading authority in developing personal and organisational capacity. In the past twenty years he has developed and implemented productivity improvement programmes for more than one million professionals and has been instrumental in assisting some of the world's major companies to get things done. His clients include many Fortune Global 1000 corporations. As a management consultant, executive coach and educator, he has given thousands of seminars and presentations and been called one of the world's most influential thinkers on productivity.

For further information, visit:

www.davidco.com
www.makingitallwork.co.uk